broken parts
missing pieces

By

Rev. Dr. Don Johnson

God Bless!
Rev. Dr. Don Johnson
2-8-14

Published by Rev. Dr. Don Johnson
3525 N 124th Street
Brookfield, Wisconsin

Cover design by Kileen Lindgren
Printed by Bethany Press International.

ISBN: 978-057811855-0

Contents

—❦—

Acknowledgements v
1.   Broken Parts, Missing Pieces.. 1
2.   Three Men and a Car... 15
3.   Generation to Generation... 31
4.   Lost Dreams 43
5.   No Choice, No Matter.. 55
6.   The Familiar to the Unknown... 67
7.   In the Shadow of the Space Needle..................................... 81
8.   Out from Under the Table... 95
9.   The Cost of Discipleship 103
10. Miracle on the Quileute... 111
11. My Greek Teacher and Me.. 119
12. The Pass Over 131
13. The Wolf at the Door 141
14. The Sacred Tree 149
15. Big Sky, Bigger Ideas 163
16. My Conundrum 173
17. The Crab Story... 183
18. Once There Was Time 195
19. My Time, God's Providence 213
20. The *Tenyu Maru*... 223
21. A Stranger in Our Midst 239
22. That's My Star!... 247
23. Missionaries, Miners, and Misfits...................................... 261
24. A Bridge to Opportunity 275
25. Escape to Freedom 287
26. The Master Mechanic... 295
Bibliography 303

Acknowledgements

———— ⟶ ⟶ ————

Ibegan writing this book in Caribou coffee houses and similar places in and around the Twin Cities; during the early morning hours mostly. My creativity was at its best then. In the six years time that it took me to complete my story, I met many good people, very often bright, young people who worked as baristas at these establishments. We became friends over time and that enabled me to try out some of my stuff on them. They are too numerous to mention but I will always remember their kindness in listening and encouraging me to finish my book, hopefully, before I got too old or they moved on to something else in life. Most of them did and I in turn got old.

There were others too, customers like me who also became interested in my book. One man, Virgil Johnson, a fine Christian man died shortly after I began my writing. I will always recall his goodness in being one of the first to come over to where I was sitting at a neighborhood Panera's to inquire about my progress. I told his wife that I would not forget his encouragement and someday, when the book was done, I would mention him in my acknowledgements.

Then there was some of my office staff like Sue Gebel who helped edit some of my early efforts. She taught me about variety in sentence structure. Kathleen Walrath, my administrative assistant working out of my Milwaukee office, however had to endure the worst of my efforts. How many times I told her to make a new file of my allegedly finished book or make corrections to my work would be too numerous to mention. The truth was, I was never done even though I would call my office on more than a few occasions to tell them that I thought I had finished. They believed me the first time; maybe even the second time. But after that, they realized this guy (me) was never going to be done.

Sometimes, a day would pass after making my latest announcement that I had written my last page; the next morning I would begin to review my supposedly completed work and realize I had not told the story the way I wanted to. Before long, I was revising again and again to the point to where people would tell me my pregnancy (the book) was way over due. "Just have that baby" they would say.

One man, David Rooke, a fellow believer and friend would constantly encourage my efforts. He knew about the writing process better than most and was always making helpful suggestions. Then there was long-time personal and family friend, Patti Heinlein. She is a brilliant person with experience in editing. She helped me organize my thoughts and provided great encouragement, especially at the beginning. Then there was Dr. Robert Hemenway, Chancellor Emeritus at Kansas University in Lawrence, Kansas. His timely suggestions and encouragement were very helpful.

Another person who helped me in the formation of the thought processes that have gone into this book is psychiatrist, Dr. Lee Griffin. Lee has long been a friend of mine and a former member of my Board of Directors for the Lutheran Association of Missionaries and Pilots U.S. His wisdom in knowing how to combine his discipline as a psychiatrist with Biblical truth has always struck me as profound. What is more, he always seemed to know what to say to me at just the right time. He, along with other of my Board members, was most gracious in offering me insight as well as timely suggestions. Some of them, especially Rev. Dr. Warren Schumacher and Reverend Harry Henneman provided excellent advice.

Of course, my greatest appreciation goes to my wife Mary for her insightful care in proofing my writings and her patience in allowing me to disappear every morning to do my writing. She even had to put up with me taking my personal computer on vacations. (I wrote early in the morning before we did anything). I told her it was fun to engage in the writing process. It was of course; writing becomes habitual, a way of discovering yourself as well as tell a story. Then too, my son Chris, an amazingly talented young writer without even trying, deserves some credit. What a creative gift for putting words together. Then too, there is my daughter Rachel and my oldest son, David. They do not live at home anymore, but they supported me in this effort and it was very encouraging.

Finally, I need to acknowledge my tribe. Much of my story originates out of my relationships within the community of Neah Bay where I spent my most significant years. And even though there is much sadness in the story I share, there is also pride of being part of a community that has withstood many forces for change. Much of what I have learned about life and the struggles we all face, comes from my interaction with the people of my hometown. They taught me great lessons and afforded me opportunity to serve; and I will always be grateful that God made me a part of them.

CHAPTER 1

Broken Parts, Missing Pieces

"This group wishes . . . to express their gratitude to you and your people for the help and assistance extended by Washington's founding fathers to the 3 survivors of Hojun-Maru.*"*
—Reiji Suzuki, Governor, Aichi Prefecture,
Japan, to the governor of the
State of Washington.
Oct. 11, 1991

It was November 3, 1832, with all hands on board that the fourteen-member crew of the *Hojun-Maru* cast off her lines and set sail from Nagoya into Toba port at the mouth of Ise Bay for Edo, or modern day Tokyo, with a load of rice and porcelain. The weather that day looked promising and the winds cooperative as the ship's sail filled to near capacity in the gentle sea breeze that would take them along the coast to their destination. As the vessel slowly maneuvered out of the bay onto open seas, moderate ocean swells caused it to gently pitch and roll to its rhythms. Meanwhile, all hands on board carried out their duties under the watchful eye of the captain. It was a good start to what would be a relatively short sail.

Somewhere, no doubt soon after their departure, the captain's attention was drawn to the horizon. In the distance, he could see the telltale signs of a storm brewing—maybe a typhoon. It looked as if they were in for a difficult sail. Already,

1

he could feel the wind quickening against his skin as he surveyed the ominous scene forming in the distance. Clouds were gathering on the horizon, and the frequency and size of the waves were beginning to increase in the stiffening wind. His crew, including two teenagers serving onboard as apprentices, could see the signs of deteriorating weather too. Soon, the captain was barking out orders to secure the cargo and anything else that could break loose in rough seas. He looked furtively to the rudder. Rudders of this type had a reputation for breaking loose in a storm. This one had better hold.

In the meanwhile, the youngest sailor aboard, a fourteen-year-old apprentice named Otokichi, looked anxiously in the direction of fellow teenager Kyukichi, who was fifteen. You could see the fear in their eyes. The mounting ferociousness of the seas and a darkening sky was like nothing they had ever experienced. Nevertheless, they did whatever they could to help the rest of the crew prepare the ship, as moment by moment, the seas grew angrier and the skies more threatening.

The helmsman, too, did his best to keep the ship at optimum position to deal with the large rollers now buffeting the ship. It was a near impossible task, though, as the mounting seas and frightening winds pushed the vessel in any direction they pleased. At some point, an especially large wave pushed hard against the side of the *Hojun-Maru*, causing it to lurch abruptly to one side. The helmsman struggled to hold onto the rudder, but the stress was too great. Above the din of the wind and waves crashing against its hull, a sickening crack could be heard. The rudder had broken loose and was now drifting off into the darkness of the storm.

For a moment, the captain braced himself against the railing in a desperate effort to assess the damage. A sickening feeling must have come over him as he watched what was left of the rudder clinging perilously to the stern of the ship. He knew what this meant, and so did the rest of the crew. They would no longer be able to hold a course and were at the mercy of the boisterous winds and tempestuous seas. They knew something else too. With the rudderless ship increasingly subject to hurricane-force winds and vicious seas on every side, everyone aboard probably would not survive. Some of them likely began to offer what prayers they could. Death at sea seemed their likely fate.

The storm seemed to last forever. When it finally subsided, the crew was exhausted but somehow still alive. And amazingly, their vessel with broken and missing pieces had managed to stay afloat. However, land was nowhere in sight. The captain had already concluded that they were in desperate circumstances. They had nothing aboard with which to fashion a makeshift rudder, and even the mast had broken off. Even more disturbing, unfavorable currents were pushing them further out to sea and away from their beloved homeland. The captain knew it was his responsibility to keep his ship afloat and his crew alive.

Under these circumstances the captain's first order of business must surely have been to inventory their supplies and develop a plan to survive, which meant rationing what food they had carried aboard and distilling water to drink—something they knew how to do. One good thing was that part of the cargo included a load of rice. However, beyond these immediate supplies, they had little else to balance their diets. They would have to make do with the food they had carried aboard and the rice they were transporting in order to have any chance for survival.

The first days of being stranded on the ocean on a vessel with broken and missing pieces are the most hopeful. Perhaps a passing ship will happen by. Or a favorable wind will begin to push the ship toward land. Maybe someone would even think of a creative way to fix the mast or figure out a way to direct the rudderless ship. However, with each passing day, the likelihood of any of these things happening grew increasingly dim. Meanwhile, the current was taking them farther and farther from home. And with it went the diminishing hopes of the crew of the *Hojun-Maru*.

Back at home, the vessel's owner, Juemon Higuchi, and the families of the missing sailors began a frantic search in every port where the vessel might have arrived. No one had seen or heard the fate of the *Hojun-Maru*. Eventually, the owner and families concluded that all had been lost at sea. A monument with the names of each sailor aboard the vessel was dedicated at Ryosan Buddhist Temple in Mihama, their hometown.

Meanwhile, the helpless sailors were trying to maintain some semblance of hope amid the desperate conditions they were experiencing, including having to endure more storms and trying to manage their health and that of their ship under duress. Their efforts surely had to have been courageous, but time and the vastness of the Pacific Ocean seemed to conspire against them. It was not long before the days turned into weeks and the weeks into months.

Before long, a new, more deadly problem began to affect the crew. Lacking vitamin C, a crucial component found in fruits and vegetables, their bodies began to deteriorate. Some began to lose their appetite and were becoming increasingly weak and listless. Others were complaining of blurred vision and of bleeding gums or recurring fever. It was only just the beginning. Irritability set in among some, and others began to feel paralysis coming on. The men were slowly dying of scurvy.

Most likely, the vessel had been at sea a long time before the first sailor died, followed by another and then another, including the captain. Finally, there were only Otokichi, Kyukichi, and Iwakichi left, the youngest members of the crew. But they were in trouble. Their scurvy-ravaged bodies were badly weakened and were literally on the brink of death like their disabled ship, which rolled and pitched and yawed its way 6,000 miles across the Pacific Ocean to a place that is now part of the coast of Washington State. The vessel had been adrift for fourteen months when the three survivors finally came ashore near a place known as Cape Alava, not far from the Native American village of Ozette. Ozette, at the time the *Hojun-Maru* crashed on its shores, was one of five native communities that make up a part of my heritage as a member of the Makah tribe.

When I was a child growing up at Neah Bay, the eventual home of the five original villages that now comprise my tribe, I had heard a brief mention of strangers who had landed among one of our villages. It had occurred so long before I was born that it seemed to have little relevance for me or my tribe. I promptly forgot who mentioned it or when or what might have happened to the strangers.

Then one day, many years later, while I was serving as the elected leader of my tribe, I returned to my office from a long week of meetings in Seattle. As I sat down to review a myriad of government documents, legal briefs, and an assortment of the daily stuff needed to provide direction for our tribal government, I was surprised to come across a stack of papers that was different from all the rest. Some of it had been written in Japanese. Why was it on my desk? What was it about? My administrative assistant had the answer. While I had been away on business, a delegation of distinguished Japanese businessmen had come to my office to pay their respects and to leave a narrative of an epic journey involving some of their countrymen aboard the vessel *Hojun-Maru*. A journey that had begun, as my reconstruction of events relates, in November of 1832, it was an incredible saga that had eventually ended up, just as I described, as a shipwreck on the beach near Cape Alava, the home of my Ozette cousins.

There was much more to the story than the narrative I created to describe their horrific drift across the Pacific. It turns out that my Ozette cousins' hospitality in nurturing the Japanese castaways back to health played a pivotal role in enabling all that would follow. The three survivors in turn would eventually play an important role in helping to shape the relationship of Japan with the west. There was a God aspect to the story as well that surprised me. Not long after they arrived in North America, the three shipwrecked sailors converted to Christianity and were instrumental in helping translate the first-ever portions of the Bible into the Japanese language. God, it turns out, was working behind the scenes of their tragic experiences and had taken the broken and missing pieces of their lives and transformed them into blessings. In the words of the late radio personality Paul Harvey, "Here is the rest of the story."

The documents the distinguished visitors from Japan left with me provided valuable information about the beginning of the journey and how these men, especially the teenager named Otokichi Yamamoto, became an especially important transitional figure in Japanese history. The narrative, however, afforded few details about what it must have been like when Otokichi and the others encountered my people. Using my imagination along with the information that the Japanese businessmen had left with me, I began to piece together what happened after they landed among my Ozette cousins.

My first thought is that it must have been a precarious landing for the survivors of the *Hojun-Maru*. The weather in early winter of 1834, when the vessel likely drifted onto the rocks near Ozette, must have made the final moments of the vessel terrifying. High winds, dangerous rock shoals, and heavy surf are a common occurrence along the coast during the winter months. It is not a place to attempt a safe landing in a storm even with the means to guide a ship.

Today, not much remains of the old village of Ozette where the survivors finally came ashore. Everything else though has remained pretty much the same—a lovely sand beach, jagged rock islands rising out of the sea, some with trees and various flora and fauna clinging tenaciously to their sides. For countless generations, they have offered both safe haven and hazard.

Then there were the people who lived there. At the time the *Hojun-Maru* landed near there, Ozette was the southern-most extension of the five Makah communities. And while Ozette is no longer inhabited, when the *Hojun-Maru* crashed on the shore, it was a vibrant community whose previous contact with foreigners had been sporadic but was becoming more frequent.

Imagining how it must have felt for these bedraggled and near-dead young men as they clung desperately to the broken pieces of what was left of their boat coming face to face with my ancestors calls to mind both terror and desperation. My people had a well-deserved reputation for their prowess as whale hunters and fierce warriors. The early English fur trader, John Meares, described an encounter with the Makahs in 1788. In his ship's log, he wrote, "Canoes came out from the island with twenty or thirty men in each who looked very savage, with painted faces and sea otter cloaks. They were armed with bows and arrows with barbed bone points and large spears pointed with mussel shell . . . ."

If Meare's account came any way near to describing the Ozettes when Otokichi and the two other survivors came ashore, they probably wished they had landed anywhere else, especially if they had known that my people had by now become increasingly suspicious of the number of foreigners sailing near their village. By this time, the Spanish, the Americans, and the English were regularly plying these waters in large boats; my people called the foreigners "Bu'buc'lids," or, "people who live on houses on the water." These early explorers were looking for trade goods and places to claim in the name of their respective countries. Their disregard for the indigenous people they encountered along the way often resulted in conflicts. My people, for example, successfully resisted Spanish efforts to settle near Neah Bay during the late eighteenth century. The Spanish explorers had selected a site near present-day Neah Bay to build a small fort, naming their new claim "Nunez Gaona" after a city in Spain. The resulting resistance by my people, however, caused the Spanish to give up their efforts and move on.

In this context, extending mercy to these survivors of the *Hojun-Maru* must have seemed to these men at the time as extraordinary good luck. Eventually, the weakened sailors began to recover as the Ozettes provided food, shelter, and clothing. Preserving their lives and nurturing them back to health would become the critical first link in the incredible legacy beginning to form around these young men who had survived such an amazing ordeal to become the first-ever Japanese to set foot on the North American continent. And this is what begins to set the stage for the remarkable events that unfolded.

According to the information provided, after the three sailors came ashore among my people, a man named John McLoughlin, who served as head of the Hudson Bay Trading Company at Fort Vancouver near the Columbia River, had gotten word of foreigners taken in by my tribe. He soon dispatched a ship for Ozette to negotiate their release. After some discussion with the Ozette leaders, the three Japanese sailors were turned over to the ship's captain and taken to Fort Vancouver. There, the young men came under the tutelage of a Methodist missionary, Reverend Cyrus Shepherd, who not only began teaching them English but shared with them the Gospel as well.

Believing that they had been spared during their horrific journey across the ocean, they professed faith in Christ. It was now November of 1834, nearly two years since their ordeal had begun.

Apparently hoping the three sailors might be useful in helping to forge some kind of trade agreement between England and Japan, McLoughlin eventually arranged transport for them to London. Soon, the three young men were aboard the brig *The Eagle* and on their way to the Sandwich Islands (Hawaii). From there they journeyed around the tip of Cape Horn, South America, to London, where they arrived in June of 1835. It turned out that the British government had little interest in a trade agreement with Japan, at least not then. In any case, even if they had, the chances of arranging one were slim to none. That is because, in accordance with the Shogun Tokugawa's policies, Japan was a closed country to all foreigners. This exclusion policy extended to the growing number of Japanese sailors who had, for whatever reason, been stranded in foreign lands.

Intending nevertheless to have the three sailors repatriated to their homeland, the British government arranged to have the men board the British naval vessel *General Palmer*, which would take them to Macao, near Hong Kong, where the British had government offices and where they would more likely find passage home. The three arrived there in December of 1835, a little more than three years since their adventure began.

Once the three sailors arrived in Macao, they were introduced to the Reverend Doctor Karl A. Gutzlaf, a German-born missionary working in the British office as a translator. Gutzlaf was pleased to hear that the men had converted to Christianity and relished the opportunity to learn Japanese from them. Meanwhile, Gutzlaf's wife taught English to the academically inquisitive Otokichi. Once more, God's grace began to be revealed in their circumstances.

Convinced that it was possible to spread the Gospel to the Japanese through tracts, Gutzlaf soon engaged the three sailors in a yearlong project to help him translate the Gospel of John and John's Epistles into Japanese. Their successful efforts resulted in the first-ever translation of God's Word into the Japanese language (May 1837). The completed manuscripts were sent to a Christian printing firm in Singapore and published.

By then, it had been almost five years since the *Hojun-Maru* had been caught in the typhoon that had begun their long trek across the Pacific and eventually around the world. The long-lost sailors were growing increasingly anxious to return home. They were not alone in this. While in Macao, the three young men had occasion to become acquainted with four other Japanese sailors similarly stranded. Together, all seven men began to work out a plan to address their predicament. Then came an opportunity. An American entrepreneur, Mr. Charles King, who was also a fervent supporter of Christian mission, had heard of their incredible ordeal. Seeing an opportunity to accomplish Christian mission through their testimony and the possible expansion of his business empire, Mr. King worked out a plan to repatriate the castaways by having them accompany his sailing ship to Japan.

Soon, all seven, no doubt joyously happy men, were boarding the vessel *The Morrison* and on their way home to finally be reunited with their loved ones. Or so they thought. According to the narrative left with me, on July 30, 1837, as *The Morrison* entered the bay near the port of Edo, the long-lost sailors were greeted not with the happy sounds of welcome but by the angry retort of cannon fire warning them not to come any closer. They were forbidden from entering the harbor! Not even with Japanese sailors aboard. Several other ports were attempted as well with similar results.

Discouraged, the captain turned the vessel around and sailed back to Macao. The firing on the *The Morrison* became known as "The Morrison Incident" and was one of a growing number of similar incidences that would serve as an important catalyst leading Japan to eventually open up to western countries. That would come a few years later. Not, however, in time for these men.

It is impossible to imagine the awful disappointment these sailors must have felt as their beloved homeland slipped once more out of sight. They had endured unbelievable hardship and traveled much of the world in their efforts to be reunited with their families, only to come so close and then to be prevented from returning. They had become men without a country.

At this point, the story is less clear in regard to two of the sailors, Iwakichi and Kyukichi. However, Otokichi would soon become a transitional figure in Japanese and English history. God was about to turn his tragedies into blessings. The story continues as follows.

Along with some of his fellow Japanese countrymen similarly prevented from returning home, Otokichi devised a strategy to change the situation. Their hard work in due course helped to eventually turn the tide of Japanese exclusion policies. In the meanwhile, Otokichi acquired English citizenship, married an English woman, and changed his name to John W. Ottoson. After his English wife died, he married a Malay woman and moved to Singapore. There, while working as an interpreter for the British Navy, he began to play a crucial role in the negotiations leading to the first-ever treaty between the English and Japan. Ironically, it was during those negotiations that he was able to gain re-entry into Japan, but only by passing himself off as Chinese. By now, however, he had established another life for himself in another land.

It was during this time of negotiation, facilitated in part by Otokichi, that Japan finally ended its isolation policies, particularly following the 1853–54 visits of U.S. Commodore Matthew C. Perry and his fleet. However, part of Japan's openness to change was due in large part to the key role Otokichi played as an interpreter for the English and as a strategist assisting other

Japanese sailors seeking repatriation to their homeland. Thus Otokichi, the shipwrecked sailor taken in by my ancestors who eventually became a Christian and helped translate the Bible into the Japanese language, became a transitional figure in history. He was still living in Singapore when he died on January 18, 1867. Before his death, he encouraged his oldest son, John W. Ottoson, Jr., to return to his homeland. John Jr. followed his father's advice, arriving in Yokahama in 1879 where he applied for and was granted citizenship.

The story of the *Hojun-Maru* has been little known throughout much of history. In recent years, however, it has taken on a new life and has inspired the Japanese to recognize the unique contributions the three sailors have made to their history, including the translation of the Word of God into their own language for the first time. It has also helped inspire modern-day Japanese efforts to encourage good will with the nations touched by the three castaway sailors including the United States, England, Malaysia, and even my tribe. However, it is most importantly the story of God's grace at work behind the scenes of history in taking tragedy, disappointment and seeming failure—the broken and missing pieces of life—and turning them into light and hope. He even used my people, primitive by Japanese standards, to keep them alive and enable all that happened next. God is always at work behind the tumultuous and sometimes tragic events of history to bring blessing out of human suffering and pain, often through the most unusual and surprising ways. I have personal experience with this.

This unusual story of tragedy turned into blessing is, in some ways, my own story. I, too, needed God to take the broken and missing pieces of my life and transform them for His good purposes. And this I needed, in part, because of what happened to my people in the succeeding years as their world was impacted by a storm of another sort that would leave them and succeeding generations adrift on a sea of change with broken and missing pieces. And just as three men and their broken boat were used of God to influence the history of Japanese and western cultures, three men and their broken car would eventually have a profound influence on mine.

CHAPTER 2

Three Men and a Car

<=eee=>

You are not an Indian if you have never owned an Indian car!
Everybody knows what I am talking about—one snow tire on
the front, a radial on the other and two different tires on the
back. The lights only work on dim, your antenna broke off, so
you replaced it with a coat hanger.

—Author unknown

It hardly seems possible that little more than one hundred years had passed from the time the *Hojun-Maru* had crashed on the shores of Ozette and my birth. A lot had changed for my people in that short time—most noticeably, our former way of life. The reason for this was that the same ocean that had brought the three Japanese sailors to our shores brought a host of foreigners from far-off lands. They eventually came in sufficient numbers to claim our lands and change our way of life. The five villages, each with its own head chief and sub-chiefs, were soon confined to one. Ozette had by now been abandoned.

Compounding our problems was the fact that we were forced to become dependent on the care of the U.S. government, which had eventually established control of the region from the Spanish and English. Taken as a whole, the rapid nature of the forced dependency and the changes that ensued had the effect of leaving us rudderless and adrift on a stormy sea of anxieties with broken and missing pieces. And like the crew of the *Hojun-Maru*, we were without adequate means of support necessary to sustain us during our transition to a new reality. Unable to process our losses effectively, we became less healthy. By the time I was growing up on the Makah Indian Reservation, many of our people were engaged in frequent drinking binges, our traditional family system was in disarray, sickness and premature death had ravaged our community, and poverty was the norm. Some in our community had responded by becoming Christians. I was one of them. What I did not understand when I first became a believer in Jesus was the extent of the deeply rooted traumas my people had endured or how these are passed from one generation to the next with tragic consequences. In my case, it affected my ability to trust God, something He would reveal to me only through time and circumstances.

I especially recall an unusual encounter with three Northern Cheyenne men and their broken car. God used these least-likely men from a very different Native American tradition to reveal a part of my life I never understood and an aspect of His grace in bringing healing and transformation to people who, like me, grow up with broken and missing pieces.

I first met these men as a young seminary student. At the time, I had just completed my second year of school. As part of my training, I had been assigned to a one-year internship in a little town called Colstrip. Located in Southeast Montana, the town was not along your way to many places. You had to intentionally want to go there to get there. An arrangement between the Lutheran church in the nearby town of Forsyth and the mining company that owned Colstrip enabled me to live in a single-story house. In exchange for the home, I was assigned to serve the small community church in the town. Following each service, I would leave immediately to drive 50 miles west to the town of Hysham where I would preach once more to a small gathering of Lutherans. During the rest of the week, I was free to make contact with the nearby Northern Cheyenne and do whatever ministry I could.

The late August sun shone brightly on the day I drove into Colstrip for the first time past the little public school located just off the highway. Except for a couple of teenage boys playing basketball on a small paved courtyard adjacent the school, the sparsely populated town seemed abandoned.

Down the street a block or two was the house I had been provided. Surrounded by an old fence, it had the appearance of all the other little homes in the community except for this: no one had lived in it for at least a decade, and it obviously needed tender, loving care, something far from my mind as I pulled up next to the fence and parked my car. As I stepped cautiously through the gate and onto an old and worn sidewalk leading up to the porch, I felt the same tinge of anxiety I always felt when facing the unfamiliar.

Ever cautious when faced with something new, I put one foot slowly in front of the other as I gingerly made my way up the steps to the front door. Fumbling with the key my supervising pastor had provided me, I finally managed to insert it into the old door lock. Entering the living room incited a range of emotions like despair and dislike. I was momentarily struck by its barren appearance and the musty smell of a long-vacant building. Except for the lone fly buzzing around the room, there were few signs of life. Not recent life, anyway, as its only obvious furnishings were a single table, some chairs, and a pile of dust that had settled into the shape of a couch. Naturally, I wanted to turn around, walk out the door, get into my car, and continue my life in some other town.

Instead, I mustered enough courage to check out the rest of the house. I began with the bedroom. It was dark and dingy with little light coming through shaded windows. The queen-size mattress and bedsprings, pushed up against the wall, had to be early twentieth century. Of course, I had to try it out to get a feel for what the next 365 nights would be like. I stretched full out on the mattress. Then I rolled onto my side. My initial assessment was not good. The old mattress, with steel-coil springs, sank unevenly with my every move. Worse, every time I changed positions, the bedsprings made a creaking sound.

Next door to the bedroom was a small bathroom with dripping faucet, rust-stained washbasin, and an ancient, discolored porcelain tub on four legs set on worn wood flooring. Imagining a bath in that tub was more than a little repulsive. I would have to improvise if I wanted to turn it into a shower.

My next stop was the furnace room located in the basement. The stairway looked like something out of an Alfred Hitchcock movie. It was dark and musty with cobwebs hanging from the support beams, a place that quite obviously was rarely visited. I knew immediately I was going to dread having to attend to the coal furnace. My supervising pastor had casually mentioned that the house was heated by coal and that I would need to learn how to operate it. Then he added, with a mischievous look, "Montana winters can get pretty cold." Meaning I had better learn fast. Viewing for the first time a coal-fired furnace was an education. The firebox, located at the base of the stairway, looked hideous. It really was not. That was just my state of mind at the time. Upon closer evaluation, I could see that it was fed by an augur system. I would learn soon enough that the augur would need regular feeding and that the furnace would require daily maintenance, things like emptying it of any burned-out coal residue called "clinkers." Failure to do so would mean a cold house. A coal bin was located in the back of the house. The company that owned the town would fill it as needed for a small fee.

Having seen enough, I made my way back into the living room and collapsed onto the old couch. Alone and feeling sorry for myself amid a cloud of dust settling around me, I remember thinking, "This is just great! It's only my first day, and I am going to have to spend a whole year of my life here!"

It was just then that my miserable musings were suddenly interrupted by a gentle knock on the door. Standing there, hands extended in friendship, was a young couple with two small children in tow. They had come by to welcome me to Colstrip. Fairly new residents in the town themselves, Mike and Judy Hayworth and another couple, Dale and Phyllis Olson, whom I would meet later, were pleased that I would soon be holding services in the community church. Theirs was one of many lasting friendships in Colstrip that would sustain me during my year of internship.

What made their friendship and that of others I would meet seem ironic was that as a Native American, I could have expected prejudice instead of friendship. A few of the long-time residents in the area had formed negative opinions about the Indians who lived in Lame Deer, twenty miles to the south. Much of their prejudice stemmed from the affects of the alcoholism they observed among so many of the native people. There were other factors entering into their opinions as well. Some of them had derived from memories of long-ago conflicts between the Northern Cheyenne and the U.S. government back in the 1870s. One historical event above all others stood out in that part of Montana: the demise of Colonel George Armstrong Custer and the men of the 7th Calvary who, on June 25 of 1876, attacked a large encampment of mainly Sioux and Cheyenne. Custer and his men, as history books relate, were subsequently annihilated along the Little Big Horn River, not much more than an hour's drive from Colstrip. The battle was a great victory for the Sioux and the Northern Cheyenne. However, it also marked the beginning of the end of effective Indian resistance to the inevitable onslaught of immigrants and soldiers who came in large numbers to claim their territories for themselves.

Like a festering wound that would not heal, the memories of these bitter encounters were still remembered by the Cheyenne. More problematic, however, was the government-imposed reservation system. Coupled with all of the injustices, broken treaties, and the like that the Cheyenne had endured at the hands of the government, the reservation system and the forced dependency that went along with it not only added to their problems, but they insured that the Northern Cheyenne would lack sufficient resources and creative energies to deal with their mounting stresses. Because the "reservation" system was a form of forced containment, I have come to dislike the term as applied to Native American communities.

By the time I arrived on the scene, poverty and general hopelessness prevailed along with a whole host of consequences that were handed down from one generation to the next. It was the same story for many Native American communities across North America. All of them were faced with government-imposed polices intended to take their lands, coerce change, and force dependence. The typical response was bitterness and a deepening sense of despair. Alcohol eventually became for many a way of escape. So desperate were their circumstances and their prospects for recovery so bleak, L. Frank Baum, the author of *The Wizard of Oz*, openly endorsed genocide. In an 1890 Aberdeen, South Dakota, newspaper editorial, he wrote, "The whites, by law of conquest and by justice of civilization, are master of the American Continent, and the best safety of the frontier settlements will be secured by the total annihilation of the few remaining Indians."[1] It was a sentiment held by many. No one, it seemed, wanted to address the terrible consequences caused by injustices Indian tribes had

---

[1]   L. Frank Baum, *Aberdeen* (SD) *Saturday Pioneer*, December 20, 1890, quoted in *One Church Many Tribes*, 38-39

endured during America's formative years. Compounding the problems were the purveyors of alcohol who were driven by greed to take advantage of Native Americans' increasingly desperate circumstances.

In the years that followed the imposition of the reservation system, it soon became common practice for liquor establishments to locate near reservations. It enabled their owners to take advantage of the power of addictions for personal profit. I was not surprised shortly after my arrival in Colstrip to come across an establishment known as Jim Town.

Jim Town tavern was along my route to Lame Deer. Still there today, it looks to have undergone a makeover and may have new owners and a new purpose. However, when I first saw its hideous form emerging in the distance years ago, I barely noted the tavern. My attention was drawn instead to an enormous pile of debris nearly dwarfing the ramshackle wooden structure. I remember thinking, "What is this? A garbage dump next to a building?" As my car drew closer, I realized to my amazement and dismay that the giant debris pile dwarfing the tavern was made up of empty beer and whisky bottles and cans of every brand piled one on another to form a great mountain! It was a sinister monument to the power of human addiction. I thought at the time that it seemed criminal to cater to the addictions of the people, and then, to further abuse them by discarding thousands of empties for everyone to see. However, because Jim Town stood just off the reservation line, it was not illegal. And while I was shocked to see the magnitude of the mountainous pile of empties, I was not surprised. Years later, while in a twin-engine Navajo Chieftain flown by one of my staff serving the Lutheran Association of Missionaries and Pilots U.S., we flew over a tavern located on a remote part of the Alaska Yukon River. Amazingly, the liquor establishment did not have road access. How and why did it get there? My pilot, Dan Treakle, explained that it had been set on a barge and had been floated to its location *to service isolated Alaska native people* living along the river.

Almost always, things like murder, suicide, fractured families, spousal and child sexual abuse, deadly car and boating accidents, drowning, and much more have been attributed in some way to alcohol sold in places like these. Still naïve in my understandings of human response to trauma, I wondered to myself, "How had our Indian people come to this?" I was about to discover a clue that would begin to answer my question.

One bright October morning, I had driven past Jim Town tavern and into Lame Deer as usual. I was two months into my assignment and had gotten over the initial shock I felt when I first spotted the enormous pile of empties. By now, I had become acquainted with some members of the Northern Cheyenne Christian community. I was pleased to see how many of them were seeking to better their community in their roles as tribal leaders, health care workers, and teachers. I was privileged to get to know some of them as my friends. They were part of a courageous group of native men and women who had risen above their circumstances and were attempting to help their people achieve the same.

But on this particular day as I was driving through the community of Lame Deer, past substandard, government-built houses and a few small cabins, I spotted three men standing next to an old cabin, chopping wood and engaged in conversation. The fact that I was driving too slowly along the potholed street in front of their home and looking directly at them caught their attention. One of the men waved me over with a sweeping gesture. I thought, "Great, this will be a good opportunity to share my faith." After carefully maneuvering my recently washed, four-door, black-and-white Ford to a wide place on the side of the road not far from their cabin, I slowly exited the car, all the while studying the men carefully to determine what kind of situation I was about to enter.

The three men looked to be in their late twenties or thirties, although hard living had made them appear older. As I drew closer, I sensed immediately that these guys were down-on-their-luck types. Still, they appeared friendly enough. After gingerly stepping around some old car parts, piles of firewood strewn here and there, and an assortment of empty beer cans, I managed to make it to where they were standing. After we exchanged names, they asked me where I lived. "Colstrip," I answered. With a great look of surprise, one of the men blurted out, "Colstrip? Indians aren't welcome there!" They looked at one another other in seemingly shocked disbelief as I explained that people there not only welcomed me, but in fact, some had become my good friends. They were not very convinced.

After more small talk, one of them invited me into their 30 by 20 foot home. It barely qualified as a house. Its worn siding and rough-hewn appearance was better suited for some wilderness setting, maybe as a hunting cabin, not permanent residency. But I was not the least bit hesitant in accepting their invitation. Having grown up on a reservation, I had been in many substandard homes. Some of my boyhood friends lived in structures that were little more than single-room shacks. They were typically small, and had little in the way of furniture, almost no amenities, and lots of clothes piled on couches and beds. The interior of this one was much like that, consisting of a kitchen and a dining/living room combination, with a place for sleeping-all in one room. A wood stove on one end of the cabin provided heat. It may have had a sink and running water, but not much else. A dingy wood table, pockmarked and un-painted, surrounded by four wooden chairs, a cot for sleeping, and an old couch like the one I had in Colstrip made up the rest of the home's furnishings. There was one other detail: a slightly askew picture of President John F. Kennedy hanging on one wall. Kennedy, during his brief presidency, had endeared himself to many Native Americans, and over the years, I had seen his picture on the walls of some of their homes.

One of the men offered me a chair, and I sat down with them around their small table. Before I could begin to tell them that I was studying to become a pastor, one of the other men hauled out a cheap bottle of whisky from somewhere and began passing it around. When it came around to me, I panicked, choking out something like, "I'm a student preparing for ministry. I don't drink." Their bewildered stares caused me to quickly add, "My father was an alcoholic and almost died in a car accident." I proceeded to explain how my alcoholic father had nearly been killed on his way home from Jack's Place, our version of Jim Town. After all the many years since it happened, I still had vivid memories of the time it occurred. He had just made "a run" to Jack's Place and had been drinking when he drove his truck off the narrow coastal road that straddles the Strait of Juan de Fuca and down a steep embankment through some brush. The truck rolled over and finally came to rest on its side, perched precariously above the ocean. His passenger, a young woman from our community, was killed. Had the vehicle rolled one more time, it would have tumbled into the sea, and my father would surely have drowned. Instead, he suffered leg and back injuries that troubled him throughout the rest of his life.

My story caught them off guard. For a moment, however brief, we were alike. The account about my father's alcoholism and near-death experience was the bridge between our up-to-now very different worlds. This conversation opened the door for me to witness boldly about my faith in Jesus. I shared with them my life on the reservation and expanded on my father's alcoholism and how it nearly destroyed our family. Then I related how Jesus had come into my life and why I was studying for the ministry. They listened politely and even affirmed that they had nothing against the Christian faith. One of the men even acknowledged that one of his family members was a "Reverend."

Then I shared how important it was for them to receive the free gift of salvation through Jesus before it was too late. Anxious to drive my point home and close the deal, I said, "You guys are living on the dangerous edge. You, too, might have an accident and die before you know Jesus as your Savior. You would have to face eternity alone."

That is all it took. Suddenly they were sharing stories of near-death encounters. It was almost as if they were trying to one-up each other with, "My story is better than yours." Finally, one of them, a man named Medaris Bad Horse, had had enough. With a deliberate sweep of his right hand, he reached down and pulled his shirt out of his faded jeans to reveal a six-inch scar across his belly. "You see this? I got this in a bar fight. I almost died." For a moment, we all sat there in silence, looking past each other. No one could top that.

My point had been illustrated. They were living risky lives. There was nothing more I could say. This presented a good opportunity for me to get up and leave. As I slowly rose from my chair, one of the men, conferring on me a designation I had not yet earned, said, "Say Reverend, can you help us with our car?" Somewhere in the part of the brain where we have our personal security system, caution lights started to blink. A small voice started saying, "Don't do it. Don't do it." I started to break out in a cold sweat. I wanted to make up something clever like, "Sorry, but I am late for an appointment." Unfortunately, I could not think that fast.

Caught between a feeling of obligation and common sense, I drew myself deeper into commitment by asking, "What kind of help do you need?" One of the men said their car had a flat tire and asked if I could give them a ride to its location so they could fix it. Once more overriding my intuition, I invited myself further into obligation by asking, "Where is your car?" Without hesitation, and in unison, they announced, "Oh, it is just a little way down the road." When I asked, "How far down the road?" they said, "Oh, not far."

Full of growing uncertainty concerning the wisdom of all this and by no means assured by their "Oh, not far," I nevertheless found myself agreeing to take them to their car. I remember thinking to myself, "What would Jesus do?" After all, I had just witnessed to them of His love, and they had been most cordial and respectful. Then another voice said, "Do you know what you are getting yourself into? You are about to make a big mistake!" Suspended somewhere between common sense and moral duty, I suspected I was about to enter the twilight zone—a new and unpredictable adventure with a questionable outcome!

For their part, my new acquaintances were ecstatic. That they were acting as if they had just won the lottery did little to relieve my stress! The next thing I knew, they were busily piling tools, an old spare tire, and some assorted things into the trunk of my car. They were giddy with excitement—bordering on joy—a reaction I could not help but find troubling. No doubt sensing my mounting anxiety and fearing I might change my mind, they quickly piled into my car, all the while laughing and exhorting me onward. Actually, there was another underlying feeling for my anxiety. My car was not really "my car." It belonged to the Lutheran church in Forsyth, Montana, and had been provided for my use during my internship. Aware of my responsibility, I was always careful to maintain it well. I did not mind that. I had always been the type to keep things orderly and clean. It was how I was raised. Order and cleanliness made me feel better.

Soon, we were winding our way on a paved road through Lame Deer when one of the men said, "Turn off here." I hesitated for a moment but did so anyway. Suddenly we were driving off road into the hills behind the town on what seemed more like a wagon trail than a road. Sweat now visibly pouring down my brow, my heart beating ever faster, and the stress surely evident, I nervously asked again, "How far did you guys say we have to go?" Once more in unison, their reply was, "Oh, not much farther."

Then just up ahead, an enormous puddle of water covered the road. "Hey, there's a large puddle!" I yelled. Just as quickly, their retort: "Step on it! You can make it!" My mind fighting panic, I pushed the accelerator hard to the floor. They roared in laughter as my car sped through the puddle, splattering mud and water in a wide swath on either side of the road. I so wanted to be free of these guys, to return to the safe and sane where everything was predictable. But then appeared another puddle and more encouragement, coupled with another furious acceleration and accompanying wide swath of water—all to the great amusement and laughter of my new friends.

I cannot remember how many puddles we drove through that day or how much time had elapsed. It seemed like hours, but in reality, it probably was not more than a half hour. Finally we rounded a bend, crossed over a small rise, and dead ahead, a car came into view. Or was it a car? As I approached the vehicle, I could hardly believe my eyes or contain my laughter. What they called their "car" looked like something out of a combat zone. The thing had obviously been scorched in a fire. There was no hood over the engine compartment. There were dents here and there. The left rear tire was shredded, the rim distorted from having been driven on for a while.

When I parked my car and walked over to where I could examine it more closely, I could see that fire had not only scorched the exterior, it had destroyed most of the upholstery as well. You could see through the floor to the road in some places. Some of the plastic was melted on the dash. Several side windows were missing. Caught up in the bizarre spectacle before me, I started to laugh to myself. Meanwhile, they were dead-pan serious. Unable to contain my disbelief, I wondered aloud, "Where did you guys get this?" Looking at me as if I were admiring some expensive classic car they had restored, they proudly explained the obvious. The car had indeed been in a fire and had once been the property of the U.S. Bureau of Indian Affairs. After the fire had nearly destroyed it, the government had intended simply to junk it. But Medaris had asked and was given permission to take it off their hands. Then the men declared proudly, "Medaris got it running. Medaris can fix anything!"

Their brief explanation ended, the men quickly went to work. Taking a rim and tire they had scavenged from their front yard, they somehow managed to make it fit their car. Then they went to work on the engine. I watched, transfixed, all the while keeping my distance as they sprayed igniting fluid into the carburetor. I wasn't sure if the thing would somehow blow up or not. Obviously, I did not have the slightest confidence they would get the engine started. But when one of them turned the key in the ignition, the car groaned and sputtered and backfired. And then, to my absolute amazement, the car wheezed and popped one more time and sputtered to life!

Realizing that this afforded me a great opportunity to escape my circumstances, I said something insincere like, "Hey, way to go guys. I have to get going now." But then one of them said, "Follow us home, preacher, just in case something happens."

Reluctant but realizing it was the right thing to do under the circumstances, I followed them back. Down and around hills, through puddles and around twisting bends, I followed them all the way to Lame Deer and pavement. I prayed the entire way, "God, please keep their car going."

Once we hit the main road, it was my turn to be ecstatic. My ordeal was finally over. Even though my car was covered in mud, I could wash it. I waved farewell to them as I drove down the road to civilization. As I approached Colstrip, I was thinking I'd likely never run into these guys again or remember the day we met. And in my mind, that was a good thing.

One week later, as I was reading a local newspaper, I noticed on the back page, in an obscure section, a fatality notice. It was for Medaris, the man with the knife scar on his belly, the man who could fix anything; he had been killed in a car accident. I sat in momentary shock, overwhelmed by feelings of discouragement.

Later, as I thought more about the whole incident, I despaired of entering the ministry. I realized that Medaris and his friends were the type of people I would most likely encounter in my future ministry. Thinking the task was mission impossible, I began to contemplate whether or not I should return to the seminary. And more troubling, I began doubting God's will to fix the most broken of people, those with addictions and broken families, the very people I thought He had called me to serve.

Then one day, something came over me. It was as if I received a message from God in the deepest recesses of my being—call it a divine impression. The message went something like this: "Don, do you remember those three men in Montana and their broken car that had been places and experienced things it never should have?" In my mind I thought, "Yes, Lord, how could I forget that?" Then it seemed as if He said, "Do you know why I permitted you to have that experience?" My immediate response was, "You wanted me to learn not to foolishly accompany alcoholic men into off-road places." Then I received this impression: "Don, I allowed you this experience not only to illustrate the brokenness of the lives of these men but their car too. Their car had been places and experienced things it should not have just as they had. And yet Medaris was able to take what you thought was beyond repair and fix it! You doubted him then, and now you doubt My will to fix the most broken and bruised of people. You have even begun to question entering the ministry. The truth is, you are just like those men and their broken car, and I have been fixing you your entire life. I can fix anyone."

The thought startled me. How was it possible that I was "just like these men and their broken car?" And that God had been fixing me all my life? These haunting questions led me to begin a process of rediscovery of my family and generational history for clues. And in the process, I began discovering His grace at work in uncovering and fixing the broken and missing pieces of my life.

What I discovered astounded me.

CHAPTER 3

Generation to Generation

———————— ⌖ ————————

*Not to know what took place before you were born is to remain
forever a child.*

—Cicero, Roman philosopher,
statesman, 106 B.C.

A t the time I met the three Cheyenne men and their broken
car, I thought of myself as a "together kind of guy." So
why was God telling me I was like them and their car? And
how could it be that for my whole life He had been working to
fix me? Or that it might be a lifelong process? I knew that part
of the answer lay somewhere in my generational history, which
was complex at best.

To better understand it, I began putting together a "geno-
gram," a process for mapping out one's family tree with special attention to any traumas my parents or relatives may have
experienced—things like the death of a child or a spouse, divorce, alcoholism, abuse, abandonment and loss of dreams. I
first learned of this approach to discovery from reading Erich
Friedmann's book *Generation to Generation*.[2] As I began to map
out my family history (I often consulted with relatives for information), I assigned various symbols to each family member
to represent different kinds of trauma. As the picture of my

---

[2]   Friedman, *Generation to Generation*, 34.

family's history began unfolding, it dawned on me that my entire family, on both sides, had experienced many traumas in a short period. One misfortune seemed to have triggered another, affecting a whole line of descendants. As the picture started to form, I could understand why my history did not favor my conversion to Christianity. Using an analogy from Jesus' parable of the sower and the seed, the soil of my generational heritage was hard, rocky ground with lots of thorns and thistles.

My research eventually took me back to my tribal roots on the northwestern-most end of the continental United States, a land of magnificent rock formations rising out of the sea, long stretches of gorgeous sand beaches, and miles of dense forest and mountains that end abruptly where the pounding ocean surf meets the shore. Before my tribe came to be known as the Makah, my people called themselves the *Qwidicaat*—"the people who live at the end of the land." It is not hard to see how they came up with this name. A short hike along a well-maintained trail leading to what is today called Cape Flattery reveals a wondrous, if not breathtaking, view.

Standing on a wooden viewing platform set on a rock ledge jutting out into the sea, Cape Flattery is the northwestern-most point of the continental United States. Less than a half mile away, at the place where the ocean meets the Strait of Juan de Fuca, is the near-barren, fourteen-acre rock island known as Tatoosh. Right in the middle of the desolate little island is a lighthouse, a lonely sentinel for safety, providing warning to approaching ships of potential danger if they wander too close to the rocky coastline. Nearby, sea birds of all kinds cavort in the ocean waves; others can be seen diving here and there for herring or some other fish. Further in the distance, and barely visible to the untrained eye, sea lions lie motionless on smaller rocks protruding out of the sea.

"The people at the end of the land" where the seabirds gather have lived in this place for thousands of years. Eventually, my people became known as the Makah. This name conveyed hospitality, as in providing an abundance of food for our guests. You need only visit during a potlatch "give-away" ceremony to see the appropriateness of this name. At such ceremonies, food and gifts are lavished upon the guests as a way of thanking them for coming to the community to help celebrate the occasion.

Life in these communities had remained undisturbed for most of the thousands of years of our existence in these parts. People were relatively healthy, prosperous, and stable up to and after the time the *Hojun-Maru* crashed on the shores of Cape Alava. However, in 1855, all of this began to change when America's territorial expansion claims finally caught up with my ancestors and they were forced to sign a single treaty relinquishing most of their land claims to the United States. The terms of the treaty were relayed to my people by a non-Makah-speaking interpreter employing a trade language called "Chinook jargon." Its limited vocabulary was useful in trade between tribes but totally inadequate for explaining complex legal terms like "the tribe agrees to relinquish [their land]" or sharing resources "in common with the citizens of the rest of the territory."[3]

Tribal leaders agreed to affix their *X* alongside their names only when they thought they had assurances that they could preserve their traditional way of life. They were especially anxious to preserve the freedom to hunt the great whales and other sea mammals that played such a significant part in the culture and also provided food for the community. Led by Territorial Governor Isaac Stevens, the government negotiators assured

---

[3] Treaty between the Makah Tribe of Indians and the United States of America January 31, 1855

them they could do so and allowed the provision for whale hunting to be included in the treaty language. However, they were anything but transparent in dealing with the Makah. The treaty was actually a surrender document intended to secure the lands claimed by the tribes and to create perpetual dependency on the government. Even the whaling provision was eventually ignored when the government forbade the taking of whales at the beginning of the twentieth century.

The treaty and subsequent efforts to enforce its terms began a process of rapid change and the systematic disintegration of the Makah way of life. Soon, longhouse communal living gave way to single family dwellings as directed by the government agent assigned to the community. The introduction of money for things like guns, sugar, and flour changed the economy from subsistence to acquisition, and this led to addictions to new kinds of food and other health problems never previously known. Diseases they had never been exposed to, like small pox and measles, began to ravage the community, resulting in many deaths and the creation of mass burial grounds that exist in the community today.

Eventually, all the villages relocated to Neah Bay, either to be near the trade store or to enable kids to attend school as required by the government. Forcing children to attend residential school was intended to teach the children to be civilized and to break them from their parents' traditions. It did all of this over time, but it also contributed to the disintegration of the family.

To insure further dependence, Indian tribes were assigned a government official known as an "Indian Agent." These representatives of the government were assigned to the tribes to oversee all their affairs. Those assigned to our tribe soon began instituting specific cultural prohibitions and requirements. Men, for example, were discouraged from wearing blankets; failure to carry groceries for their wives after shopping at the local trade store could result in a fine of ten cents. The tribe was also prevented from celebrating the potlatch, a give-away feast and a vital part of the tribe's cultural expressions. The limits of the Makah land base under the treaty meant former hunting grounds were lost. A people who had once been rich in natural resources were eventually stripped of their way of life, their wealth, their health, and their traditional songs, all the while being made to become more dependent on the government. All of this was especially hard on the men, who no longer could provide for their families.

Dependency-creating policies like those imposed on Native Americans exact their own deadly toll. They erode self-determination, tend to destroy initiative, kill spontaneity, and have a cumulative effect of suppressing the overall ability of people to creatively solve their problems.

Overwhelmed by these sudden forces of change, my people began to grieve their losses. Like Jesus' reference to "a house swept clean" in Luke 11:21–26 and Matthew 12:43–45, we also became increasingly susceptible to dark and disruptive spiritual forces that entered in to create further havoc and destruction. Our house of core values and the traditions that once served to guard our way of life had been brutally attacked, leaving a vacuum for demonic influences. Grief at our mounting losses was soon accompanied by alcoholism and despair. The consequences of all that my people had endured were passed on from one generation to the next, and that part of my tribe's history and its influence on me were part of the person God saw when He assessed the broken and missing pieces of my life.

Many of these radical changes had occurred roughly over ninety years, less than three generations before I was born. One might think we would have gotten over our sense of loss and moved on with life. After all, setting aside the past and moving on with life is deeply rooted in the American ideal. But in reality, the unresolved disappointments, indictments, and abandonment that any people group or individual experiences in one generation are more often than not passed on to the next through a complex process of transference of anxieties.[4] I suspect this process of transmission of unresolved anxieties from one generation to the next is not only true for families but communities, churches, and even nations like our own. Each has its own history of disturbance of one kind or another and susceptibility to the consequences of unresolved traumas and rapid change. Hence the wisdom of Cicero uttered many years earlier: "Not to know what happened before you were born is to forever remain a child."

My family history is evidence of this phenomenon. As I began to uncover it, I recalled a particularly painful family trauma that had an important influence on me and the rest of my family. One day when I was a small boy, my mother made an offhand comment about my grandmother's death at the hands of a young, evidently inexperienced intern doctor the government had assigned to our community. As she began to relate this story, I could see her demeanor change. She was grieving and seemed to be reaching out to me for emotional support. Sensing that she was drawing me into a deeply painful place, I became ill at ease. She must have noticed this and abruptly ended our discussion; I quickly excused myself from the discomfort of the moment to go out to play with friends.

I did not realize at the time how close my mother had come to telling me of the most difficult experience in her life and by extension, my own. She was a young teenager, when her mother, Alice, became pregnant with her seventh child. Toward the end of the pregnancy, the baby breached. Worried, my mother's father summoned the government-assigned intern

---

4   Friedman, *Generation to Generation*, 31–32

to their home. The intern decided to perform an operation right then and there to remove the baby, with my grandmother's bed serving as his operating table. Utilizing forceps, he began an excruciatingly painful and crude surgical procedure to remove the baby from her womb.

The effort was ill conceived, and the situation quickly deteriorated. Whether the intern panicked, was incompetent, simply did not care, or all of the above, the procedure quickly degenerated into brute force removal, resulting in the baby being killed in the womb, leaving my grandmother screaming in pain and everyone in the room distraught. The loss of blood and the infection resulting from the flawed procedure soon became critical. Because a road had not yet been built from our community to the outside world, my grandmother was taken by boat to a hospital in Port Angeles, fifty miles east along the Strait of Juan de Fuca. Authorities there, however, refused to take her in as a patient in spite of her deteriorating condition. Instead, they insisted she should be transported to Tacoma, where there was an Indian hospital. The delay was critical. By the time she finally arrived at the Cushman Indian Hospital in Tacoma, my grandmother's state was dire. She died shortly thereafter.

The horrific deaths of mother and child had an immense impact on all of the family, perhaps especially so on my mother. At a crucial time in her young teenage life, a time when she needed her mother's counsel, she had lost her youngest sibling and her mother. Moreover, as I look back on her life and my own, it now seems to me that she lost her sense of innocence as well.

It took me a long time to figure out the implications of this trauma. Let's fast forward some sixty-plus years after my grandmother's death. My mother was then living in Tacoma, Washington. She had left the reservation many years before to live in the city. She was in her mid-seventies and greatly weakened due to kidney failure. Her kidneys had never been healthy, and while in her thirties, her doctor had concluded she would soon die as a result of a kidney infection. He advised her to go home to the reservation and put her affairs in order. I was but a boy of eight at the time, but I still remember the long ride home from the doctor's office as she searched for words to explain the hopelessness of her situation to my older brother Leonard and me. Subdued and choked with emotion, she tried to help us understand that she would be leaving us soon and that we should look after one another. Perhaps unwilling or unable to comprehend the enormity of her sad declaration, I sat quietly in the back seat of the car and starred at the nothingness of the passing landscape.

Not long after we returned home, some elder native women in the community who heard of her desperate circumstances came to our home and prescribed for my mother a natural tea remedy from the bark of a wild crab apple tree native to the area. Boiled in a pot of water for a set time, the tea was then strained. It was bitter to the taste, but she drank it faithfully three times a day, just as they had instructed her. Amazingly, the curative properties of the ancient Indian remedy worked to cleanse her system and heal her infected kidneys. Her doctor was so surprised when she returned to his office for another check up that he nearly fell back in shock. It was like he was seeing a ghost. He quickly ushered her into his office and said, "What happened to you? We thought you would be dead by now."

But that was a long time ago. Now she was on dialysis, and her kidneys were shutting down once again. It was obvious she didn't have many days left. Realizing this, I had made a point to come home to see her one more time. At the time, I was living nearly 1,500 miles away in Minnesota.

It was difficult to see how she had changed. She had lost a lot of weight, her complexion was ashen, her hair whitened. As we sat in her living room, a sense of imminent death enclosing around her, my mother reached out to me one more time for emotional strength. She began sobbing quietly.

Thinking she must be in pain, I asked her if I could do anything. What she said caught me totally off guard. Tears streaming down her face, anguish pouring from her soul, she managed a muffled confession, declaring, "I was in the room when the doctor took out the baby. I watched as my mother screamed out in pain!" Although I didn't appreciate the significance of her statement at the time, I later realized that this was a crucial detail from the story she had tried to tell me years before that had caused me to feel so ill at ease. I held her hand and offered what comfort I could. Troubled by her sudden confession, I could only think to offer a hasty prayer. That afternoon, I left her home deeply disturbed. Why had she shared this? Her mother's tragic death was a long time ago. Why did it matter at this point in her life?

One day I happened to mention my mother's baffling behavior to a Christian psychiatrist who had also served as a spiritual mentor to me. He explained, "When a child in their formative years experiences a severe emotional trauma or is part of a stressful family situation like a divorce, they will often assume blame for what has occurred." Pondering his words for a time, I remembered another comment my mother had made many years earlier. Following her mother's death, she began to assume responsibility for her siblings. I could feel her frustration relived as she related how difficult it had been to get them to take more responsibility for the care of their home now that mom was gone.

It all made sense now. Witnessing the heartbreaking death of her mother at such a vulnerable age had caused her to feel as if she had something to do with it. Her resulting sense of obligation, born out of misplaced guilt, caused her to take on responsibilities that were not really hers. The fact that she did not understand what was happening to her meant that her life would forever be shadowed by a dark event. As I began piecing together more and more of my mother's life, I could understand how the death of her mom could affect her in this way. Because she was so young when this darkly tragic event occurred and had been traumatized by actually witnessing her mother's excruciating pain, she was unable to deal with her loss properly. With no one to help her process what she had witnessed, she began assuming responsibility she never should have. This irrational but understandable reaction to a horrific event affected the rest of her life and would eventually impact all of her children as well.

When this revelation began to unfold, I started to form a picture of how my mother's hidden anxieties, based on her reaction to tragedy, had transferred to me. Through a process of transference of emotional stresses from parent to child, it could be said that the wheels of my life had begun to fall off long before I was born. I was only just beginning to understand why God would tell me, "You are just like those men and their car, and I have been fixing you all of your life." God knew that my life had already been affected by things outside my control, even before I was born because of a family tragedy that had not been successfully resolved.

As I thought about my family's sad history, I found comfort in this: the principle of transference of anxieties from one generation to the next can also be applied to blessings as well. I learned from talking to different people that my grandmother, Alice Penn, whose tragic death had triggered my mother's emotional reaction, was a devout Christian, one who was known for her kindness to strangers and generosity to the poor. She even named my mother, Harriet, after a missionary friend who apparently served in our community.

As I thought about my grandmother's faith in her moment of darkness, I was tempted to conclude how unfair it was for her to die that way. Then I thought of a familiar Bible verse from Psalm 112:4: "Even in the darkness light dawns for the upright, for the gracious and compassionate man [or woman]."

I was reminded that when things seem darkest and beyond hope of redemption, God's grace is present, able to bring out of the darkness hope for redemption, even though it may not be evident until the blessing appears in the following generation.

Chapter 4

Lost Dreams

———————————— ⎯⎯⎯⎯⎯⎯⎯ ————————————

I said, "How are you guys going to get that car running?" And one of them said, "Medaris can fix anything."

At an age when my mother was most vulnerable, she had witnessed the horrific events leading to her mother's death. Unable to process her loss, she began believing that she was responsible, resulting in deep emotional scarring and unresolved feelings of guilt that followed her throughout the rest of her life. In matters pertaining to her home, she became a perfectionist. Her responses to her trauma would impact my life years later. However, both she and her siblings faced immediate challenges.

When people are traumatized by unexpected events, they often react in predictable ways. Some recede deeply into themselves where they bury their hurt in some remote place in the mind. Others flee as far away from the pain as possible. Others escape by immersing themselves in relationships, maybe even by engaging in alcohol or other mind-altering drugs. My grandfather's initial response following his wife and baby's death at the hands of the incompetent intern was rage. Normally one of the kindest and gentlest of men, he had to be restrained by other men from the community from doing harm to the intern doctor. Soon after that, his anger was replaced by overwhelming grief and a determination to do something. Of course, he had an immediate problem. How was he going to manage his family that included his eldest, a son, four girls nearing or in their teen years, and a toddler? His son was evidently so overwhelmed with grief he decided to leave town. He sold his prized horses and moved to the small Quileute Indian community of La Push where his father was from. He never returned to live in Neah Bay.

Sometime later, my grandfather apparently believed evil spirits had cursed the house where the tragedy took place. He borrowed a tractor, pushed the house onto the beach, and torched it—an ancient purification ritual in many cultures. About the same time, he decided to wed a woman in the community who had never been married, no doubt hoping a new mother for his children would help to lighten their darkness and provide them stability. It may have provided some permanence, but his new wife, perhaps feeling theirs was more a union of convenience than love, had little patience with her ready-made family. She subjected my Aunt Shirley, who was the youngest, to severe punishments like locking her for hours in a dark shed. My mother, who had married shortly after all of this had begun to unfold, escaped this. Unfortunately, there were deeper issues in my mother's life.

Her response to her mother's death, as I have already related, was to assume the role of responsible adult. Driven by a need to bring order back into their lives, she began telling her siblings to pick up after themselves and to do chores around the house. This did not go over very well. They either ignored or resisted her efforts. Her attempts at mothering having failed, she turned her attention to her recent marriage; seeking the security she had once known in her mother's presence in a relationship with my father.

My mother must have been barely fourteen when they first noticed each other and fifteen when they got married, which was not that unusual in our traditional culture. However, since she had only recently endured the horrific death of her mother that left her with unresolved feelings of guilt and loss, she likely saw my father as someone who could fill the empty feelings deep inside and perhaps provide a way of escape from her grief. Not long into their relationship and her mother's death, they had their first child, a son they named Ben. Hardly more than a child herself, she was now beginning to raise a family.

Their relationship, tainted in part out of lost childhood dreams, was at risk from the start. It turns out that my father's background was similar to my mother's. Like her, he too had lost something vitally important during his youth. His story begins not in Neah Bay but in the small city of Port Angeles.

Built initially on the promise of wealth from the emerging logging industry that fueled much of the early development in the Pacific Northwest, Port Angeles was a mostly Caucasian community nestled in the shadows of the majestic Olympic Mountains and adjacent the Strait of Juan de Fuca, the fifteen-mile-wide waterway that separates the Olympic Peninsula from Vancouver Island. My father's family, along with a few other Indians, lived along the shoreline next to the present-day marina.

Husky of build from an early age, my father appeared older than he really was. He got that from his Makah mother, who was stout, broad shouldered, and strong in appearance. His father, a Jamestown Clallam Indian with a little Swedish ancestry mixed in (I would discover this later), was more of a smallish, wiry man. For some reason, I was always somewhat afraid of her but really liked him.

Curious to know something of my father's childhood, one day a few years before his death, I asked him to share something of his days growing up in the small city. He recalled how as a boy of ten, he used to paddle a small dugout cedar canoe a mile or so out into the bay in front of his parent's home where he would hook huge King salmon with a hand line. I could sense his excitement as he described how the large salmon would pull him around the bay until they finally tired to the point where he could then haul them into his canoe. His eyes especially lit up as he related how much he enjoyed playing sports in school, especially baseball. He always had exceptional eyesight and good reflexes to go with his strength and weight; he was 170 pounds by the time he was thirteen. People could see how his size and strength translated into athletic potential and would tell him, "You have a chance to become really good." Those highlights of his childhood were about as much as I could get from him. That is until one day, in a candid moment, he provided some important details that would greatly affect his life and eventually set the stage for my own.

The year was 1930, and America was in the throes of the Great Depression. Families all over America were struggling with unemployment much as they are today and facing difficult decisions that would have long-term impacts on their children. Like so many others in America, my father's parents were struggling to manage the diminishing resources needed to put food on the table. They decided on a plan to have the two oldest boys leave home and school and find work. My father was just thirteen and his oldest brother eighteen when their father told them to gather their things together so that they could go to Neah Bay to find work.

At the time, the government responded to the deepening economic crisis by creating work projects through a job program that put unemployed men to work. One of the proposed projects was to build a rubble mount or rock breakwater in front of Neah Bay. The exposed harbor in front of the small community was often subject to large wind-driven waves, making it difficult to protect boats moored there. Job prospects looked favorable.

Leaving family, friends, and school behind at such a youthful age to work in a man's world would have terrified me but hardly seemed to have fazed my father as he casually described what would be a momentous life change. Nevertheless, I have formed an enduring picture of my grandfather and his oldest boys piling into a hand-carved cedar dugout canoe, along with what meager possessions they must have accumulated at the time, and paddling out of the harbor and on to what would become the rest of their lives. As they made their way along the strait, I can picture my father asking, "Dad, how long will we have to live in Neah Bay?"

I never knew my dad's father, Ed Johnson, very well. From what little I was able to discern about his family history, he was born around 1891 to Henry and Emma Johnson. I was never able to discern much more than that except to learn that Ed's father's history seems to have predated the early census efforts on the Olympic Peninsula. Gaps in history aside, on those few occasions when I did have opportunity to talk with my grandfather, he always seemed kind and pleasant, a good man at heart. I suspect having to take his sons out of school, especially my father, must have been a hard decision for him. Still, these were terribly difficult times for many families, and having two fewer mouths to feed would make things easier for the rest of the kids. From my grandfather's point of view, his oldest boys were the most likely of all the children to make it.

As they made their way westward along the strait, with the current behind them to make the journey easier, I am sure that my father's mind was on anything but the world he was leaving behind. Caught up in the novelty of it all and the chance to be independent had to have been one great adventure. In the distance, he could see the beginning of the vast Pacific Ocean, a scene so breathtaking, it must have seemed to him like one great playground. Surely, his thoughts were consumed by the prospect of wonderful opportunities for great salmon fishing he knew would abound. After all, if he could catch large salmon in the bay in front of his parents' house in Port Angeles, imagine how many large salmon could be caught fishing on the ocean?

In later years, salmon would not be so readily harvested. Expansive electricity-producing dams, extensive tree harvests, foreign fish viruses, ocean pollution, over-harvesting, and urban sprawl would collaborate to kill off many salmon runs. In 1930, though, there were lots of salmon and halibut that, for someone like my father, who loved fishing, made Neah Bay a veritable fishermen's paradise.

In my mind, I can see my grandfather and his two boys as they beached their canoe on the sandy shore at Neah Bay and began the short trek up the beach and across the road past humble, rough-hewn, wood-frame, single-family homes. Only a few years before, these would have been traditional cedar long-houses. The 30-foot by 60-foot long-houses with their roofs constructed from cedar logs and hand-hewn cedar shakes were intended to house extended families. The government, in its effort to force cultural change through architecture, had made the people take them down and build individual family dwellings.

I can remember the pride on my father's face as he described his first job interview. The project foreman looked him up and down, probably a little skeptical. The strapping boy standing in front of him appeared to be too young. Pointing to a cement sack on the floor of his makeshift office, he said, "Son, if you can pick that up, you're hired." My father lifted it easily. And just as his own father had calculated, the people managing the program were more than ready to believe he was eighteen. My dad then filled out the form, lied about his age, and was assigned to live in a barracks with men twice his age or more.

Soon, my father had a job as a powder-monkey, a task that involved drilling holes in big rocks for explosive charges. Later he worked as a choke setter in the forest, setting steel cables around trees that had been cut and trimmed for removal. When he was an older teen, a construction contractor who had been impressed by my father's work ethic hired him to help build a house for the lighthouse keeper on Tatoosh Island, the vital navigation aid situated at the entrance to the Strait of Juan de Fuca. His new job required unloading boats by hand and carrying heavy bags of cement to the construction site. My father, broad shouldered and husky for his youthfulness, was more than capable.

As he related stories of his life during these times, his countenance seemed to warm to the memories. He proudly described how he was strong enough to do hard work and how much he enjoyed the camaraderie in the company of older men. And then there was plenty to eat. My father especially liked that. And the friendships, the freedom, and the money were great—$45 per month—heady stuff for a young teen and big money for the times. But there was a down side my father had no way of understanding, a hidden cost even a strong, independent man would have to pay that would likely contribute to his eventual alcoholism, ruin his marriage, and cost his family immensely.

Through the years, I began to pick up vague hints that the relationship between my father and his dad lacked a certain level of trust. For the most part, I knew he loved his parents and had nothing but good to say about them. Nevertheless, there was something missing. Where I saw this most evident was in a single, albeit rare opportunity I had to go salmon fishing with my grandfather.

My father, like so many Native Americans, was a careful observer of nature. He understood ocean currents, their interaction with the tides, when and where the fish bite best, and the tell-tale signs of approaching weather. His trademark comment to me and my brothers through the years was about the ocean:

"There are never two days alike." One day the ocean is placid and the fish are biting, and the next, the wind comes up, the seas are rough, and the fish have moved on.

Eventually, his affinity for understanding the rhythms of the natural world made my father an excellent fisherman. He invented clever "hook-ups" and ways to cut bait-fish that would cause a herring attached to hook and line to mimic a wounded herring. It worked well because salmon feeding on herring often strike first with their tail to cripple them before quickly turning around to devour them. Using my father's fishing techniques meant you would catch large salmon while other fishermen looked on. I retain vivid memories of times fishing with my father in his open boat when he would be catching one large salmon after another while other fishermen, skunked and anxious to catch a fish of their own, would try to come as close to our boat as they could to see what we were doing. Of course, he shared his secret techniques with us while giving us strict instructions not to show anyone what we were doing.

One day, I mentioned to my father that I had been invited to go salmon fishing with his dad. It was a rare opportunity for me to get to know my grandfather, and I looked forward to going with him to a place called Spike Rock, some fifteen miles distant along the coast from Neah Bay. When my father learned of my intent, he instructed me not to show my grandfather the style of cutting bait-fish that he had taught my brothers and me. I thought it unusual and asked him why. He explained that he didn't trust his father with fishing secrets that had taken him years to develop. He believed his father would tell all of his friends. Knowing my dad's directive in this regard caused me to feel anxious. How do I help my grandfather while being true to the promise I made not to share my father's secrets with anyone? I remember deliberately cutting the bait-fish in a different style than I had been taught while my grandfather looked intently at my every move. I don't remember what I did that was different than what my Dad taught me, but whatever I did, it still worked well enough that we caught fish anyway.

To his credit, in later years, my father felt bad about not sharing his secrets with his own father. In a candid confession many years after his father had died, he confessed to my brother Ben how much he regretted not sharing these secrets with his dad.

There were other consequences of his early trauma as well. The fact that he had abandoned his childhood so abruptly contributed to his inability to remember important occasions, like our birthdays, or provide gifts for Christmas or any other type of family event. I know he didn't mean to forget. Things like Christmas and birthday celebrations had not likely been a part of his life either. After all, celebrations like this were new to his generation of Native Americans. Moreover, and perhaps more importantly, like my mother, he had been forced to become an adult early in his life; thus, he had never truly known childhood and could not understand why his children should not be as self-sufficient as he had been.

Then, there was perhaps the most costly of consequences— one that I was able to discern only through rare comments he would offer in passing. For much of his older life, my father seemed to have had an enduring sense of having lost what could have been. Occasionally this would surface in two haunting comments: "I wonder how good I could have been if I had been able to continue playing baseball?" and "I think I could have done well if I had stayed in school."

For all of his self-sufficiency, my father, too, was this broken-and-missing-pieces person that had been places and experienced things he never should have. The cumulative sense of having lost something precious and irreplaceable contributed to a disquieting sense of not fulfilling his potential that would follow him through the rest of his life. And this would have a huge impact on us, his family.

Not long before he died, I had asked my father to write down the details of his early life. In response to my request, he wrote a long letter in which he shared how he began drinking to dull the inner aloneness that marriage to my mother did not fill. He never knew why he was lonely or why marriage did not fill this void. Before long, his drinking became an addiction, then a compulsion, and finally an obsession. I had first-hand knowledge of some of this.

Some days he would come in from a week of successful fishing and then blow all the money he had made in raucous partying. Afraid his drinking buddies were stealing his money when he was passed out, he would sometimes hand one of my brothers or me his wallet full of cash from a recent fishing trip and instruct us to keep it for him while he kept just enough to set out on another drinking spree. On occasion, my mother would bitterly recount stories of my father's drinking bouts. If his alcoholic friends happened to come around, the drinking fests would sometimes degenerate into loud, boisterous, and even dangerous situations. She once confided in me that she even hid us in a closet during one particularly wild time to keep us from being harmed by some of his drinking buddies.

Listening to my mother recount these difficult times made me uncomfortable. I did not want to believe anything negative about my father. My father, for his part, never acknowledged these behaviors, except ever so briefly in his letter to me. Yet I knew he felt much guilt for not being the father he should have been. At the same time, I felt my mother's deep hurt. Her marriage had not filled the void she desperately craved to have filled after she lost her mother. Nor had it fulfilled the sense of lost potential in my father's life. Sadly, disillusionment in relationships and lost dreams not only left both of them bitter and unhappy, but the pattern followed them throughout their lives. I was beginning to learn that marriage does not fix our broken and missing pieces. Only God can do that. It brought to mind something St. Augustine wrote: "Our hearts are restless until they rest in Thee." There is within all of us a God-created space that only a relationship with Jesus can fill.

Their failed relationship had an effect on all of the children—maybe more upon me than my siblings. Caught between the tensions of the two people I loved the most, my physical and emotional stability began to be affected. The consequences of the broken and missing pieces of their lives, reflected in their hidden anxieties, had begun to transfer to me.

By the time I was four, their relationship had deteriorated from desperate pleadings on my mother's part to angry arguments leading to a bitter divorce and custody battle. Theirs was a familiar story of paradise lost. It was becoming mine as well. I, too, was losing something in the drama unfolding in my parents' lives. There was no security in their home. I responded by retreating into a dark hiding place of my own. I became inhibited in my physical and social development. I was already becoming a broken-and-missing-pieces person.

How could God fix the broken and missing pieces of my life already forming through my fractured family and generational history?

Chapter 5

No Choice, No Matter

The most important nanosecond in each of our lives is also the nanosecond over which we have no control. [. . .] It's the moment we're born.
The Generational Imperative—Chuck Underwood

I was the last child born to my parents before their divorce. In my efforts to uncover my generational history, I remembered something my mother shared regarding problems she was experiencing during her pregnancy with me. Seven months into the pregnancy, she began having trouble with severe cramping. It may have been related to the increasing tension in her failing marriage. Family members took her to a hospital in Port Angeles where a doctor recommended an immediate abortion. In those moments of my mother's indecision, my life literally hung in the balance.

Then a nurse who had overheard the doctor's recommendation discretely pulled my mother aside and told her not to go through with it. The nurse had even arranged for a cab to transport my mother to another hospital. And that is how I entered the world—in another hospital, two months premature but alive, the beneficiary of a courageous nurse's last-minute intervention.

My mother never knew who the nurse was or ever saw her again. Whoever she was, I owe my life to her timely intervention.

Having been born a "preemie" was challenge enough. More problematic, however, were the anxieties rampant in my home at the time and my apparent response to them. The stresses in our home seem to have played a significant role in delaying my physical and emotional development. I did not talk or walk until I was four, yet there appeared to be no physiological reasons for this delay. However, when I finally took my first steps, something in my brain seems to have engaged my conscious awareness as well.

By this time, my parent's marriage had come to an end, and they were fully engaged in a contentious divorce and child custody proceeding. Sadly, members of a local church where my father's family had been members took sides against my mother as the rift grew ever wider. She never forgot what she considered the lies they told the judge to persuade him to award custody of the children to our father.

At the height of this bitter debate, while our destinies were still being argued in a court proceeding, my father decided to take my siblings and me away to his parents' community. While my mom was away at work, we were driven to the little native village of Elwah, some fifty miles from Neah Bay.

By this time, my father's parents had moved from Port Angeles to Elwah where they resided in a two-story, wood-framed, 1890s-style home set in a field below a green hillside. Situated off the main road in a sparsely populated community, the house sat alone in a field next to a small barn. Well-worn wooden steps led up to a porch and the entry way to the living room. Two ancient cast-iron wood stoves sat at either end of the house, barely providing enough heat against the damp winter cold. Midway between the kitchen and living room, a dark and narrow stairway that creaked with each step led to the second floor. I remember crawling up those stairs on hands and knees. An outhouse, partially obscured by small trees and brush, was situated behind the house. I have a dim recollection that the trail leading to the toilet was enclosed with low-lying brush or small trees.

If my description of the house and its immediate setting seems less than appealing, it was more than likely a reflection of my state of mind at the time than reality. The truth was, there was beauty all around. Standing sentinel-like over a vast region of magnificent forests and lakes, the snow-capped Olympic Mountains were easily visible through the living room window. To the north and east, easily visible as well, lay the beautiful Strait of Juan de Fuca separating Vancouver Island, British Columbia from the U.S. mainland. Set in such natural beauty, it was, in fact, an ideal setting for a home. Yet my memories of my life there seem shaded more by darkness than light, possibly shadowy indicators of my emerging worldview. This seems to have been borne out by four visual images that form my most important memories of life there.

The first is of a small single engine plane that crashed nose down in an open field near my grandparent's house. Face bloodied and head resting against his chest, the barely conscious pilot sat slumped over next to his aircraft. I do not remember what happened after that. The next recollection is of crawling or walking out into the darkness of the night along an overgrown path to use the outhouse while hearing the voices of people behind me laughing and cajoling me to overcome my fear of the dark. They were likely impatient with my inhibited development. The third is of my crawling on hands and knees up the dark and narrow stairway leading to an attic with a low ceiling. This was where I slept with my siblings. My final memory is of cowering under a table, afraid of having to leave my grandparents' home with a stranger.

The "stranger," it turns out, was none other than my maternal grandfather from Neah Bay. His name was William Penn or, as most knew him, "Big Bill." He wasn't really a big man. He was just bigger than another man with the same name from his hometown of La Push on the Quileute Indian reservation. Dark hair, of medium build and a well-formed physique, Bill Penn stood out in a crowd. When I was growing up, I can remember women telling my mother how handsome they thought her father was.

In spite of his rage at the time of his wife Alice's death, Bill Penn was known mostly for his kindness, generosity, and the capacity to convey genuine warmth to complete strangers. I still have fond memories of my introducing him to a friend and having him smile broadly and literally tear up with unbridled warmth of affection as he reached out with oversize hands to grasp the hand of whomever it was that I was introducing. It mattered not who you were or what you needed, he was the type that would gladly give you the shirt off his back. He was also an expert fisherman and hunter, schooled in the tradition of his forefathers. He combined this with a great sense of humor.

One story reflecting his prowess as a hunter and his sense of humor has remained with me through the years. According to the account, several sports writers from a national sporting magazine decided to do a story on deer hunting on the Olympic Peninsula. They wanted an experienced guide to show them where to hunt. Somehow, they learned my grandfather was the best around. They soon arranged to have him accompany them as a guide along with an Olympic National Park Service employee. The park bordered some of the best hunting areas as well as the reservation. Having a park service ranger along would insure that they kept from straying into the park.

There was reason for their caution. From time to time, park service employees suspected local Indians were occasionally sneaking into the park to take a deer or elk. There were also disputes over the boundary. Some of the local native men were still feeling resentment over the loss of much of their traditional hunting places. It led to tension and threats to prosecute violators. Needless to say, knowing where the park ended and the reservation began was no small thing. And of course, deer typically moved in and out of the park with no regard for boundaries. On this day, though, the deer were scarce in spite of my grandfather's best efforts to take the writers to a place where they could successfully complete the hunt. The writers remarked how tired they had become after a long day of climbing up and down and along heavily forested hill and dale and how they were barely able to keep pace with my grandfather. At some point, according to their narrative, he turned to them and said, "I know where we can find a deer." Exhausted because of their tiring efforts to keep up with him and anxious to finish what they had come across the country to do, they all nodded as if to say, "Well then, let's go."

Soon, they came to a clearing where, just as my grandfather had promised, there stood a buck. Nodding to the park service employee as if to say without actually saying it, "Go ahead, take the shot," the park service employee took aim and, with one shot, dropped the deer where it stood. With a mischievous smile and a twinkle in his eye, my grandfather turned to him and said, "We are in the park."

It is the first of many fond recollections I have of this kind and gentle man. However, my initial encounter with him conveyed none of this. I was afraid of him when he drove to Elwah in his pickup to take me away from my father's parents. Not even the promise of toys or pop was enough to cause me to leave my hiding place under the table in the dining room. At the time, I didn't know why he had come to take me away. It was only later that I learned that he had come to Elwah to retrieve my siblings and me because the judge in the custody hearing had ruled in my mother's favor. Once persuaded to come out from my hiding place, I was headed back to Neah Bay in his pickup truck with Hires orange pop, candy, and toys to ease my journey.

Neah Bay, on the Makah Indian Reservation, would be the place where I would spend the next decade being found by God. It was no simple thing for God to find and fix the broken and missing pieces of my life. The task had been complicated by the fact that I was already exhibiting unhealthy emotional behaviors. It appears that I had responded to my parent's anxieties and the bitter acrimony between them by withdrawing into the deep recesses of my mind, a secret hiding place that inhibited my physical and emotional health. It is possible my retreat had actually begun in my mother's womb during those times when she was increasingly distressed by her failing marriage.

This raises an important question. How does God go about repairing the damage when we respond to anxiety by fleeing into the deepest places of the mind? My experience would suggest that He does this a little at a time and ever so gently and perhaps not unlike my grandfather, who had so patiently persuaded me to leave my hiding place under the table with a friendly smile, a tender voice, and some treats for the ride home. I would experience some complications along the way to being found by God, though.

About a year after my siblings and I moved back to Neah Bay, my mother married a man who was not from our community. Was this a marriage of convenience? Was it another effort at finding escape in a relationship? I don't know for sure, but I do know it would have a large impact on the rest of my formative years.

At the time of their marriage, I was five and only just beginning to emerge out of my inhibited emotional development. My stepfather, who was of Caucasian descent, had been assigned as an airman to the small U.S. Air Force radar squadron located on the reservation when he first met my mother. With roots in the upper Midwest and East Coast, being assigned to a small radar site on an Indian reservation must have seemed to him like being sent to a foreign country. In a way, it was. After all, we were a people with a culture rooted for thousands of years in a vastly different tradition from his Scotch-Irish roots.

Had it not been for the small air force contingent in our community, of course he would never have met my mother; a military base located on an Indian reservation such as ours was rare. In an increasingly dangerous world, however, our strategic location at the "end of the land" had made it necessary.

When World War II broke out, the U.S. government established a small radar facility adjacent to a beautiful stretch of ocean beach, staffing it with enough men to maintain and sustain its operations. Temporary at first, it consisted mostly of several corrugated steel Quonset huts and towers for the radar and provisional housing for the few men assigned to operate it. After the war ended, however, the government decided to make the base permanent by relocating to a different part of the reservation.

Some of the local tribal members, still nursing bad memories of tribal lands taken by the government in the wake of the treaty of 1855, were upset that land allocated to their families by treaty were once again being confiscated with little or, as it turned out, no compensation. There was little chance the government would change its mind, however. The location had been deemed strategically important to America's security. Thus, by the early 1950s, the small grouping of Quonset huts originally set up along the beach had become a permanent radar installation and eventually relocated high atop Bahocus Peak, a place with a sweeping view of the Pacific Ocean. A small complex located below the hill, complete with barracks and support buildings, housed the small contingent of men assigned to the installation.

Naturally, tensions existed between tribal members who had lost some of their land and military personnel, but some of it began to dissipate when men from the community took on civilian jobs with the government. Eventually, a few of the service men married local Makah women as in my mother's case, further blending the military community with the tribe.

Soon after my mother remarried, I began my first year of school. My emotional stability was still impaired, and I did not do well. I "flunked" first grade. How does one fail first grade? My teacher explained to my mother, "Your son is socially and academically immature." The proof was that I did not relate well with other kids and in the course of the year had not learned to read or even to recite the alphabet. My only recollection of my first year of school is of sitting in a school hallway outside the classroom, my pants wet with urine because I did not know enough to ask where the bathroom was. My teacher was right.

That following summer, something like a miracle happened that changed everything for me. With no prompting from anyone at all, I slowly began to walk myself out of my inhibited academic and social development. While this may seem strange, and it remains a mystery, one night, while I was lying alone on my bed in a dark room, a sense of well-being encompassed me. The entire room seemed to fill with a comforting presence. For the first time, I felt safe in the darkness, and somehow I concluded that the presence I felt was God. I have no other rational explanation. But from that time on, I knew God existed.

During this same summer, for no known reason and with no prodding or tutoring from anyone, I picked up an old, worn hardcover English book of short stories and started reading it. I devoured that book repeatedly. By the time I returned to repeat first grade, I had made a remarkable turnabout, quickly learning my ABCs and becoming one of the best readers and spellers in my first grade class.

How was this possible? More importantly, how critical was this episode to my development and eventual course of my life? I am absolutely convinced that if I had not learned to read at that point, I would have continued to fall further behind in school, without hope of redemption. This was a reservation school, after all—underfunded, sometimes understaffed, and without a special needs education program. It is also likely that I would have eventually dropped out of school. Surely my mounting academic failures would have reinforced feelings of inadequacy and aloneness and increased the likelihood that in later years I would turn to alcohol or some other form of addictive behavior to dull the sense of lost potential.

Except for the grace of God quietly unfolding in my life through all of my circumstances, my life surely would have mirrored the lives of the three men I met in Montana, and I could have easily ended up living my life from bottle to bottle instead of from day to day. This unusual summer of spiritual and academic enlightenment was a turning point. God had begun sifting through the damaged emotions of my life, working some preventive maintenance along the way and doing repair work ever so gently. Not all at once—just a little at a time and as much as I could handle. And since He was doing this in the often-hidden world of His Spirit, I didn't even know who He was or realize that it was His work that was carefully drawing me to Him.

You might well have drawn a different conclusion had you been observing our family life at the time. Just as some semblance of normalcy was beginning to attach itself to me and the rest of my family, a new cloud was forming on the horizon of our family life. My mother's recent marriage was already beginning to lose some of its intimacy, and I soon found myself caught in the middle of their disappointment.

A contributing factor was my stepfather's inability to relate well to his new family—which would have been a challenge under even the best of circumstances but was made all the more difficult because his world and ours were so vastly different. In Neah Bay, he was far removed from his culture, and living on an Indian reservation must have seemed strange. Add to this the fact that he was overly strict, possibly a reflection of his own upbringing. He never revealed much about his relationships with his parents. My suspicion is that there was likely a trail of broken and missing pieces in his family relationships as well. His reaction to such things as our failure to say, "Please pass the salt," or to hold a fork properly could trigger a sharp rebuke, maybe even a jab in the hand with a fork.

My siblings and I had never experienced formal dinner times during the previous chaotic years. Table etiquette was lost on us. The anticipation of a demeaning criticism or a jab in the hand with a fork when we made the wrong move made family dinner gatherings in our new setting altogether unpleasant. My mother did her best to ease the tensions. She became especially overprotective of me, possibly because of my slow emotional and physical development. Maybe she felt guilty for that too. In any case, she began rearranging dinner times so that my siblings and I ate before our stepfather came home.

Feeling the distancing from his wife and seeing how she tried to protect me, he seems to have seen me as a rival for her emotional support, which only intensified his criticisms. Over the course of my life in his home and for years after, I sensed his animosity and disliked being in his presence. Thus, I could never force myself to call him "Dad," even though he was married to my mother and provided for us. I know my mother felt the increasing stress of this during the course of our life together in these early years. In her mind, I suspect she felt she had few alternatives. At best, the circumstances were tenuous and remained so through all the years I lived in their home.

When things would become particularly intense, my mother would threaten to leave him. By now, however, their relationship had become one of co-dependency. He would promise to change— she could not imagine how she could manage apart from him—and they would resolve to work things out once more. However, the good intentions lasted only for a short while, and soon, our family would return to the familiar pattern of dysfunction.

The cumulative effect of the negative atmosphere in our home seems to have had serious consequences for me. The constant tension coupled with an atmosphere of criticism eroded my self-confidence. I began to have strong feelings of inadequacy and an attitude of disappointment. Before long, I began to develop a habit of giving up whenever I encountered disappointment. This eventually was reflected in my inability to trust God when things did not go as I expected. This tendency was manifest in the way I reacted years later when I encountered the three men in Montana and heard about Medaris' death. My lack of self-confidence and dark-side sense of things not working out became a pattern in my life. I clung to my familiar because things seemed safer and I could manage things in a predictable way. It likely affected spontaneity in my life as well. Even to this day, I struggle with allowing naturalness in my life—that is, the willingness to do things on the spur of the moment, to have fun by doing something completely unexpected.

In later years, I discovered my tendency to cling to my familiar can also inhibit the work of God in my life. I eventually came to understand that throughout the whole of my young life, I had learned to resist change and hold on to the familiar because of the illusion of safety familiarity affords. Hiding under the table in my grandparent's home was one expression of this. What I did not know, of course, was that what I thought was a safe place under a table was not safe after all. To begin to find healing for my already broken-and-missing-pieces life, God needed to get me out from my hiding places to a place where He could begin to deal with me; God needed to take me from my familiar to the unfamiliar where He could begin to talk more directly with me and begin to lead me out of my darkness. This was no simple task, though. I was about to discover that there are many kinds of hiding places where I could cling to my familiar. I stubbornly resisted change.

Nevertheless, I was about to discover that God in His graciousness would leave me with no choice in the matter.

CHAPTER 6

The Familiar to the Unknown

Be kinder than necessary. For everyone you meet is fighting some kind of battle.

—Author unknown

I never thought about this while growing up, but I was not the only kid in my community feeling the effects of a fractured home life. At least seven homes within a block or two of mine were places where the parents were alcoholics. Sometimes I would hear yelling and laughing long into the night, especially if others showed up to party with the patrons. Many of my classmates were experiencing varying states of emotional distress because of homes in crisis. Some were living in family systems so torn by alcoholism that they often came to school without breakfast or adequate sleep. I discovered many years later that some of the girls and maybe even some of the boys had experienced sexual abuse. Sadly, I know the pain that can result from this too well.

One day in a coffee shop while attempting to recover stories from my youth for this book, my mind's meandering over the mundane of my life took a sudden off-road journey into a part of my mind I had not visited for many years. It was a deeply painful and dark place, a place of secrets, shame, and hurt. As I approached this long hidden memory, tears suddenly welled up in my eyes. Before I could summon enough composure to forestall my runaway emotions, I found myself ducking behind my computer screen to avoid being seen. As I did so, the memory of a name from my past, someone not from my native community, suddenly came to mind. It was an adult who had been too willing to baby sit me as a small child and had been the cause of my pain. Sitting there in that coffee shop nearly 1,600 miles and many years removed from where this took place with my eyes welling with tears was an overwhelming experience. An acquaintance of mine, the late Bill Sandberg, who at the time was mayor of North St. Paul, was sitting across the room from me and had noticed my abrupt change in behavior. He immediately came over and inquired, "Are you okay?" I nodded my head as if to say, "Yes." Stunned by the suddenness of my emotional release and unsure of my feelings, I could not bring myself to explain the reason for my sudden change in temperament: my realization that I, too, had been a victim of sexual abuse. I cannot remember what excuse I offered. In any case, it's the kind of thing you never want to tell anyone, and very often, as in my case, the people who are victims tend to bury the memory deep within. This often becomes the seed for other dysfunctional behaviors later in their lives and can even lead to thoughts of suicide. Some of the victims of sexual abuse may find it difficult to find meaning in life or they may struggle with acceptance of themselves, occasionally experiencing outbreaks of emotional distress without knowing the reasons. Fortunately, that did not happen in my case but may have contributed to my social maladjustment in my first year of school. It was certainly what God saw when He assessed my life after my encounter with the three men and their car.

Most, if not all, in my community had been made especially vulnerable and affected by traumas initially rooted in the rapid changes the previous generations had endured. The resulting vacuum created by the growing disparity between our ancient traditions and their relevance in a modern world and the restrictions on hunting and fishing and other aspects of our traditional way of life were especially hard on the men, who were no longer able to provide for their families in traditional ways. Accompanying these, as previously noted, were more physical illnesses increasingly manifest in our community, such as diabetes, arthritis, heart disease, cancer, and alcohol-related problems like fetal alcohol syndrome. The truth was, we were increasingly susceptible to many kinds of illnesses as well as abuses of all sorts. We were in a bad way and getting worse, and no one knew what to do about it.

When you live long enough in a community thus affected, the resulting pattern of dysfunction becomes the new norm, and behaviors once deemed unacceptable in the old culture become tolerated in the new. This is not just true of the Native American experience. All people, regardless of ethnicity, have experienced rapid cultural change to some degree and are paying a price of lost traditions and values that once provided community stability. Sometimes the causes that result in rapid cultural change are rooted in technological advancement or some traumatic event on a national scale that increases anxiety or appears to make past wisdom and knowledge irrelevant. And that, too, can contribute to societal illness, depending on the response. I have more to say on this in a later chapter.

Long before anyone understood the effects of too-rapid change and its potentially damaging effects on humans, well-intentioned Christian missionaries had come to our community to offer salvation and to encourage culture change amid the unfolding chaos. Attempts to persuade my people to give up their cultural traditions in exchange for "civilization" further reinforced the idea that the old ways were irrelevant.

Some interesting inconsistencies grew out of this dialogue. One respected female missionary, a trim, rather well dressed

woman from Quebec named Helen Clark, who lived in our village around the close of the nineteenth century, encouraged the
Makahs to give up wearing the masks and feathers that were a
part of their ceremonial dress. According to the story, a Makah
man responded, "Miss Clark, whenever you put away your
feathers, I will put away mine."[5] At the time, she used to wear a
hat with an ostrich feather. The missionary and the men likely
laughed about this contradiction. However, I suspect that their
friendly dialogue hid a resentment festering deeper under the
surface, especially among the men.

The truth was, the men were increasingly unhappy with
the government for placing their children in residential schools,
seizing their lands, and forbidding more and more of their traditions, especially the practice of hunting the great grey whales. It
meant that Makah men were not too anxious to embrace Christianity if it meant having to give up more of their traditional
heritage. Unfortunately, Christian missionaries' efforts to force
cultural change led to an untenable and unnecessary choice:
being Christian or Indian. One could not be both.

To make matters worse, several of the denominations
present in our community in succeeding years taught that participation in school athletics was "worldly" and forbade their
youth from participating in football and basketball. Many of
the young men, myself included, developed a love for athletics
in part because it provided a badly needed way to express our
maleness. The softer, feminine side of Christianity emphasizing
the church as the bride of Christ, often articulated by women
missionaries like Helen Clark or male pastors with little interest in sports, reinforced in our minds that Christianity was for
women and children. These things conspired to make me an
unlikely candidate for the Christian faith. And this perception

---

5   The Makah Cultural and Research Center, *Portraits in Time*, 58

would likely have remained with me except for an encounter with a certain female Christian teacher.

When I repeated first grade and began to progress normally along the education track, I began to develop a different point of view on Christianity—one I did not expect and from a source I could not have possibly anticipated. One of my primary grade teachers was a woman who probably came to teach in our community because of her commitment to God. Her name was Miss Helen Sachs. She was a most unusual lady. Never married and not a likely candidate any time soon, she always dressed the same way: slightly graying blond hair with a tinge of white pulled back tightly in a bun, wire-rimmed glasses, print dresses halfway down to her ankles, and old-fashioned shoes. She looked harmless, but behind her kindly appearance was a formidable disciplinarian with a no-nonsense approach to teaching. I suspect we were a little unruly and needed her discipline to keep us in line.

Her insistence on proper classroom decorum extended to the lunchroom, where we had to eat everything on our lunch tray, including tomatoes, which I didn't like, and beets, which I hated with a passion. Lunches were provided free of charge to Makah tribal members through a shared tribal/ U.S. government subsidy. I remember sitting at my desk, tray of food set before me, trying to figure how I was going to get the hated beets and tomatoes past her inspection at the doorway. She probably thought some of the kids might not be getting adequate food at home, and that was true for some, although not for me. When I thought she wasn't looking, I would deftly slip the offending vegetables onto a napkin and slide the soggy mess into the pocket of my jeans, where they might stay for a few days. My mom, who washed clothes in an old-style upright ringer washer, never quite figured out why my pant pockets always seemed to have dried tomatoes and beets, and fortunately, Miss Sachs never caught on either.

At the same time, Miss Sachs was an excellent teacher, and now that I was more socially adjusted, I was beginning to enjoy school, and that really helped. But what impacted me most was realizing how passionate she was about her faith in God. She did not force her beliefs on us, but we all knew that she attended the local Presbyterian church every Sunday without fail. From time to time, she would pray with us about something we might all want—a day of snow, for example. Living close to the ocean meant snowfalls were relatively rare. To this day, I marvel how her prayers seemed to have been answered. Her singular devotion and the sense we had that she truly believed in a powerful, living God made an important impression on all of us, especially on Mondays.

Monday mornings were a kind of day of reckoning. I can still see her standing there, surveying the class of maybe twenty-five mostly Makah kids and asking the dreaded question, "How many of you went to Sunday school yesterday?" Feelings of guilt arising from somewhere, I and the others in my class would quickly avert our eyes from her penetrating stare while we shifted nervously in our seats. Eventually, I ended up attending Sunday school at the Presbyterian church where she worshiped. I did not attend every Sunday, and I did not go for the lessons. Mostly I went to play with my friends and to collect bulletins for use in making airplanes. A typical Sunday was often spent fooling around, distracting our teacher from the day's lesson by asking him questions about World War II, and then running home to have more fun.

Nevertheless, a few Bible stories, the familiar ones, were sprinkled into my experience. The Jesus forming in my mind in these early days was the guy in flowing white robes illustrated in the large picture hanging behind the altar in the sanctuary at the Presbyterian church. Hands folded in devotion, kneeling before a boulder, face turned to the heavens, and heavenly light from above illuminating his peaceful countenance, Jesus seemed like a kindly man who did some good things once. It was not much to go on, but attending Sunday school and getting this glimpse of Jesus was a step toward being found by God and being healed.

Now that I was more socially adjusted, my life on the reservation took on the familiar routine of school, playing with friends, and enjoying the pristine beauty all around. Although Neah Bay at the time was gradually looking more like a typical American community, meaning pavement, cafés, a general store, and several gas stations, and even a movie theatre, there were still lots of forested areas all around us. It was a great place for boys to play war games. We especially enjoyed games like Cowboys and Indians. Arguments would ensue about who got to be the Indians. In a way, it was an idyllic time, a time to be wild and free with little to worry about except one thing: how best to avoid conflict at home. By now, I had learned how to avoid my stepfather whenever possible. Still, there was a time or two when our stressed relationship became especially toxic.

One year, there was a big fire in our town that completely destroyed the corrugated metal and wood building along the front street that housed the huge diesel generator that provided our small community with electricity. Within a week or two, a large barge was floated into the bay in front of our town with a portable generator on board that could provide enough electricity for the entire town. A work crew began immediately to set it up.

My stepfather, obviously aware of my youthful naiveté, told me that if I took an empty bucket to the men working to set up the generator and asked for a bucket of electricity, we could then throw it on the side of the house and our lights would work. I felt a little uncomfortable. It didn't seem to make sense. However, he was an adult, and I believed he must know about these things, and besides, I wanted to please him. I can still see myself, bucket in hand, standing in front of a rather large man wearing a yellow hard hat and asking, "Sir, may I have a bucket of electricity?" The man looked down on me with a puzzled expression, and then looked toward my mother and stepfather who were standing a little way off. Then everyone began to laugh. They thought it was funny, and it was—to everyone but me.

Negative comments reinforced by stupid acts had more than the usual impact on my self-esteem. I began to believe things about myself that would plague me throughout much of my life. Early on, I pictured myself as inadequate and stupid. For many years, especially through high school, I experienced a painful lack of confidence in any social situation. It was especially apparent when I would try to talk to a girl I liked. Most of the time, I would try to avoid eye contact, and when those frightening occasions came when I actually talked to some reasonably attractive girl, I would become so nervous that my face twitched, my throat became dry, and my words came out a jumbled mess of nonsense. Or there would be moments of embarrassing and awkward silence that would make the girl extremely uncomfortable as well. It happened with other people, too, and teachers and other adult acquaintances usually thought of me as painfully shy or overly self-conscious. I was all of these things, for sure, but mostly I was a badly broken person with missing parts in need of a spiritual and emotional makeover, even if I wasn't aware of it at the time.

Strange as it sounds, I have come to understand in retrospect that the gracious finger of God was involved in my life all along, preserving and shaping my life so that I could be of use to Him and His purposes. One of the ways God was doing this was by minimizing the effect of negative experiences in my home by balancing them with some good times with my birth father.

The divorce had been a type of abandonment by our father. Even though we all lived in the same small town, we did not see him very often, and for the most part, he was absent from our early lives, with the exception that my oldest brother Ben chose to live with him. As I grew older, I would walk the short distance across town to the place where my father lived. By now he had become a commercial salmon and halibut fisherman—something he would do for the rest of his life. And he was good at it. As I grew older, of course I not only longed to get to know and to spend time with him, I desperately craved the father/son relationship that was absent with my stepfather. Even though my real dad had done little to help my mother with clothes or toys or anything else we might need through the years, I would find my way over to his house, without my mother's knowledge, and ask if I could go fishing or hunting or cutting firewood with him.

I quickly discovered him to be easy going and fun to be with. Sometimes he would reach into his pocket for a dollar and hand it over. In those days, a dollar would buy a candy bar, pop, and even get you into a movie with change left over. What I really wanted though was fatherly companionship. He never once rejected my requests to go with him to hunt or cut wood or fish, even though I was often more a hindrance than help. I took special delight in the few times I went with him and my brother Ben to rocky areas, during low-tide, to catch "devil fish". My father would typically use a long stick with something called "blue-stone" (copper sulfate) attached to one end that caused the *"fish"*, when prodded by the stick, to come out from its hiding place under the rocks. They weren't actually fish at all but giant octopus with (eight) four-foot or longer tentacles with powerful suctions, about the diameter of a quarter that could wrap around your legs once cornered. My dad would then somehow manage to grasp them by the head and with a quick motion that I could never quite discern, disable them so that they could not use their beak to bite. My father thought of these giant "calamari" as a real delicacy. I wasn't so sure!

Going out on the ocean with him in his little boat presented a special challenge. I had a tendency to suffer motion sickness. There were times when I would become so deathly seasick that I would spend much of the time hanging over the side. It was not a pretty sight, and it threatened to disrupt his fishing efforts. Imagine having to pick up your fishing gear at a time when fish were biting as fast as you could get your line in the water because your son is seasick? Even now, I can see myself lying prostrate in the front of his boat, weak and tired and barely able to hold up my head, while my father pulled in one big salmon after another. Every now and then, he would holler out to me above the din of the engine and the sound of the waves lapping against the hull to take a look at a particularly large Chinook salmon on the line. On occasion, he'd ask me to hand over a gaff, fish club, or net so he could land the fish. I would then make another feeble effort to comply while fumbling around to find the landing net or whatever else he needed and hand it over. I would then flop back down to rest to the steady staccato sound of the motor and the smells of the engine fumes that contributed to my getting sick in the first place.

Through all of those times though, my father never once criticized or made fun of me. Instead, he did his best to be the kind of father I could love and appreciate. In later years, I overcame my tendency for motion sickness, eventually bought a small salmon troller of my own, and learned to have the same love for fishing on the ocean that he had.

My experience relating to my father in this good way suggests that God is never far from any one of us, working through all of our relationships, even broken ones, to help shape and mold us. In retrospect, it was an aspect of preventive maintenance for the Holy Spirit to rekindle my relationship with my birth father in this way. Sometimes it is hard for people to trust God the Father if they have not had a good relationship with the most significant male figure in their lives. A restored relationship with my father was a step toward getting to know God the Father. A genuine encounter with Him, however, would require something more dramatic. I was about to learn that for some, God's greatest revelation of His Person occurs when we are placed in situations outside our comfort zones, a place in the desert or some other wilderness. Maybe even on a stormy sea in a broken boat. There, separated from our familiar, our vulnerabilities (the truth about ourselves) are exposed and God can reveal Himself to us in a unique way. A forced move from the reservation to a desert of a different sort would provide a place for me to meet Jesus for the first time.

My journey from my familiar to the unknown started with an opportunity and a circumstance. The opportunity came when my stepfather was offered a job at McChord Air Force Base in Tacoma, Washington. By this time, he had ended his military obligation and was employed as a civilian employee with the government. The move to Tacoma would mean a job promotion.

Fourteen years old by then and beginning to feel independent, I vigorously protested any move from the reservation. I liked my familiar, even if it was at times dysfunctional. But then this circumstance conspired with my stepfather's job opportunity to add further incentive to move. My older brother Leonard had contracted rheumatic fever as a child, and his illness had severely limited his early childhood education. His lost school time coupled with our chaotic home life greatly inhibited his ability to read. For reasons I do not understand, the school simply passed him on from grade to grade each year even though he couldn't read the simplest of books.

My mother was deeply troubled by this but never knew how to address it. His situation, like mine had been, was especially critical. If he failed to learn to read soon, he would face the same fate I might have faced if I had not learned to read. My mother knew that his only chance to escape poverty and likely alcoholism was by taking advantage of the job offer. Moving to a far-away city school would mean an opportunity to get special education help. It would be my brother's last chance. And for my mother, it would mean that she could finally escape the place where she had endured so much disappointment. Everyone could see the advantages in a move but me.

All of this meant that I had no allies in my resistance to the move. Realizing the hopelessness of my cause, I desperately pleaded to stay in Neah Bay. My mother would have let me if I had found a way.

My first choice was to move in with my older sister, Yvonne. She was an attractive girl with lots of promise, but she eventually paid a large price for living in our dysfunctional home. She was the second oldest, and I still have memories of the loud arguments she would have with my stepfather followed by the slamming of the door and my sister running from our home in tears. She couldn't have been more than eleven or twelve at the time. Her eventual response to our unhappy home was to seek escape in relationships. And just like our mother, she looked for it in male companionship. Against my mother's desperate pleas that she not wed, at the age of seventeen she did it anyway, dropping out of school to wed an older man who was completely unsuitable for her.

Not surprisingly, their relationship quickly deteriorated. Bitter arguments and threats of bodily harm soon became part of their life. I was no more than twelve or thirteen when, during one of their frightful arguments, I dared to grab a two by four out of her husband's hands just as he drew it back to hit her.

Her husband was an athletic, muscular man who could have easily dispensed with me but, fortunately for me, did not. My sister, too, had been a casualty of our family's dysfunction, and now with three kids and a marriage headed for shipwreck, she was experiencing broken dreams. Needless to say, staying with her was not an option. Sadly, my sister ended up experiencing a series of failed male relationships, eventually dying at age forty-nine, due in part, from injuries sustained in a car accident that had occurred years earlier.

Moving in with my father as my older brother Ben had done years before might have been my next best hope. But my father was drinking heavily once again and was living with a woman he would eventually marry and with whom he would begin another family. Besides that, the house they were living in was little more than a barely habitable shack, small, dark, and dilapidated. Another possibility was to move in with my oldest brother, Ben. He had a stable marriage, but with a growing family, he was barely making it financially. I could not stay with him.

All my escape routes to remain in the community had been cut off. I remember the sad day when that realization finally hit me. My heart heavy with sadness bordering on despair, I took a slow walk along the beach one last time, trying to come up with some final option that would afford me a way to avoid the inevitable. With the familiar sound of waves lapping on the shore along a stretch of lonely sand beach that had often served as one of my favorite playgrounds, I quietly let go of my stubborn resistance to the move. I couldn't think of any more alternatives. Resigned to my fate, I said goodbye to some of my favorite friends.

It was a bright, sunny morning the day we all piled into the family sedan and headed out of Neah Bay for a city two hundred miles away—a place with concrete high-rise buildings, stop- lights, lots of cars, big schools, drive-in theaters, hamburger joints, and thousands of well-maintained houses with manicured yards and fenced areas. We were headed for modern suburbia. It was "civilized," it was unfamiliar, and I was already homesick.

CHAPTER 7

In the Shadow of the Space Needle

———————————— ⟨⟨⟨⟩⟩⟩ ————————————

Jesus Christ is the same yesterday and today, and forever.
Hebrews 13:8

It was late August 1960, and I recall seeing our new home in Lakewood, a suburb of Tacoma, for the first time. It was a 1950s-style, white three-bedroom rambler with an attached double-car garage, floor-to-ceiling front windows, and a partially fenced and manicured yard—all nestled beneath five or six large evergreens towering one hundred and fifty feet or more over the house on maybe a half acre. At the very back, a small rock garden formed one corner of the fenced property. There were other homes on the sides and in the back and across the street, mostly hidden by carefully groomed rhododendrons and small flowering trees. In the front was a busy two-lane road, partially obscured by trees and shrubbery. It was the typical highway through modern suburbia. A little more than a mile down the road were a recently completed, state-of-the-art strip mall, health services, a hospital, schools, and multiple grocery and drug stores. We had access to anything one would ever need or want. And there was this: our new neighborhood was not like anything our family had ever experienced. It was clean, it was middle class, and it was more home than we had ever experienced. And while I am sure my mother must have welcomed this, in my sorrow at the loss of my familiar, I hated it.

That first day, I spent the initial hour in my new surroundings working through my grief. Making my way around to the back of the house, I found a secluded spot under a tall tree and threw myself onto the manicured lawn. Feeling discouragement and self-pity, my new friends, and despairing over my loss of forests, sand beaches, and the wild, I felt hemmed in, lost and abjectly alone. I longed for my familiar. I wanted to return to the well-known land of my tribe. I wanted to find myself in a walk on the beach. Adjusting to this was going to be a big challenge, maybe an impossible one.

My first day of junior high school a few days later was terrifying. Sensing my mounting insecurity, my mother drove me the three miles to the school and dropped me off at the front entrance. My sweaty hands trembled as I slowly grasped the door handle of our white 1957 Chevy. I wanted so much to fake illness. Somehow, I managed to fight the urge and slowly exited the car.

As I stood there next to the sedan, transfixed by the scene, the number of students immediately struck me. There must have been a thousand young people (as many as the entire population in my hometown) and not one Indian in the mix, anxiously awaiting entry through the doors of newly constructed Iva Alice Mann Jr. High. Set in front of a tree-lined clearing with ball fields on the side and back and modest homes in the front, it was the first day for the brand new school as well. Momentarily dazed by unfamiliar sights and sounds, I was awakened from my stupor by my mother's voice: "Don, close the car door! I know you will be fine." I doubt if she really believed that as I watched her slowly exit the parking lot past the buses and cars unloading in front of the school. Alone now in my strange new environment, I forced one foot forward and then another and then slowly worked my way through the throng.

As would become a pattern, my self-consciousness and anxiety beat me to the double doors of the school entrance. My only thought, "What do I do now?" Had anyone even noticed me? I must have looked like the proverbial deer caught in head-lights. Somehow, I was able to summon enough composure to get through the day. While there were a few moments of panic at not being able to find my next class and not having the cour-age to ask, I got through the morning classes. During the noon lunch break, I found my way to the cafeteria where I choked down lunch at the end of the bench in a lonely corner. It was like being in first grade once more.

It wasn't easy being me then. An intense feeling of being alone in an alien and foreign land prevailed. It didn't get better any time soon. Most days during the lunch hour, I retreated to a discrete corner in the back of the cafeteria to quickly devour a sandwich, a cupcake, and anything else my mother might have packed. On a few occasions, I would quietly slip behind the school and find a lonely place to wolf down my lunch. As far as I know, no one ever noticed my strange conduct.

Getting home from school was no fun either. When I lived in Neah Bay, I had always walked less than a block to get to school. Now I was getting on a bus that stopped at many places along the way, and all the bus stops seemed alike. I experienced something like a desperate panic at each one. Not wanting to seem stupid by asking questions, it took me awhile to finally muster enough boldness to ask the bus driver for pertinent in-formation about my bus stop. Naturally, I got off at the wrong place several times and ended up having to walk a mile or two before eventually getting home.

After several months of this painful behavior, I began to adjust. Eventually I began to relate to others and even joined the regular lunchtime crowd in the cafeteria. I didn't talk much, though, since most of my thoughts were consumed by homesickness and feelings that as a black-haired, brown-skin guy I stood out like a sore thumb. Each day at school could not end soon enough for me.

Ironically, the move to the city seemed problematic only for me. My brother Leonard, whose illness and learning disability had precipitated our move in the first place, adjusted to suburban life much easier than I had. Older by almost three years, in spite of his learning disability, he was better adjusted socially. Whereas our new environment seemed to bring out my dysfunction, he seemed to flourish, revealing both resilience and determination to rise above his circumstances. He even managed to overcome the stigma of being a "special ed" student and any feelings of inferiority he might have had because he was Indian in a mostly white environment. He made friends easily, and for the first time I saw him pick up a newspaper and begin to read it. The move for him had paid off.

It was beginning to pay off for me too, although I did not recognize it. Without a hint of God working in my life, I was now at a place where He could begin to reveal myself to me, a most frightening thought, especially with all the emotional baggage I was carrying. Even more importantly, God was about to make known more of Himself to me— His grace and mercy in taking us with all of our past curses and turning them into blessings. Experiencing a gracious and merciful God was the key to my healing. God was still a distant concept, not someone I felt I could call on to help me through my awkward and difficult times. And of course, I was still a self-conscious and self-absorbed person.

While my new environment was good for me, I little understood this at the time. In hindsight, I can see what it accomplished: it helped to surface the deeply rooted anxieties that life on the reservation had concealed. The intense feelings of aloneness, inferiority, and lack of self-confidence were certainly present in Neah Bay too. But since my failed first year of school, living among my own people in familiar surroundings had provided a level of comfort and reassurance that prevented me from having to face those feelings. Without symptoms, I had no need of a cure. In truth, if I had not moved from that place of comfortable complacency in the land of the familiar, it is likely my peculiar behaviors would have surfaced in some other context. I might have experienced something similar to what my father had gone through when forced by his circumstances to forego his childhood. His sense of not being all that he could have been followed him throughout his life.

My new setting afforded another quite surprising, if not unexpected, circumstance that would serve as a catalyst to faith in God. Because of the large military community in the Tacoma area, McChord Air Force Base, Fort Lewis (now referred to as Joint Base Lewis/McChord) and the nearby Bremerton Naval Shipyard, I became increasingly aware of America's crucial role as a counterbalance to communism.

My interest in international affairs had actually begun to develop in 1957, the year that the USSR launched *Sputnik* into orbit. The successful launch of the Russian satellite caught America off guard and ignited the race into space that culminated with the United States successfully landing men on the moon in 1969.

Even though I was living on an Indian reservation far removed from the world of politics and space technology, for some reason I developed a keen interest in books about military rocket science and satellites. Perhaps my interest in military hardware was influenced by the disproportionate number of Makah men and women who had served in the U.S. military. It is also possible that my interest in military space technology was spurred by the small U.S. Air Force early warning radar site located in our community. I have fond memories of opportunities afforded community members to tour the complex, situated on a hill high above the village, during Armed-Forces Day. Before long, I had become familiar with the U.S. military rocket arsenal, including Redstone, Atlas, Titan, Polaris, Jupiter, Thor, Minute Man, and other rockets, eventually memorizing their engine thrusts and range. Sometimes, I would set my alarm to wake up early in the morning to watch the first televised launch of rockets carrying American astronauts into space. Through the years my interest in this never dissipated. Quite unexpectedly, a friend who worked with NASA, got permission for me and a co-worker to watch the launch of STS-72 (shuttle Endeavour) from a special viewing area located barely three miles from the launch pad in late January of 1996. Experiencing the intense roar of millions of pounds of rocket engine thrust and the concussion it produced while sitting in a viewing stand so near the launch pad was an experience I will never forget. (I eventually had opportunity to witness a night launch of Discovery from the same location several years later.)

At some point, this interest in the race into space spilled over into international politics. This was not such a big leap. Even though I was by now a young teen, it was a growing concern of mine that the Soviets were not only sending men into space; more ominously, they were also building a powerful nuclear arsenal of their own. Caught up in Cold War tensions of the times and fully aware of the range and horrific destruction a nuclear–tipped, intercontinental ballistic missile (ICBM) could do, I began to question what the future might hold. Then an event occurred that further added to the world's stress and mine. On October 30, 1961, the Soviets detonated a mammoth, 58-megaton thermonuclear bomb, the equivalent, by some estimates, of 100 million tons of TNT. It was and remains to this day the largest man-made explosion ever achieved. It is not hard to imagine what a bomb of that size would do if it were dropped on New York City or any other American city for that matter; it would likely vaporize ground zero for miles around. Compare that to the 15 kiloton bomb (15,000 tons of TNT) estimated to be the destructive power of the bomb that destroyed Hiroshima and you can get a sense of what I mean.

Determined to use Soviet military and space accomplishments as a means of promoting the superiority of communism over capitalism, then Soviet Premier Nikita S. Khrushchev boldly predicted that one day the Soviet Union would "bury the U.S." His bluster seemed to have merit. Already, the Russians were expanding their political and military influence throughout Southeast Asia and were seeking to accomplish the same in South America. I was convinced that our country and way of life was at great risk.

The growing tensions between the super powers eventually reached critical mass in October of 1962, a little more than a year and several months since we had moved to the city. Labeled "the most dangerous moment in world history" by Arthur Schlesinger, historian during the Kennedy presidency, the Cuban Missile Crisis almost ended life on earth as we know it. It began when the Soviets secretly placed nearly 43,000 troops on Cuban soil and began installing intermediate range, nuclear-tipped missiles.[6]

Only ninety miles from Key West, Florida, the discovery of Soviet ballistic missiles so near the U.S. mainland meant that the entire eastern seaboard of the United States was only minutes away from potential nuclear annihilation. Once discovered, President Kennedy was faced with risky options. He could order an immediate airstrike and maybe an invasion of Cuba and possibly begin World War III. Instead, he chose to respond to this growing threat by ordering the Soviets to remove them.

---

[6]   Dobbs, *One Minute to Midnight*, 66

When they refused, he acted immediately to impose a military blockade, pitting U.S. warships against Soviet freighters carrying more missiles. It was, in his mind, a safer option but obviously a still dangerous one.

Few people living at the time will forget the intense drama portrayed on nightly newscasts as American and Russian warships were set on a collision course while the entire arsenal of nuclear-tipped missiles and nuclear bomb–carrying aircraft of either country were only a momentary decision away from being launched against pre-selected targets. Living in Lakewood with two key military bases no more than a mile or two from our house meant we were literally at ground zero if all-out war were to break out. An eerie pall of doom seemed to hang over the pre-dominantly military community, especially felt in public schools, shopping centers, or wherever else people gathered. War seemed imminent. Then, unbeknown to most people at the time, a near-tragic event occurred that could have been the spark that ignited worldwide destruction.

On October 27, at the peak of the Cuban Missile Crisis, an especially dangerous moment began to unfold on a day that has become known to historians as "Black Saturday." On that near-fatal day, an American U-2 spy plane flying out of Eielson Air Force Base near Fairbanks, Alaska, had gone missing, and it was feared that it had strayed into Soviet territory. A navigation error was responsible. At the height of grave tensions, nothing could have been more dangerous. Especially since earlier that day, another U-2 reconnaissance aircraft had been shot down over Cuba by a Russian SAM missile and the pilot had been killed. President Kennedy was immediately informed about the situation occurring over Russia by Secretary of Defense, Robert McNamara. The Russians were also tracking the errant plane and had scrambled at least six fighter jets to intercept and shoot down the plane. The U.S. Strategic Air Command had, in the meanwhile, responded by scrambling its own fighters. What made the incident especially dangerous was that communications in those days were primitive by today's standards. Battlefield commanders sometimes did not know what was happening and were susceptible to making decisions without appropriate authorization. To make matters even more dangerous, during the heightened tensions, military leaders of both countries had increased their military readiness to their highest state. The Soviets had even moved nuclear-tipped cruise missiles to firing positions only fifteen miles from Guantanamo Bay. Meanwhile, the U.S. military had previously initiated DEFCON 3, just two-step short of all-out nuclear war.[7] It effectively meant that the entire U.S. nuclear bomber fleet, along with intercontinental ballistic missiles, could be launched within fifteen minutes of a presidential order.

Nearly fifty years later, we know from the information available that at the height of the tensions, the U.S. military had targeted nearly 3,000 nuclear bombs for delivery to pre-selected Russian targets.[8] The Russians, although with fewer warheads and the means to deliver them, had responded accordingly. A decision by one or other of the parties to the conflict, sparked by something as inadvertent as a plane straying into one or other's territory, or the provocative act of downing a plane, could have easily triggered the initiation of the missile launch sequences that could have ended much of civilization as we know it. Fortunately, and at the last minute, the pilot of the errant plane flying out of Alaska realized his error and managed to correct his course in time enough to elude Russian interceptors. He glided his out-of-fuel aircraft to a safe landing on Alaskan soil.[9] And, perhaps more significantly, the U.S. military did not

---

[7] Ibid., 51

[8] Ibid., 276

[9] Ibid., 274

launch a retaliatory strike against the Russians for shooting down the U-2 spy plane over Cuba.

For my readers who were born in a post-Cold War era, you might have difficulty grasping the intensity of the fears of that time or understand how close we came to ending civilization. At one point in his shortened presidency, a greatly troubled President Kennedy had serious concerns about mankind's future. And so did many others. A popular song of the era being played on the radio echoing this fear was Barry McGuire's haunting, "The Eve of Destruction."

Soon thereafter, sanity prevailed, and President John Kennedy and Premier Nikita Khrushchev reached an accommodation resulting in concessions on both sides and an agreement that ended the threat. Modern efforts to reduce the numbers of nuclear warheads were born out of this near catastrophe. This is not the whole story, though. The Cuban Missile Crisis demonstrated that humankind's technological advancements can take on a dark side, often triggering unpredictable, chaotic events that can lead to catastrophic consequences. Things in a fallen world can get out of hand very quickly. It nearly happened then with all of the accidents and near accidents, disruption in communications, and the inability of political leaders of either country to communicate on a timely basis. If you add to that mix the egos of the respective leaders and their tendencies under duress, you can easily imagine how dark spiritual forces working in the hidden world of the spirit likely worked hard behind the scenes of human frailty to push mankind over the abyss. I am convinced that except for a slim thread of restraint guided by a powerful unseen force working inside the scenes of history, the end of all things, as we know it, would have already occurred. And, if that had occurred, I would not have been around to write this book. I would eventually learn a vitally important truth: that it is for the elect's sake (those called to faith in Jesus) that God restrains cataclysmic events from occurring prematurely.

Just as importantly, I would come to understand that the Holy Spirit, functioning behind the unfolding scenes of history does this. Nevertheless, all of this was happening during an impressionable period in my life, a time when I did not know God or His sovereign authority over all things, and that led to my anxiety. I was not the only one. Many Americans who could afford it had installed underground fallout shelters in their backyards. Part of the yard work my brother Leonard and I did for a widowed lady who lived close to our house included climbing down into her underground fallout shelter to recycle fresh air by turning a manual crank. Interestingly enough, in our present age, with terrorism the new threat and political instability across the world on the rise, there has been a renewed interest in the construction of fallout shelters in the United States. Fear and anxiety regarding our future is once again on the increase.

Amazingly, all of this worked to my benefit. The mounting anxieties of the times along with my loneliness eventually led me to a place and time where God could speak to my heart, and I would listen.

I was about to enter tenth grade when I found myself occasionally lingering over late-night religious programs, especially one hosted by the well-known evangelist Billy Graham. One evening, I heard him declare that God would have the last word to say about world history. History was God's domain to determine, in accord with His timing and purposes, not man's. I wanted to believe this. But where was God in a world seemingly bent on destruction? And who was Billy Graham anyway? Was what he preached true? I was about to find out.

It was July of 1962, the time I believe that God had intended for me to have an encounter with His Son, Jesus. It had been almost two years since we left the reservation, and by now, we had settled into life in suburbia. As a family, we had gotten into a weekend pattern of sleeping in, mowing the yard, or taking car rides out into the country, which I looked forward to with some anticipation. Some days we would drive to Mount Rainier, called "Tahoma" by the local Indian tribes. Only a two-hour drive from our home, the great 14,000 foot mountain, a dormant volcano, stood out on a clear day like a giant ice cream cone, beckoning one and all to come and enjoy its flavors.

On other weekends, we raced go-carts with my stepfather. By this time, he and I had reached some kind of accommodation. While it was not the ideal relationship and I still felt uncomfortable around him, we maneuvered around the stresses that had inflamed our relationship through the years. Home life was still intense and times around the dining room table uncomfortable, but my mother and stepfather had adapted to their new life together and I to them. I think my mother was especially pleased to be free of the reservation community where so much of her pain had originated. Of course, she was very pleased that my brother Leonard was doing so well. The summer of 1962 was a turning point for all of us.

On July 8, an especially bright and warm day in the Pacific Northwest, our family chose a weekend outing that would forever change my life. During that summer, Seattle was host to one of the last great World Fairs in the United States. With the far-reaching theme "Century Twenty One Exposition," the Seattle World's Fair had, as its most noted attraction, a 605-foot tower with a rotating restaurant at the top called the Space Needle. Also featured were exhibits intended to showcase future achievements in: the World of Science, the World of Communication, the World of Commerce and Industry, and a futuristic monorail system from downtown to the fairgrounds, along with large exhibit halls with the latest displays in technology. A football stadium sat right in the middle of it all.

When we arrived at the fairgrounds, I took a step back to get a better view and then craned my neck as far as I could to look up at the Space Needle, the crowning icon of the fair. The Space Needle was more than a marvel of technology and engineering; it was a magnificent symbol of promise for a better world tomorrow. Technology promised to solve all of mankind's problems. I remember my excitement as we walked through the turnstiles past uniformed employees, many of whom were dressed in exotic colors and representing many nations, the voices of excited children on the roller coaster in the background. People were everywhere, and I could feel their excitement.

Then, just as I was about to start toward one of the exhibits, someone handed me a bookmark with the invitation, "Come and hear Billy Graham today, 2 P.M. at Memorial Coliseum. All seats free." Printed on the bookmark was a picture of a fortyish Graham—resolute, piercing eyes, Bible in hand—and a Scripture verse from Hebrews 13:8, "Jesus Christ is the same yesterday and today and forever."

I was surprised; Billy Graham was at the World's Fair? Immediately, my curiosity was piqued, and I was determined to go and listen to the famous evangelist whose messages had captivated me during my late-night trysts with the radio. It took a little negotiation with my parents, but they relented and let me go.

I arrived at least an hour early at Memorial Coliseum. According to the notation on the bookmark I received as I entered the fairgrounds, Graham's message would be "Man in the 21st Century." As I sat down, I wondered, "Is there really going to be a twenty-first century?" I was not so sure. I was never more ready to hear his message.

For the very first time I was about to meet Jesus in, of all places, the shadow of the Space Needle. I was soon to learn that He not only held the future of the world in His hands but mine as well.

CHAPTER 8

Out from Under the Table

———— ⟨∞⟩ ————

When Christ calls a man, He bids him come and die.
—Dietrich Bonhoeffer

Imagine a teenager going to a stadium and choosing to listen to a sermon over all of the enticements of a World's Fair! This sounds strange even now, especially given how unsettled my spiritual and emotional states were at the time. If anything, I felt alienated from God. I was aware of Him, to be sure, but I did not know Him as my Savior.

In retrospect, I am convinced that I did not go to the Billy Graham event of my own accord. Instead, I had been drawn by a Divine power that had orchestrated all of my circumstances to bring me to this place in time. My experience was comparable to the time my grandfather summoned me to go back with him to Neah Bay. I did not know who he was or where he intended to take me and because of that, I was afraid. However, his kind smile and gentle voice persuaded me to crawl out from under the table that had been my hiding place. It seems as if all along God had been carefully preparing me for this moment, often through circumstances I could not possibly understand. These included the witness of a teacher, little-understood Bible stories, and disappointing conditions, even through my stepfather's job opportunity.

Placed in another context, it seems as if God had been gathering and assembling bits and pieces of broken relationships and difficult conditions to lead me to this moment in time and place. It was something like Medaris Bad Horse and his friends, who had gathered broken car parts and collected an assortment of rusty old tools from the refuse that had collected in their yard to fix their broken car. The occasion for beginning my assembly, however, seems ironic. The Seattle World's Fair on July 8, 1962, at 2 P.M., Memorial Stadium. The person God would use to introduce me to Jesus was the most famous evangelist of the twentieth century, Billy Graham.

With a sense of expectation bordering on excitement, I arrived at the twenty-thousand-seat football stadium earlier than most. Small by today's standards, the sports facility was built long before the fair itself, mostly for high school or semi-pro football games. The fair planners had simply made cosmetic improvements and built around the existing structure so that it fit the fair's futuristic decor.

As I ascended the aisle to mid-level, eventually selecting an aisle seat, I could not help but wonder how I ended up here. Meanwhile, ushers were preparing for the crowd. The choir, assembled from an assortment of local area churches, began practicing their hymns under the capable direction of Cliff Barrows, Billy Graham's long-time associate.

Soon, the stadium began to fill with a diverse collection of people, young and old. Clearly, Billy Graham's reputation as America's leading evangelist was a big draw. As I sat there in my faded blue jeans and a long-sleeved blue shirt, a little inappropriate for that warm July day, I began to feel that I was in the right place at the right time. Somehow it felt like I was meant to be there. Before long, the choir began in earnest to sing a medley of Christian music, followed by welcomes and greetings from local Seattle officials. Then Billy Graham stepped up to the podium. Bible in hand, hair pushed back, his presence conveyed the same authority that first attracted me to his late night radio messages.

Once Reverend Graham began to preach, I sat there hanging onto his every word. It was as if he knew I was in the audience with all of my fears and anxieties and designed his message accordingly. As he began to expound on the text, he deftly painted a picture of the world I had been increasingly aware—a world with broken and missing pieces and therefore headed for destruction. Because of human sin, modern technology—heralded as the promise for a better world to come—was susceptible to a dark side. Technological advances made it possible for an enemy to make a nuclear device small enough to fit into a suitcase, be discretely transported, and casually left behind in a city like Seattle or New York. Detonated with some kind of timing device, the resulting explosion would likely kill thousands, maybe even millions of people. This was 1962, no less! Today, something like this scenario is considered a likely objective of terrorist organizations.

Then, Reverend Graham added something I had not considered. Apart from a saving relationship with Jesus Christ, there could be no hope for a world with broken and missing pieces. Not now and not in the twenty-first century. Not ever. I carefully weighed his words as Graham explained that Jesus loved us and that He had died on the cross for our sins. His subsequent resurrection was hope for eternal life. He emphasized that Jesus alone could offer the security and the hope the world so desperately craved.

His message concluded, Billy Graham gave the invitation to come and receive Jesus Christ as Savior and Lord. He explained that counselors were standing by in the field below to pray with those who came down. Everyone was asked to bow in prayer as Graham renewed the invitation to come forward and receive

Jesus. The choir began to sing softly while the pianist began to play the words to the famous hymn, "Just as I am."

For an entire minute, I sat there wondering if I should go forward. In the midst of my indecision, I happened to notice the man next to me. We had been sitting side by side for the better part of an hour and had not so much as acknowledged one another. Out of the corner of my eye, I could see the man looked to be in his fifties, was casually dressed, of medium build, and had his head bowed in fervent prayer. The sight of his devotion sparked two questions: "Are you certain of your salvation? Do you know where you would spend eternity if you were to die?" While I did not realize it then, I came to understand that it was the Holy Spirit speaking to my conscience through the preached Word and the pious demeanor of this stranger.

This was all the motivation I needed. Rising from my seat, I surveyed the scene below before descending the aisles toward the stadium floor. Then I took my first steps of faith. Each step along the way was reminiscent of my crawling out from beneath the table where I had hid from my grandfather years before. This time, it was God issuing the invitation. Once again, a court decision was the primary impetus forcing me out of my hiding place. It was a court like none other; it was the court of God. The Great Judge of the Universe had ruled in my favor through His Son Jesus and elected me to salvation. The custody battle over whose child I would be had been settled once and for all; I was now one of God's children. I soon memorized John 1:12: "Yet to all who received Him, to those who believed in His name, He gave the right to become the children of God." What I would learn later is that my election and adoption into the family of God had been determined from all eternity. Roman 8:29 says, "For those God foreknew, He also predestined to be conformed to the likeness of His son, that He might be the first born among many brothers."

Explaining the spiritual transaction that had just taken place was impossible. All I knew was that I was a sinner and Jesus loved me and had offered to forgive my sins. As I worked my way through the gathering of a thousand people, a college-age man of Asian ancestry approached me. He introduced himself as one of the counselors and asked if I was a Christian. I told him I didn't think so, but I wanted to be. He proceeded to explain the way of salvation and then prayed with me to receive Jesus as my Savior. Reaching into a satchel he was carrying at his side, he pulled out a packet of Bible study lessons and handed them to me. He encouraged me to fill out the study and mail it to the Billy Graham Evangelistic Association in Minneapolis. With each completed lesson, they would send additional lessons to help me in my walk with Jesus. He then encouraged me to pray and read God's Word and to find a church home where Christ was honored. Mulling this over, I slowly worked my way out of the stadium to the place where my parents and I had agreed to meet following the service. By now, I was growing anxious. The service had lasted longer than I had anticipated. Of course, I had not expected I would be meeting Jesus that day. How could I explain that?

I was relieved to see them at the appointed place. They were waiting patiently, obviously more than a little concerned. My stepfather was the first to notice something had changed. He had a quizzical, slightly suspicious look accompanying his question: "What happened to you?" I was unaware that there was a big grin on my face. It was the first external evidence of the miraculous transaction that had just taken place. Five words tumbled out of my mouth, ones that even surprised me: "I just became a Christian." It was the first acknowledgement of my newfound faith. From the moment the words came out, I could see the look on my parent's faces of surprise and maybe even a hint of concern. I was surprised, too. What had just happened?

Once past that nervous moment, we quickly resumed our activities for the rest of the afternoon, enjoying the sights and sounds of the fair. It was still a beautiful, warm July afternoon in Seattle. The fair was full of exciting attractions and brilliant sunlight. Then there was this added feature: now the Son was shining in my heart as well. Wherever we went, I had a great new sense of God's purpose and presence. The fair's underlying theme, "Man in the 21st Century," had taken on an entirely different meaning. For the first time in all of my young life, I had the confident assurance of knowing that no matter what happened, I had a blessed future because of Jesus. My often-chaotic life of seemingly random acts of disappointment, going back at least a generation to my grandmother's premature death, had suddenly been transformed. In an instant, the Great God of the Universe, the Master Mechanic who can fix anything, had made me one of His children.

There was much for me to learn. I was still the insecure, lacking-in-confidence person I had always been. Like Medaris's broken car, there were broken parts and missing pieces to my life, and I needed a lot of repair work. There were things about my generational history and my response to it that would need to be uncovered and dealt with. For now, though, I was running on the good road of life in Christ. More importantly, I had a Friend, an Advocate whom I could look to for help when life took unexpected turns, as it surely would. In relationship to Him, I had significance as a child of God. My worth was not in my goodness but His. My relationship with God was rooted not in my flawed life but in Jesus' perfect life. I soon memorized Ephesians 2:8– 9: "For it is by grace you have been saved through faith—and this not from yourselves, it is the gift of God, not by works so that no one can boast." Another familiar verse summarized the whole of my experience. It was John 3:16, which I committed to memory immediately: "For God so loved the world that He gave His one and only Son that who-soever believes in Him, shall not perish but have eternal life."

Something else may have happened that day in the shadow of the Space Needle, something connecting me to an event that had occurred long before I was born. I believe that when Jesus came into my life that day at the World's Fair in Seattle, the barely smoldering ember of light from God that had been nearly extinguished in my family the day my grandmother died could now be seen dimly shining through the darkness in me, her grandson. Could my coming to faith be an answer to her prayer for her family? Was there some connection between her faithful-ness and my new faith? I will never know for sure, at least not on this side of eternity. However, it does seem to me that God was addressing something terrible that happened in my family a generation before that had precipitated so much suffering. Per-haps the psalmist was acknowledging this hope for good out of evil when he wrote Psalm 112:4: "Even in darkness, light shines for the upright . . . ."

Chapter 9

The Cost of Discipleship

—◦◦◦—

"But God chose the foolish things of this world to shame the wise; God chose the weak things of this world to shame the strong."

1 Corinthians 1:27

Remembering the early days of my faith relationship with Jesus as I began the Bible study correspondence course brings a smile to this day. With each new insight, I would run to my mother and share my latest revelation. I was especially excited to confirm through my own studies the truth of one of the things I had heard Billy Graham say: that while the world's powerful leaders might think they were directing history, God, not leaders or the devil, would have the last say. Chaotic and out of control as it all seemed, a macrocosm of my life up to that time, God was working behind the scenes of history to insure final outcomes, and that every moment, Jesus was holding together the universe. And there was one more all-important truth: Jesus would be coming once again to establish His Lordship over all of His creation and cause all authorities to come under His dominion. This was great assurance in light of my former conviction that the world was spinning out of control and well on its way to oblivion.

My mother listened politely, if not patiently, to my daily discoveries of Bible truth. It was becoming apparent that something had taken control of my life and I wasn't just going through a phase that would soon give way to some other interest. She, however, remained cool to it. The Christian faith had never seemed to be light for her darkness. The vivid memories of her Christian mother's horrible death surely must have affected her trust. And then there was her failed first marriage and the bitter custody hearings to determine who would get the children. Where was God in all of that? It is also possible she recalled how members of my father's church had deliberately miscast her as the villain in those custody hearings. God seemed nowhere in sight. Christianity and blessings did not go together in her mind. Nevertheless, she was happy for me.

None of us were quite prepared for the next intrusion of God into my life. Shortly after my call to faith, we returned to the Makah reservation at Neah Bay to visit family and friends. Word by now had somehow spread around the community that I had become a Christian at a Billy Graham meeting. One day Ruth Ward, a highly respected elder woman from the community and a long-time family friend came to me and said, "Donnie, you should become a Reverend and come home to help your people." Her comment struck a sensitive chord, triggering an immediate revulsion that surprised me.

The truth was, I had not given the pastoral calling the slightest consideration. In fact, from childhood, I was convinced that the ministry was effeminate. Clearly, it didn't seem to work in my native community. Even the church buildings reflected disinterest and lack of money—another version of Medaris' broken car. More importantly, even though I was just 16, I wanted to do other things with my life. Quite frankly, although I had just had a wonderful conversion experience, I had no natural affinity or interest in the ministry. A little embarrassed by the discomfort her suggestion had suddenly aroused in me, I responded to the native elder with a polite, "No, I don't think so."

However, the words had barely escaped my lips when I felt an unusual sensation. It was as if the peace with God I had so recently known simply evaporated. It started with a deep inner conviction that my rejection of the elder's suggestion was also a repudiation of God's plan. Worse, my inner feeling of discomfort wouldn't go away. The question kept repeating itself. Had I just said no to God? Did He want me to enter the ministry? Finally, after struggling internally for several weeks and after much thought and prayer, I resigned myself by saying to God, "If you want me to go into the ministry, I will do it. I'll do whatever you want."

Immediately the peace and joy returned. I knew then that this is what God had planned for me. And I was now committed to obeying His call.

The clarity of the message didn't make any sense though. My past had seemingly done little to prepare me for service in God's kingdom. The circumstances I faced growing up in an unhappy home and the way I responded to them had deeply impacted me. Lack of self-confidence and feelings of inadequacy were present in nearly every social setting. In summary, as a result of my childhood experiences, I had come to believe lies about my life that kept me from trusting God, and these influenced some of my beliefs and behaviors. How could I ever be useful to God?

In time, God's and not mine, I would eventually come to understand that it is not who we are or what we may have experienced that qualifies or excludes us from service in God's Kingdom. It is about His grace and power to take our broken and missing pieces, reassemble them, and transform them for good. God can do this for anyone!

It would also take time for me to determine that genuine discipleship is ultimately a breaking away from our natural understandings and assumptions about the world and ourselves and conforming to God's. My experience called to mind something Dietrich Bonhoeffer had said in his famous treatise, *The Cost of Discipleship*; in it, he makes this point: "At the very moment of their call, men find that they have already broken with all the natural ties to life. This is not their doing, but his who calls them. For Christ has delivered them from immediacy with the world and brought them to immediacy with himself."[10]

In my heart, I had now made the commitment to do whatever God wanted me to do, no matter what the cost. In responding to His call, I was figuratively out from my hiding place beneath the table once and for all. I had been brought from my familiar to the unfamiliar place where God could begin to fix my life and where faith is required.

Nonetheless, from the beginning, my calling should have discouraged me. The fact that I was Native American posed immediate challenges for my faith. As I discussed previously, the linkage between the church's activities in support of government's goals to civilize Indians had been especially demeaning to Native American men. Church was for women and children. I was now beginning to struggle with how to reconcile these past perceptions with the call to the ministry.

One insight from my Bible readings helped to resolve some of the internal conflict that I was experiencing. Shortly after I began my Bible study, I discovered that the cost of discipleship had a warrior appeal to it. There was, at its fundamental core, a very masculine side to the Christian faith that required sacrifice and the denial of self for the good of others. I first noted this emphasis during the Billy Graham correspondence course. Luke 9:23 was one of the verses I studied: "If any man will come after me, let him deny himself and take up his cross daily and follow me."

---

[10]   Bonhoeffer, *The Cost of Discipleship*, 105–106

As I became more familiar with the Bible, I began to understand the soldier-like demands of the faith modeled by Jesus. This warrior Jesus could not have risked more than He did or chosen a manlier fate than to submit to ridicule, abuse, a horrific death on a cross, and all that this entailed in order to accomplish our salvation. This Jesus had now called me to follow Him, and that would mean having to go off road from time to time and experience difficult circumstances for the Kingdom's sake.

I was further motivated when I came to understand that the God we serve calls us to join Him in the fight against the darkness of this world. Men and women are expected to live their lives after the model of Jesus, who gave his life for the Church. I didn't understand what this might require of me immediately, but through the years, I began to appreciate that following Jesus would result in battle scars and suffering for the sake of the Gospel. And the cause, as I would also discover, was well worth the price. I eventually understood that being a Christian meant we were at war with Satan and that the war is ultimately against principalities and powers of the spirit world that contend for the eternal destinies of the souls of men, civilizations, and the world. And these evil beings would align themselves against anyone who dared to take up the cross for Jesus's sake.

What more noble cause than to serve God in this Great War? What greater calling than to enlist as a frontline warrior for the kingdom's sake no matter the cost?

The importance of the ministry was beginning to make sense to me now. But I knew that from the world's point of view, and especially that of my fellow native brethren, my decision would be viewed as foolishness and perhaps even as a betrayal of my native heritage. That being the case, I was right where God wanted me. To accomplish His purposes, God often uses that which is not the norm—what we least expect. That's the reason I believe He chose me for the ministry in the first place. I was the most unfit, the least likely. He knew He could fix me and make me useful in His Kingdom and for His glory.

What I needed next was a church to attend. But which one? There were so many. I tried several. I even invited a pastor or two to come visit me. For whatever reasons, the two I selected seemed intent on discouraging me from my commitment to God's Word. I soon devised a litmus test consisting of two questions to determine if what they believed matched my recent discoveries in the Bible. One, did they believe the Bible was God's Word? That was something I believed strongly. And two, were they convinced that Jesus was coming again to set the world aright? This question was especially relevant since I had been led to faith in Christ in part because I had been so conscious of world issues threatening our security.

Eventually I settled on a Lutheran church just starting up near us. I did not go looking for this church. It came looking for me. One afternoon, the opportunity presented itself with a knock on the door. When I opened it, there stood a tall, bespectacled man in a suit and tie, with a smile on his face, thinning hair, a pleasant demeanor, and brochures in hand. My mother and I invited him in. I wondered to myself, "Did God send this man to our house?" He shared with us that he was starting a new church not far from where we lived and we were welcome to join his fledgling congregation. On a follow-up visit, the pastor affirmed my views on the second coming of Christ and assured me he believed the Bible to be God's Word. There was one small, seemingly insignificant caution light that flickered on an off during our conversation. He was less than enthused when I shared with him that I had recently met Jesus at a Billy Graham meeting. His lack of interest following my statement troubled me, but I quickly dismissed it. I now had a church home!

Almost immediately, I began attending his church. As I got to know him better, I learned that he had been a combat veteran who had seen significant action in Europe during World War II. His lack of enthusiasm for crusade evangelism might have been a little disconcerting, but this military veteran, now a pastor, was just the masculine influence I needed. He took me in and began to mentor me.

Unfortunately, my interest in attending church was not shared by my mother or anyone else in my family for that matter. But since she wanted to encourage me and could see I was excited by my new faith, she came along. In spite of her many disappointments, my mother was really a courageous person, a survivor who had learned not to permit her disappointments to destroy her optimism. Noting a tendency on my part to expect the worse, to imagine the dark side of everything, she was always exhorting me to see the positive in every negative and never quit on anything worthwhile—character values no doubt distilled from all the adversity she had encountered since childhood.

Early on in my Christian faith, I was beginning to discover a God-blessed irony in all of my mother's travails. I had suffered emotionally from some of her choices, born out of her own setbacks. Yet it was out of her pain and failed dreams that I gained some of the most important core values that would help me throughout my Christian life. This was not an all-at-once revelation, but over time I was able to see that all along, God had been collecting the bits and pieces of the shattered parts of her life, using them to mold her character, and then taking what she had learned to counter some of my worst tendencies. Obviously, she had needed to meet the same Jesus who had revealed Himself to me. However, she had a difficult challenge. How could she trust God after all that she had been through? All of that was about to change in a most dramatic way. A seeming miraculous intervention on a dark river late one night would play a major part. The event took place a little more than a year after I had become a Christian.

CHAPTER 10

Miracle on the Quileute

———— ◈◈◈ ————

"When you pass through the waters I will be with you; and when you pass through the rivers, they will not sweep over you. . . ."

Isaiah 43:2

My mother was related to two tribes: the Makah on her mother's side and the Quileute on her father's. Her Quileute tribal ancestry through her father, Bill Penn, permitted her to fish salmon returning to the Quileute River in the fall of the year from their nearly three-year sojourn on the Pacific Ocean.

Salmon returning to their rivers of origin usually wait for the first good rain of the fall, called a "freshet," before beginning their journey up-river. The females, by now beginning to lose their silvery coloring and becoming increasingly emaciated, know they will die soon. Some powerful instinct, however, causes them to persevere in their effort to find the ideal places to lay their eggs, usually in gravel areas. Once they spawn, they offer a final sacrifice. Their decaying carcasses provide nutrients for the next generation. The males, similarly disfigured, then fertilize the eggs and then they also die. Their decaying bodies contribute to the cyclical ritual of birth, life and death and rebirth that, for thousands of years, has provided the native people with an appreciation for the cycles of life.

The often fast-flowing Quileute River, where this spectacle has been repeated for thousands of years, has its origins in the abundant rain and snowmelt of the Olympic Mountains that form the backbone of the lush, thickly forested Olympic Peninsula of Washington State. The clear, cold waters, flowing down from the mountains, past rocks and boulders to the forested valleys below, provide excellent habitat for several varieties of salmon. It had been a key source of food for the tribe for thousands of years.

The Quileutes lived at an ideal location near the mouth of the river. Through the eons of time, they had devised clever ways of harvesting the salmon. Utilizing small cedar dugout canoes along with gill-nets fashioned from nettle roots or other natural wood fibers (and in modern times, nylon mesh), they harvested an abundance of salmon. They did it this way. With one end of the net tied to the canoe, the nets were set perpendicular from near the shore to the middle of the river. Hardened Styrofoam floats spaced every few feet held up the top of the web, while a weighted line fixed to the bottom of the webbing enabled the shallow draft nets to hang straight down without sinking to the bottom. This allowed the net to fish with maximum efficiency as canoe and net drifted with the swift-moving current. Unsuspecting salmon would then swim into the net and become "gilled."

Typically, this type of net fishing, called "drift netting," occurred in the evenings in the fall of the year. Usually, when the river was high with recent rains, the nights were dark, the sky overcast and often rainy, and the fish runs at their peak. I participated in this type of fishing only a few times. It was exciting to hear what you could not see: the splash of a big salmon, twenty pounds or more, swimming into the mesh and being caught in the webbing.

One Friday in late fall, my mother and older brother Leonard decided to drive to La Push, the home of my mother's relatives, to fish on the river. They wanted me to go along with them to help operate the boat. The community of La Push is nearly 200 miles from where we were living in Tacoma, but only a little more than 30 miles along the coast south of Neah Bay.

The journey to the community of La Push on a bright, sunlit day is a feast for the senses. As you drive past vivid greens, browns, and oranges adorning flora and fauna crowding the narrow two-lane highway and descend into the small town nestled along the shoreline, an incredibly gorgeous vista opens up. It's the kind of beauty that will take your breath away. There, in all of its magnificence, is the vast expanse of the Pacific Ocean, long stretches of sand and pebble beaches, and James Island, just a stone's throw from the community. A short distance farther out, rock-like islands of no more than an acre or two, some with trees clinging tenaciously to their sides, rise out of the sea— all of this resplendent in the brightness of the sun glistening on placid waters. If you look carefully, you will certainly capture a glimpse of gulls, sand pipers, and sea puffins. If you are really blessed, you might even catch sight of a sea lion or a gray whale or two cavorting about in the surf. In that moment, whatever else is on your mind dissipates in the magnificence of the beautiful scene before you. Maybe heaven looks a little like this.

My Quileute relatives, who have lived here for countless generations, know that there is another, darker side to this place as well. Winter storms, their legendary fury a wonder of nature, sometimes ravage the region, very often littering the shoreline with a debris field of great logs and stumps and anything else caught in the fury of a storm and tossed onto the beach. Many a boat and a few lives have been lost in the tumultuous waters in front of the community. The *Hojun-Maru* crashed on the shoreline only fifteen miles or more further to the north.

I would have liked to have accompanied my mother and brother that late fall day to La Push. I enjoyed the few opportunities I had to fish on the river. Seeing the ocean again would replenish, however temporarily, my longing for the familiar places of my youth. I could also see that my mother was anxious for me to accompany them. However, I did not want to miss church on Sunday. I did not want to disappoint her, but God was now my first priority, and I was determined not to establish a precedent of missing church worship for a personal pleasure. When I explained my thinking to her, I could see that she was visibly let down. She had been counting on my help. "Couldn't you miss just one church service?" she pleaded.

But I had another reason for saying no. For some reason, I had a strange sense of foreboding. Something was not right about this trip. I wanted to say something about this to her, but my sense of imminent danger was effectively obscured by the uncomfortable feeling that I had made her unhappy. Unable to separate my conflicted loyalties to her and to God, I said nothing.

While I remained at home agonizing over my decision, my mother and brother drove to La Push, a long and tiring drive lasting far into Friday evening. A sixteen-foot, outboard-powered, wood-hulled boat with a gill-net piled inside awaited their arrival. In my absence, they recruited my mother's nephew Earl Penn Jr., who was my age and lived in La Push. He was a far better choice because he knew the river well and had lots of experience as a fisherman.

Soon, the three were motoring up river in the darkness, employing hand-held spotlights to illuminate the way. The river width varied, ranging from 150 to 200 feet or more in places, and there was always the risk of some hidden log or tree in the way. Adding to the isolation, darkness, and possible danger was the dense underbrush and a variety of trees that seemed to crowd the riverbank. Here and there, an old snag or two protruded upwards from the river bottom, withered and worn by the rushing water. Some places along the river had shallow spots where boulders and hidden debris made it risky for outboard motors, often causing damage to the propellers. All factors considered, though, this was a good night for fishing.

Once at the right fishing hole a few miles upriver from the community, they set the net from near the shore toward the center of the river, taking care to avoid any snags that might be in the way. Then, for no particular reason, my cousin did something uncharacteristic. While momentarily pausing from his work of setting the net, he tied the boat end of the net onto his leg instead of fastening it to the bow. The river, swollen from recent rains, was flowing rapidly, and so were the boat and net. Without warning, the net became ensnared in a snag hidden under water. The net end tied to my cousin's leg went taut immediately, causing him to be jerked out of the small boat. He uttered a terrifying scream as he felt himself being thrust overboard by the pull of the net and into the frigid waters. As he flew through the air, he somehow managed to grasp the gunwale of the boat, causing the boat to flip on its side at a dangerous angle. My mother clung desperately to her seat in the bow. Meanwhile, the boat was now at a near-critical state, tipped precariously on its side and beginning to swirl around the snag like it was being drawn into a vortex, susceptible at any moment to being sucked under the cold and dark river.

In a matter of a few microseconds, my brother, who had been seated near the motor in the back of the boat, had managed to reach out with one arm to grasp his cousin, while with the other he somehow burrowed under layers of shirt, sweater, and rain jacket to unsheathe the hunting knife he happened to have with him. In a single motion, he reached out to slice the taut rope with the blade of his knife. Instantly the rope snapped, and the boat, dangerously close to being pulled under, immediately righted. My brother, his adrenalin flowing, somehow pulled his cousin on board and then collapsed to catch his breath, exhausted from the stress.

For long moments, they said nothing. They had been wearing thick coats, heavy sweaters, boots, and layers of clothing. No one had on a life preserver. My mother could not swim, and I don't believe my cousin could either. The river was cold and swift, and the night dark and unforgiving. There was no one around to help them. Were it not for my brother's instinctive action, they would have all drowned.

They made their way to the riverbank, shaken and frightened, and began to reconstruct their near-death experience. Thinking back to the scene, they all remembered one important detail. In the midst of the unfolding drama, with the boat spinning around and darkness all about them, a mysterious light had illuminated the darkness around the boat. It enabled my brother to see what he was doing. Where had it come from? Not the spotlights—they had disappeared in all the chaos. How had my brother, in a matter of microseconds, been able to grasp his cousin with one hand, reach through many layers of clothing with the other, and then cut the rope attached to the net while somehow maintaining his balance in the boat? And why hadn't the water flooded the boat when it was on its side? And how fortunate was it that my brother had only recently honed his knife to razor-edge sharpness?

They sat there quietly for a moment as they contemplated the improbable conditions that had just transpired. They should have drowned. This was apparent to everyone. Why hadn't they? My mother had the answer. It was, she offered, because they had not been alone in their struggle. God had somehow intervened. It was a miracle.

My mother offered a prayer of thanks that night on a lonely beach next to the river that might have been their grave. For the first time since darkness had enshrouded her life with her mother's death and the many other disappointments she had endured, it seemed as if light from God had shone on her and spared her life. From that time forward, my mother began to seek God and eventually became a member of the church we were attending.

There was, however, a sad postscript to this story. A little more than a year later, my cousin, who had also been spared that night on the river, was killed in a horrendous car crash along with two other boys from the community. The other boys were good friends of my cousin and had been drinking. They decided to invite him to join in their fun and had gone to his house to persuade him to go along with them. He was in the back seat when their car, traveling at a high rate of speed, hit a concrete bridge abutment along Pacific Coast Highway 101. My uncle and his family, including my mother and me, were devastated by the loss.

After the funeral service and the traditional dinner customary in such circumstances, at the urging of my mother I got up and spoke to the hundreds of mourning family members and friends about the importance of having a faith relationship with Jesus Christ. It may have been my first public effort to proclaim faith in Jesus as an antidote to drugs and alcohol and, of course, premature loss of life. Unhappily and during the course of my ministry, I would give the same message in similar situations far too often. It was discouraging at times. As I acknowledge earlier, after hearing of Medaris's death, I even considered giving up ministry preparation. But God reminded me how I was like Medaris and his friends and told me He had been fixing me all my life. If He could fix me, the least likely, He could fix anyone.

A week after my cousin's funeral, I was off to Bethany Lutheran Junior College, a small Lutheran liberal arts college in Mankato, Minnesota. The small school was connected to my pastor's denomination. Now that I was a member of his church, it seemed the logical place to begin college and preparation for the ministry. God was not only at work fixing the missing and broken parts of my emotional life; He also needed to prepare me for use in His kingdom through the academic process. I was now facing a new kind of challenge. I had thought of myself as only an average student, maybe even a little below. But now I found that if I did not pass Greek, I could not enter the Lutheran ministry.

God needed to fix that too.

CHAPTER 11

My Greek Teacher and Me

And we know that in all things God works for the good of those
who love Him, who have been called according to His purpose.
Romans 8:28

Random tragedies, like my family experienced when my grandmother died, often leave us not only with grief at our loss but struggling to find answers as to why they happen. I have occasionally wondered how different my life might have been if my family had drowned in the Quileute River that night. How would I have responded? Looking back to that time with the perspective only later years afford, I am convinced God's grace is sufficient for all of our circumstances, no matter how tragic, and that He would have provided sufficient grace for me. Nevertheless, aware of the vulnerability of my new faith at that point, I can see how a tragedy like this could have easily tested my faith to its limits. Instead, their near-death experience and my mother's sense that God had saved them accomplished another purpose. It strengthened my conviction that when a person becomes a believer in Jesus, what seem to be random disappointments of life are joined to the eternal purposes of God. And when this happens, the Holy Spirit takes painful events, even those from a preceding generation, and uses them for good. Of course, we must trust Him. The proof was that my mother's near tragic death inspired her to turn to Jesus. But even before this, God was at work in our family.

This was not an all of a sudden revelation. However, as I began piecing together the broken and missing pieces of my family history, I could see places where God's Holy Spirit had been at work behind the scenes of our lives all along, quietly orchestrating preventive maintenance here, making a little alteration there and replacing a missing part as needed, and perhaps just as importantly, allowing only as much stress as we could deal with at any one time. And as I noted previously, God even seemed to use my mother's difficult experiences born of her own sadness and lost dreams to build in her the character that she in turn used to help shape my life, taking from the broken parts of her life to fix parts of mine.

All things worked together for good.

Still, I had many things to work through—my lack of self-confidence for one. Now, as a result of my pastor's recommendation, I was in Minnesota, the heartland of America, attending a small Lutheran college surrounded by Midwest youth, many of Scandinavian or German ancestry. Of all places to find myself! Nearly 1,500 miles from the Pacific Ocean, I was out of my familiar once again. And that meant that I was just where God could continue to fix aspects of my life.

The small Lutheran school located in Mankato, in southern Minnesota, stood on the edge of a hill high above the town where a little more than one hundred years earlier, on December 26, 1862, thirty-eight Sioux men had been hanged as a result of something known as the Dakota Conflict. It was the largest public lynching in the history of America and would have been much larger had not President Lincoln acted to reduce the number.[11]

---

[11]   Gilman, *The Story of Minnesota's Past*, 120

The events leading to the conflict were rooted in the long history of broken promises made to the Indians to coerce them to move off the land. Sparked by corrupt government officials fraudulently stealing what was promised the Indians, a common practice in those days, the resulting violation of treaty promises of food and medicine reached a crisis point. Some of the younger Sioux warriors decided to take matters into their own hands. Settlers were killed, soldiers sent in, and suspects rounded up and eventually hanged. When I arrived in Mankato, the event was still recounted as part of the orientation of newcomers. Fortunately, I never had to hear about it. In any event, while I was interested in learning more history, even its painful aspects, I had come to learn the disciplines necessary to qualify for becoming a pastor. Bethany Lutheran College seemed an ideal place for this to occur.

Situated on a hill above the town amid tall maples that turned a gorgeous gold and orange in the fall, Bethany Lutheran College, a two-year liberal arts school with fewer than 250 students, was an ideal place for me. It was small and user-friendly for someone with little self-confidence. Although it had the look and feel of architecture left over from the nineteenth century, the five-story brick building that served as the main structure was highly utilitarian, housing administration, a chapel, classrooms, and even men's and women's dormitories.

Shortly after my arrival, we were assembled in the chapel for orientation and election of student officers. Located in the basement of the building, the chapel served as a worship place and a classroom for music. It had seating for maybe three hundred people. When nominations were requested for class officers, someone in the back of the room nominated me for freshman class president, a position mainly intended to coordinate student social activities for the year. Why me? Perhaps my dark complexion caused me to stand out among all the blond, blue-eyed Scandinavian and German students.

Caught off guard by the nomination, I sat in my seat in the back of the room dumbfounded. Obviously, they did not have a clue that I was not exactly the life of the party in any setting. I was still socially reticent and lacked the self-confidence to lead others. How was I going to manage the affairs of my class for an entire year when I was barely learning to manage my own? Before I could open my mouth to object, the nomination was seconded and a vote taken. Suddenly, I was thrust to the front as their elected leader. I swallowed hard and then gave a lucent acceptance speech stating how pleased I was to assume my new responsibilities. In truth, I was full of anxiety. I did not have a clue what my new responsibilities would be. Nevertheless, I adjusted to my new status, even though it took me awhile to learn what I was supposed to do.

As my classmates became more acquainted with me and I began to adjust to classroom routine, I soon developed a comfort level with my new circumstances. Ever so slowly, I began to emerge from my self-consciousness, in part because classmates would draw me out of my self-imposed reticence to talk. Occasionally someone would ask, "If you are an Indian, how is it that you have a last name like Johnson?" With hint of a smile and a sense of humor beginning to grow out of my usual reserve, I would tell them, "Well, actually I am a brown sheep in my Scandinavian family." No one believed me, of course. The truth was there were many people in my native community with the last name "Johnson." When I inquired from an elder in our community how we happened to have names like these, I was told that government agents assigned to our community imposed anglicized names on Makah families by having them select a name out of a hat. To this day, names like Smith, Green, and Johnson are common in my hometown. This has always been my understanding of the origin of my obviously Swedish-origin name until one day, while attempting to uncover my family history, I discovered that I actually had a great grandfather on my father's side whose own father appears to have been of Swedish origin. When he may have immigrated to America or why he ended up on the Olympic Peninsula is hazy at best. It appears, nevertheless, that my last name likely had its origins not in some government official's hat but in Sweden many years earlier and had survived several generations through my ancestry.

After I got over my initial surprise over this discovery and connection to a distant land and people, I began to consider how important even this small part of my heritage had been to my life purpose as God's child. Even though the percentage of my Swedish heritage seemed minimal, it was important in God's design for my life. Had this person with the last name Johnson never immigrated to America or married into my native heritage, I would never have been born. I quickly discerned that God's good and gracious purposes in our lives are revealed in part from all eternity in connection with all of the people in our generational history. It is in the composite of the DNA from all of our ancestry, whoever they may have been or from wherever they may have come, that contributes to all that we are and can be as God's children. This is an insight that is best understood in light of the Apostle Paul's comment: "From one man He made every nation of men that they should inhabit the whole earth, and He determined the times set for them and the exact places where they should live. God did this so that men would seek Him and perhaps reach out for Him, though He is not far from each one of us." (Acts 17:26, 27) Think of the diversity of the people of America and how each people group has made a valuable and unique contribution. And then remember God's ultimate purpose in bringing us together. He wants us to experience His grace and love in the person of Jesus Christ.

Sadly, some people, including many with Native American blood in their heritage, have been made to be ashamed of their ethnicity and may even deny some aspects of it. Through the years, I have been approached by people with Native American heritage somewhere in their genealogy who cannot discover their native roots. One of the reasons is that having an Indian in the family tree was considered an embarrassment. Families often covered it up. Prejudices against one ethnic group or another have long contributed to this. When that happens, there are generational consequences that may even affect our relationship to our Creator. The perception we have of ourselves often affects how we relate to God. Part of the work God was working in my life was to help me resolve to appreciate and embrace every part of my heritage as part of His blessing, even an investment, which He expects me to use wisely. Of course, as I would learn ever so slowly, we cannot become all He intends unless we submit to His working in our lives.

At the time of my election, I was experiencing feelings of inadequacy for reasons other than my heritage. I had a problem. How was I supposed to lead my class? Thankfully, an older student who had served in my position the year before took me aside and helped me see how to accomplish the tasks I had assumed. What seemed a random act, my election, worked for my benefit. My new responsibilities kept me from retreating off into a corner somewhere. I was forced to step out of my usual hiding places and work with others in planning fun social activities. Unfortunately, because I had been socially inhibited much of my life, fun and me did not seem to go together in the same sentence. Nevertheless, as the year progressed, I began to develop the confidence in personal relationships that had eluded me all through high school, and I started to actually experience fun.

In the ensuing years, I would be elected to serve in a number of leadership capacities for my tribe, for the school district, for my denomination, and eventually for the ministry I currently serve. But none was more surprising or came at a more important point in my life than this one election. Once more, in retrospect, I could see God at work turning seeming insignificant events into important ones, chance and circumstance into order, and a formerly chaotic life into one that was beginning to have purpose. He did this so I could better serve Him and, in the process, honor and glorify His Name.

My greatest challenge at Bethany, however, was not leading my classmates to a happier social life. Overcoming my self-image as an average or even below-average student was. Throughout many of my high school years, I had struggled to maintain a C average. I was capable of much better but did not believe it. My self-imposed limitations on my academic performance had to be overcome if I was to succeed in life.

Part of my problem was rooted in my poor academic history. Reservation schools where I had spent the first seven years of my educational life typically do not attract the best, most conscientious teachers, although there were exceptions as borne out by my experience. The best teachers often leave after a short term. Inadequate housing is one of the problems that contribute to the high turnover. Then there is the challenge of teaching in a reservation environment, where divorce, alcoholism, and poverty are so prevalent. For most of my academic life on the reservation, as I related earlier, I had been surrounded by similarly affected youth whose home lives were often dysfunctional. Coming to school tired and anxious from some family disturbance did not translate into academic success. One boy used to walk by our house on his way to school with torn and shredded trousers, and sometimes my mother would intercept him and give him a clean pair or sew up the holes, maybe even give him something to eat.

In an atmosphere like this, I did not think of education as a key to anything. If I gave thought to the future at all, I visualized working in the logging industry or as a commercial salmon or halibut fishermen—things I could do in our own community without having to attend college. Only five years removed from this setting and now living in a more rigorous college academic setting, I worried that I would not be capable enough to get through the course work necessary to enter the seminary.

I hit the wall of my dire self-assessment soon after beginning my first Greek language class. There were probably twenty other students in the class, all intending to become pastors. Many of these students had attended some kind of Lutheran prep school. Naturally, I was full of fear and trepidation as the professor explained his meticulous expectations. My Greek teacher was a small man, probably in his fifties, and balding. His perpetually exuberant expression went along well with his enthusiasm for the subject. But he had a serious and stern side. We all knew the rule. If we did not pass Greek, we would be ineligible for seminary following college.

It was my misfortune to sit next to the brightest guy in class. Sitting next to this genius was a temptation for me to occasionally look over at his scores to compare my progress with his. Not a good idea. He was an outstanding student who seemed to memorize the Greek alphabet easily, including all the assigned tenses and vocabulary assigned each day. Meanwhile, I struggled mightily.

At the end of each class, our professor handed out a new assignment to memorize more vocabulary words and translate classical Greek sentences out of Homer's *Iliad*. My classmates' translations always seemed so refined. Mine were often stilted and halting at best. The truth was, I sometimes mangled the classics into comical renditions of what was actually written in the original. More than once, other students laughed aloud at some of my efforts at translation. Actually, I did too.

My progress was obviously discouraging and led me to question my call. Was I in the wrong place? Had God missed the fact that I might not have the talent needed to go into the ministry? It sure seemed that way. There were times when I would receive a score of sixty percent on an assignment—the equivalent of a D minus, on the edge of failing. I expected to be told at any time I would have to drop out of the class.

But then something unusual happened that was critical to my eventual success. Alongside each low grade I received, the teacher would write something encouraging, like "Good work. Keep trying." Then, on my next assignment, I would receive something better, like a seventy percent. He would then add, "Excellent. You're improving." And so on until I was consistently averaging eighty and ninety percent on all my work. He then added "Outstanding!" or "Excellent!"

His little encouragements may have seemed a small thing. But what if he had never encouraged me? What then? His comments helped me rise above my self-defeating self-assessments and kept me going. One day, at a time when I felt I had reached a place of success, my curiosity prevailed over my self-restraint. If my teacher was writing nice little notes to me, what wonderful things must he be writing to the genius student next to me? I leaned over to glance at his graded work. His usual "A" paper had a one-word comment from the professor: "Good." I suspected that this was the only comment he ever wrote on my neighbor's perfect papers. It dawned on me then that my Greek teacher had been carefully nurturing my positive self-assessment and gradually building my confidence until eventually I believed I could improve. He knew I needed encouragement. The smart student already had overflowing confidence and did not need much encouragement or prompting. God was working to repair the damage of my lowered expectations by giving me self-confidence so that I could be of use to Him. In this situation, He used a wise teacher to instill in me the self-assurance that I badly needed.

Through the years, I have met many people like me—people who set for themselves low expectations, often based on someone else's opinion or repeated disappointments. Sometimes, Satan is only too pleased to reinforce our feelings of self-recrimination and self-doubt. It amounts to a lie that, if internalized, limits our ability to achieve all that God intends for us.

Sadly, many Native Americans have had to contend with a long history of having been marginalized. It was a way to justify all the injustices that had been visited upon them. In fact, only recently has Hollywood stopped reinforcing negative stereotypes of Native Americans popularized especially in John Wayne movies. For far too long, Native Americans have had to endure dark stereotypes even though they have contributed greatly to America's formation, medicines, food groups, and more. Consider just one of many contributions. Long before the formation of the American constitution, the Iroquois Confederation of nations had developed a government system of checks and balances in their relationships with one another. That model eventually served as an example for the American constitution writers.[12] Instead of credits for providing a foundation for America's rise to greatness, the constant barrage of negative rhetoric against Native Americans has made the climb out of dependence and despair much more difficult.

Aware of the danger of diminished expectations growing out of the Native American experience, I try instead to encourage people, regardless of ethnicity, to keep their goals in front of them. I tell them not to give up on themselves and to discover how God has gifted them for use in service to others. Somewhere in our dreams of what we'd like to be, our experiences, our talents, and even our lineage are keys to what God would have us become.

---

[12] Johansen, *Forgotten Founders*, 9

My Greek professor's careful use of encouragement helped me to rise above the boundaries I had unconsciously set for myself. I could accomplish a lot. I just did not believe it. In order for me to be useful in God's kingdom work, it was necessary for Him to have that part of me fixed. Otherwise, I could not fulfill His expectations for my life if I was fixated on my failed self. For me, this has been a lifelong struggle in every new situation. Even now, I find myself from time to time needing someone to come along side me to encourage me when my tendency for self-doubt arises. Along the way, I have discovered that old habits of thinking and doing die hard.

The call to discipleship is in part a call to persevere in becoming the unique individuals God has intended us to be from all eternity. When we answer His call, we are led by the Holy Spirit to discover that we are born with certain gifts and talents and experiences, including our generational heritage; together, these makeup God's design for our lives. When these are yielded to God, they are transformed for good. Thus, we need not be satisfied with our limiting self-assessments nor should we permit disappointment to become a curse. God has a different plan for us. We are called to become something different than what we were. That realization has come to be one of the most important insights that has served to guide my life purpose and informs a key goal of the organization I currently lead, Lutheran Indian Ministries.

Chapter 12

The Pass Over

*When we in darkness walk and no longer feel the heavenly
flame, then is the time to trust the Lord and rest upon His name.*
—Author unknown

I truly enjoyed my time in Minnesota, managing even to adapt to the sometimes bitterly cold winters. In spite of having to leave the ocean, mountains, and lush evergreens of the Pacific Northwest far behind, the little school in the land of ten thousand lakes turned out to be a good place. I soon achieved a comfort level with other students in my role as freshman class president, and thanks to my Greek professor's encouragement in helping me improve in class, my confidence and my overall course work were going better than I expected. Eventually, I even overcame my tendency to become anxious around girls, thanks in no small part to several young women students at the school who worked me out of my initial shyness and into their world of serendipitous fun. They were my first meaningful female friendships and enabled me to begin to gain self-confidence in more social settings.

As my first year rolled into my second, my world seemed to continue on an upward, positive trajectory. It seemed as if God favored me, and I loved the college experience. So much so that upon graduation with a two-year associate of arts degree, I was really sad to leave my friends and the little school on a hill behind for the continuation of my life back in the Pacific Northwest. Since Bethany had only been a two-year school, it was necessary to transfer to a four-year college to complete my four-year degree. I chose Seattle Pacific College, affiliated with the Free Methodist Church.

Located next to the Ballard ship canal on the north side of Seattle's Queen Anne Hill, Seattle Pacific had a good reputation for preparing Christian young people for public service, and the school was only a short distance from the Space Needle where I had met Jesus. In spite of my familiarity with Seattle, my new school seemed intimidating. I did not know anyone, and it was situated in the middle of a large metropolitan area. But I quickly adjusted to my new setting and began making new friends. I was growing increasingly confident that things in my life would only continue to get better and better. However, curious behaviors began to surface in my life that reflected the pain my mother had experienced in hers. It would have a bearing on my trust in God when things did not go so well.

My mother had developed certain responses to the adversity in her life that attached to me over time. For one thing, she was a perfectionist when it came to cleanliness in the home. She insisted that everything be in its place and immaculate all the time. Sometimes the dinner dishes were washed and put away before we had even left the table! She could not stand things in disorder; and that meant the sooner things were cleaned up, the better. Naturally, her house was always spotless, even the substandard one we lived in on the reservation. Most people in our community were not as attentive in such matters.

Part of this was likely rooted in our recent past. Only seventy years earlier, we were still living communally in cedar longhouses with dirt floors and wood fires issuing smoke out of holes in the roof. In fact, some of our people were only just now beginning to get used to the single-family wood-frame houses, which were usually simply constructed, inadequately wired, and not very well insulated. Most people in our community did not have the kind of money needed to afford expensive homes. In any case, the idea of saving for bigger, better, more expensive homes and pursuing the American Dream had little appeal to the average Makah. Most probably would have preferred the older dream of their parents' generation when they could practice their traditions and live off the provisions of the sea and the land.

My mother was the exception. At her request, my brother Leonard and I regularly buffed her linoleum floors. Not many homes even had linoleum, much less waxed and buffed linoleum. We, however, managed to make a game of it—climbing into cardboard boxes set on top of old towels and using our hands to pull ourselves along the floor as if driving a car. We would not end our game until the waxed floor was buffed to a brilliant shine. This was simple fun for sure. At the time, we did not have television to compete for our interests.

There was nothing wrong with a clean house, of course, especially a house that needed all the help it could get. Cleanliness and things in place provided security, particularly in a community where there was so much disorder in people's personal lives as a result of the forced changes we had endured. My mother's effort to keep her world free of clutter was her way of controlling the chaos for her benefit as well as ours.

Somewhere along the way, I picked up on her habits, perhaps more so her anxiety over things disordered. Unfortunately, my roommate in college was comfortable with clutter. He would leave clothes, books, and papers strewn across his side of the room. It was strange to walk into our dorm room with one side very ordered and the other chaos. His lack of concern for cleanliness resulted in conflict between us. It was like a marriage going bad. I was always trying to tell him to clean up his messes.

I would even threaten on occasion to find a new roommate. He would in turn plead with me to reconsider and promise to change. Then I would grant him forgiveness and allow him one more chance. I do not remember how many times I gave him one more chance. We lasted the whole school year.

It seems strange behavior now that I think about it. I can even laugh about it now. At the same time, I have come to realize that my angst over disorder was symptomatic of pain in my family's past. This seemed to surface in my life in other ways as well.

Through the years, I found myself noticing little specks of dust and lint here and there on the carpet or other places. They seemed conspicuous to me but invisible to others, and I would not feel comfortable until I had reached down to pick the offending miniscule speck off the fabric. Eventually, I began to notice this bothersome tendency intensifying when I was going through some difficult challenge. At such times, I would organize my office or clean up a room. I was a good guy to have around at such times if you needed a room cleaned up. It seemed to do something for me as well. My efforts to exercise control over the things I could seemed to relieve my anxiety over the things I could not. It is amusing in retrospect, of course, especially when I think of the silly things I have done. However, compulsive behaviors like this can sometimes indicate a lack of trust in God as well; they are a way to manage outcomes when we think God is not doing a good job of it. They may also be a symptom, as in my mother's case, of unresolved trauma.

Finding ways to maintain control of life's sometimes-chaotic circumstances occurs naturally in a world where political events, catastrophes, and even natural-world upheavals rock our sense of security. Think of the massive amounts of money we have spent on achieving security since 9/11 and all the rules we have put in place to manage the increasing disorder of our present age. In retrospect, my encounter with the three alcoholic men and their broken car was a microcosm of life. I remember my initial anxiety as the three men piled into my car. I had lost control. My feelings only intensified as we drove off the paved road onto unfamiliar back roads, around hill and dale, and through deep puddles to the place where their wreck of a car sat disabled. I had not planned on this. When the car I kept spotlessly clean became covered with mud, I agonized over it and could not wait to clean it up. All that I wanted to do was get far away from them and the anxiety I was feeling at the time.

Behind all of this, though, was something profoundly significant. I did not trust God in all of my circumstances. Behind my efforts to manage disorder were issues hidden deep within my own life yet unresolved, woundings and hurts that I had not acknowledged and dealt with in accord with God's will. I became discouraged and wanted to give up the ministry. It was my way of taking back the controls of my life. Looking back, I can see that God was giving me an illustration, teaching me that life is often uncertain. Not just for me but also for most of the people I would meet. The pathways to trust in Him and the reasons for our inability to do so are often revealed in off-road experiences, sometimes along twisted trails, with deep puddles and hidden surprises around the next bend. My difficulty in trusting God in all of my experiences eventually called to mind my finiteness and God's infinite wisdom as revealed in Isaiah 55:8: "For my thoughts are not your thoughts, neither are your ways my ways." And, of course, the truth that God sometimes uses disorder in our lives to teach us valuable lessons on trust in all of our circumstances.

I would be tested on this lesson many times throughout my life. I remember one time in particular. I had just graduated from Seattle Pacific College and was planning to return to Bethany Lutheran Seminary in Mankato, Minnesota, to begin my theological training leading to ordination in my pastor's denomination. I had already forwarded my college transcripts and been accepted. Up to this point, things in my life since I became a believer had been going along quite well, meaning I had not had to go off road or face any strange twists or turns.

One day, shortly after I completed my college degree program and while I was getting ready to enter the seminary in Minnesota, the pastor who had mentored me and been my friend since shortly after I had become a Christian decided it was time to settle a matter that had long been lying dormant. He called me into his office shortly after my graduation to discuss his concern. I didn't know it at the time, but the issue he wanted to talk about was a doctrinal matter rooted in his belief, and that of his denomination, that having fellowship with Christians from different theological perspectives was not biblically correct; the association would send a wrong message, implying somehow that I agreed with all of their doctrinal teachings. This explained my pastor's skeptical comment when I first mentioned to him that I had received Jesus as my Savior at a Billy Graham meeting.

During the years of my association with my pastor's denomination, I gradually understood their teaching on this and should have made the decision long before now to find a church where I was more in agreement. I had slowly come to the understanding that absolute adherence to this doctrinal view was essential to ordination in their church. Instead of leaving of my own accord once I understood this, I ignored my intuition, perhaps hoping that it was not that important. Looking back, I think that since my association with their denomination had been mostly a blessing to my life, I simply suppressed any thoughts of finding another church. In any case, God had provided me many good things through the many fine people I had gotten to know. The pastor had been so supportive. Nevertheless, now that I had just completed my four-year degree in a Free Methodist college, he apparently decided it was time to resolve the issue once and for all.

Walking into his office that June day with apprehension surely written on my face, I managed to offer a greeting. After we exchanged a few pleasantries, his demeanor became very serious as he began to outline his concern. He quickly introduced the subject by telling me that we needed to resolve the issue of doctrinal fellowship with other denominations. My Billy Graham experience notwithstanding, he explained it was a violation of biblical teachings on association with other denominations. Our discussion became intense at times as he tried to persuade me that my understanding was wrong. I told him I could not deny my faith experience or agree with his narrow interpretation of the biblical teaching on Christian fellowship. The discussion finally ended with me simply reiterating that I could not agree with him. The following Sunday, he decided to draw a line in the sand. He drew this line during the communion service.

As usual, I went forward to the altar rail to receive the Lord's Supper. He paused momentarily to look down on me, kneeling before the altar with hands out in expectation of receiving the bread and the wine. Then, with his face resolute with solemn determination, he turned his attention to the next person and passed over me. In his mind, I no longer met the standard of doctrinal purity and hence was not worthy of the bread and wine. As I knelt there, palms extended but empty handed, I felt a flush of emotions I could not have anticipated. His refusal to commune me was his declaration that I was unworthy of the Lord's forgiveness. This ended my relationship with his denomination. It meant I could not attend their seminary in Minnesota.

It felt like I had been denied entry into God's Kingdom as well.

Deeply hurt, confused, and overwhelmed by feelings of rejection and embarrassment, I slowly rose from my kneeling position along with the other parishioners. I half stumbled back to my pew, barely able to comprehend what had just happened. How could our friendship end like this? What was I going to do now? For the past six years, ever since I had first met this pastor, I had been planning to attend the little Lutheran seminary in Mankato, Minnesota. It was the only place I had ever considered. Sort of like having all your eggs in one basket. It meant that I had no alternatives in mind. The dream instilled in me by God to become a pastor seemed to have died that day at the altar of God's grace in a little Lutheran church.

Hurt feelings and all, I slid into the pew next to my mother, who had communed before me. She had seen it all. Anger, hurt, betrayal, and disappointment were deeply etched on her face. Would she ever attend a church again? The rest of the service was a blur. We probably should have gotten up immediately and left. Instead, we stayed until the end. A few people came to our side but said little. They were dumbfounded by what had just transpired.

By the time we got home, I was angry with my former pastor and with God. Why had God taken me to a place He had determined was right for me, only to pull out the rug from underneath me? How could He do this? Wasn't it He who wanted me to go into the ministry in the first place? Didn't I tell Him I did not want to go into the ministry? And when I finally agreed, hadn't He led me to this pastor and his denomination? I had other similar vexing thoughts like this. Mostly, I was deeply depressed. God seemed so unfair and now so very distant when I needed Him most.

The disappointment affected my mother as well. She was a new Christian and had only recently begun to understand what it meant to be a follower of Jesus. She had developed a high regard for the pastor. But his seeming rejection of me shook her faith. It seemed like one more example of God failing her family, going back to her mother's death. Both of us were at a crossroads in our faith. We decided never to return to that church. But we were in danger of turning away from God as well. The resulting anxiety began to trigger efforts in me to control the world around me as best I could. Mostly, I did little things like straighten out my room and pick up things others hardly noticed. I was also very depressed. I seem to have entered a dark place with no way out.

Of course, there was a God-purpose in my disappointment. I began to understand that when devotion to doctrinal purity is not joined to acts of grace and forgiveness, there is usually a problem with the teaching or the practice or both. On the other hand, my response to this adversity underscored my tendency to retreat from my problems and to fall back into the old habit of believing that things never work out and to seek solace in the familiar. As was my habit, I hid in the face of adversity. It was the old me with all the unresolved generational wounds and hurts, still buried deep within the sanctuary of my mind and heart. It was important for God to work me through this in order to teach me trust. He had chosen this occasion to begin this process and to remind me once again that "all things work together for good" for those who love and are called of God. Once more, He had used a circumstance to break me away from my familiar so that He could change the direction of my life.

Had I understood it better, I would have seen that my experience with the small Lutheran denomination had accomplished the good God had intended. It was the right place for me at the right time. The truth was, I had met many people there who helped me grow. Now, He had another place for me. It took a painful experience, even a broken relationship, to move me on to His next best place for my life. However, in the midst of this dark moment, it did not feel like that.

Then, at the height of my confusion and with my future seemingly in doubt, someone who heard of my circumstances called to tell me of a new Lutheran seminary located in Tacoma that would be opening its doors for the first time in September. Why not check it out?

The little seminary turned out to be the faith venture of a medium-sized Lutheran church on the other side of the city. Classes were to begin in the fall. The teaching staff was made up of pastors and recently retired professors from several Lutheran colleges and seminaries. Most importantly, it was accredited. Encouraged by this unexpected information, I hurriedly drove across town to meet with the seminary dean of students. He was a balding man with a genuine warmth and smile to go with it. I soon filled out the enrollment application, forwarded my college transcripts, and was accepted. By early September, I was attending classes with six other men.

Although this was not what I had planned, I was on track once again to realize my goal of becoming a pastor. My nearly lost dreams were being reborn in a most unexpected way. God had provided me just what I needed at the right time to take me from despair to the next step along His path for my life. My anxiety ended. My tendency to straighten and put things in order dissipated. And the God who had led me off the road and down a twisting trail was large in my life once again. Things were going well once more.

Or were they? I was about to go off-road again, down another twisting trail. More disappointment was just around the next corner. This is a story you are not going to believe.

CHAPTER 13

The Wolf at the Door

—⊙⁄⊙⁄⊙—

If the wolf is not knocking on your door, it would pay you to hire one.

—Bob Gorman, retired Seattle banker

It was quite a transition from a four-year college setting to a tiny seminary in an upper room of a church. For the past six years, I had planned to attend a Lutheran seminary in Minnesota—until my pastor had denied me communion and, in effect, excommunicated me from his denomination. Cut off and my plans thrown into disarray, things looked bleak. But here I was in the presence of six other men attending Faith Lutheran Seminary, a small, independent, startup school. Sitting at my desk and looking around at my classmates in the little room that served as our classroom, I recall thinking, "How in the world did I end up here?" Then, perhaps more importantly, "Where will I be going from here?"

My classmates, mostly second-career guys, had to be thinking the same thing. It seemed so surreal; seven of us trying to balance the excitement of pioneering a brand-new seminary with its obvious liabilities: small staff, limited library, and, more troubling, no denominational affiliation. Nevertheless, it had afforded me a soft landing at a critical time in my life. In spite of our differing backgrounds and the pathways that got us there, the seven of us formed a strong bond. How could it be otherwise? We shared every class, daily chapel, and generally worked in concert to sustain collegiality. My college Greek served me well in classes requiring translation, and as the weeks turned into months, I settled into a routine of classes, study, and adjusting to apartment living.

I gave little thought to this initially, but I soon realized that since the fledgling seminary had limited affiliation within the broader Lutheran community, we would likely have difficulty finding a place to serve once we graduated. Its only accreditation with the larger Lutheran world hung by a slim thread of academic recognition from the Lutheran Church Missouri Synod's Concordia Seminary in Springfield, Illinois. How had the little seminary managed to achieve this? In any case, this slimmest connection would have significance for me sooner rather than later. In the meantime, we were encouraged by the efforts of the dean of students to find places for us to serve once we graduated.

I am not sure when my classmates and I began to understand that all was not well at the new school. Somehow, we discovered that a growing disagreement was festering among the members of the recently formed seminary board and the dean of students. There was talk that the dean would soon be relieved of his responsibilities.

This news disturbed the order and delicate symmetry that held the little school together that first year. Already feeling the seminary was at risk with little or no support from the general Lutheran community, we students agreed that the departure of the dean would further jeopardize our chances for placement as pastors. After much discussion among ourselves, we made the decision to leave the school at year's end. It was not an easy decision for any of us. The seminary had been a place to realize our dreams, and none of us knew where we would end up. But we were unanimous in our intent to drink of the same cup of resolve regardless of the consequences. At the end of the academic year, all seven of us terminated our relationship with Faith Lutheran Seminary by simply conveying to the authorities that we would not be returning.

Within weeks of the end of classes, I was once again adrift on a sea of indecision and doubt. Barely less than a year had passed since I had graduated from college and been forced to leave my former denomination. Once more feeling as if I were the victim of circumstances, I had become like a rudderless ship in the midst of a thick fog. Things were chaotic once more. Once more, it seemed to me as if God was silent. Why was He silent at a time like this? I had an even more troubling question: how could these things be happening to me if I was doing His will? Didn't He know I did not like uncertainty?

I lacked trust, but at least I had perseverance—I did not quit. I sent an application to a seminary in another denomination far across the country. And another to a Bible school much closer to home. My discouragement left me indecisive and confused. I lay on my bed for long hours, not knowing what to do. I tortured myself with thoughts like, "Have I missed God's will? Should I be doing something else? Why are things so chaotic?" I reminded God that I had not wanted to go into the ministry in the first place. Once again, He did not respond. Why didn't He listen to me? I was all the more agitated because since I had become a believer, it seemed as if I was on a journey on which Jesus had sent me to cross a body of water. I got into the boat just as He had commanded and started out on a journey just and He had told me to do. Now that the sea was getting rough and the wind stronger, He had decided to take a nap! Obviously, I was in a state of total despair. More importantly, I lacked faith. By late August, I had not committed to go anywhere or be anything. Once again, my dream seemed to be coming to an end. I lay on my bed dejected and discouraged.

Then one day, in the midst of my deepest depression, the phone rang, disturbing my self-pity. It was one of my classmates from the little seminary, calling me from Springfield, Illinois. He had good news. His transcripts from the seminary in Tacoma had been accepted by Concordia Lutheran Seminary, and he was now on campus. He had more good news. He had spoken to the registrar. If I came immediately, the school would accept me as a second-year student. My transcripts could follow.

The call came on a Wednesday; I was in class the following Monday. The seminary was located in Springfield, the state capitol of Illinois. It was the home of Abraham Lincoln. Once more, I was in unfamiliar territory. I did not know it then, but I was exactly where God intended. Once more, He had moved me from my familiar to the unfamiliar through circumstances beyond my control. In all that I had just experienced, I could hear a gentle voice saying to me much the same as Jesus had said to His disciples upon calming the storm, "Why are you so afraid? Do you still have no faith?" (Mark 4:40)

For much of my early life, I lived with unpredictability and chaos. My personality reflected the tensions of our family situation. Then, I became a believer in Jesus, and all the disorder of my past seemed to come together in a good way. Now, in just a year's time, my life seemed to have entered once more into chaos and confusion. This seemed to trigger the old habit patterns. When overcome by adversity or disappointment, I longed for the familiar and the safe, and I focused on things I could control. I fell into depression. I complained to God. Then something amazing would happen. Just when it seemed I had reached the end of my tolerance for disorder, the Holy Spirit would come once more into my life and provide order and purpose to my chaos through some new opportunity. My faith was rekindled once again.

You might think, since God knew my past, that He would let up on me—give me a break, so to speak—and sort of feel sorry for me for all the struggles I had incurred in my earlier life. He does not behave the way we expect or even want. Instead of removing chaos and unpredictable events and circumstances from my life, He permitted me to experience *more* uncertainty and chaos. He seemed always to be taking me from the familiar to the unfamiliar, from the safe to the edges, where it was easy to fall off. Through the myriad confusing things that occurred in such a short time, He seemed to have had a singular purpose: to teach me how to have faith no matter what and to trust His love under *any* circumstances. He also wanted me to learn to expect adversity as part of my Christian walk and to profit from it. It was a key to everything He intended to accomplish through my life. Had I thought more carefully, I would have understood that following Jesus meant I would experience uncertainty and risk. It would require a willingness to die to self and trust Him. Disturbing to our sensibilities, death to the self is risky. I would eventually learn that what we experience as disappointment in our efforts to follow Jesus is but a tiny reflection of what He endured in coming into our world and suffering and dying in our place. If we would follow Him, we must understand this. It is the only way to be of use to God.

This is not how I had thought Christian life should be, of course. I wanted everything to be painless and predictable, and usually that meant that I was in control of at least some things. But my life was never that way, at least not for very long. Had I been a little more astute as a student of the Bible, I might have seen that the same pattern occurs in the life of all of God's people. They all bore scars and bite marks, if you will, in their struggles to learn obedience to the call of discipleship. It calls to mind something we can all identify with, a story from childhood.

Remember the story of the three little pigs? The big, bad wolf arrives at their residences and begins pounding on their doors, threatening to "huff and puff and blow their house in." Sometimes during my efforts to fulfill God's purposes for my life, it seemed as if I were regularly receiving a visit from one sort of wolf or another, pounding on my door. Every unexpected challenge was like a predator wolf threatening to blow my house down. Through the years, it has become apparent that God had *allowed* the wolves to knock on my door, but it is important to note that He didn't *make* them come to my door. They just did. And sometimes, my own sin behaviors even invited them. That is the way life is for most people. At the same time, He wanted me to understand that if I trusted Him, the wolves could huff and puff and threaten all they wanted, but they would never blow my house down. In truth, their presence, however threatening, maybe even painful, could have positive, transformational benefits such as changing the direction of my life or teaching me patience or developing in me compassion for others in their sufferings.

Of course, I did not like having wolves beating on my door any more than the three little pigs. Nevertheless, the more I experienced blessings out of adversity, the more I could appreciate that the wolves God was permitting in my life could be made to grow my faith and understanding. Hence the wisdom behind the statement, "If the wolf is not knocking on your door, it would pay you to hire one."

The wolves knocking on my door on this occasion had served to change the direction of my educational track. On the campus of Concordia Seminary in Springfield, Illinois, for the first time, I felt I was finally where God intended all along. The place had a sense of permanence, of stability and connectedness. Its brick-and-mortar chapel, a familiar-style dormitory such as I had known in college, and the newly constructed library in the center of the campus were comforting assurances that things were going to work out after all. I was in my familiar once more!

My new setting brought to mind a verse I had once memorized from 1 Corinthians 10:13: "No temptation has seized you except what is common to man; and God is faithful; He will not let you to be tempted beyond what you can bear. But when you are tempted, He will also provide a way out so that you can stand up under it." It was great assurance in times of difficulty and seeming chaos. It had this meaning for me.

When the wolves arrive at your door and threaten to blow your house in, as they most assuredly will, God will provide a way of escape, and for me, that was perhaps the biggest lesson of all. Trust Him!

CHAPTER 14

The Sacred Tree

Then I looked . . . and in the center stood the holy tree, the land about was all green. [. . .] [We were] all walking in a sacred manner on the good road together.

—Black Elk, Sioux prophet

A little leery at first that more wolves might be lurking around the doorways of my life, and the lesson of trust in all of my circumstances still in its early stages, I began my first year at Concordia Seminary in Springfield with some trepidation. Soon enough, however, as I began classes and meeting new people, I started to feel that I was once again walking the good road.

Shortly after my arrival, a fellow student gave me a copy of *Black Elk Speaks,* a book written in the 1930s by John Neihardt, a professor from the University of Nebraska. Neihardt's book was based on interviews he had conducted with a famous Lakota Sioux man named Black Elk. Black Elk's childhood experience of being transported into the heavens to view vistas and hear prophetic utterances was acknowledged as legitimate and held in high regard by his people. There was a danger, however. If someone did not record the aging warrior's story soon, his remarkable vision would be lost to history.

With his daughter at his side to record Black Elk's amazing story, Neihardt began meticulously interviewing the elder Sioux warrior through an interpreter. He soon discovered a remarkable man with a real-life story exceeding Hollywood's fictitious Forrest Gump. During the course of Black Elk's early life (in the 1860s and 1870s), he had witnessed his people increasingly harassed and driven from their lands by a U.S. Army intent on genocide and placing the survivors on reservations. As a young teen, he had even been a participant at the historic Battle of the Little Bighorn that took place on June of 1876. Later in life, he had witnessed the deadly outcome of the massacre that took place at Wounded Knee, South Dakota, in late December of 1890.

At still another point in his fascinating life, Black Elk had traveled to Europe as an actor in Buffalo Bill Cody's famous Wild West shows. While in England, he had occasion to meet the Queen of England. For a time, he had even served as an evangelist for the Catholic Church.[13]

Nevertheless, it was more his vision than his fascinating life that captivated most people. Its imagery seemed to encompass the difficult history of his people in conflict with the U.S. government through the 1870s and 1880s.

Once I began the book, I couldn't put it down. Full of symbolism and powerful imagery of Plains Indian culture, it read something like John's Revelation.

In his vision, Black Elk describes how, as a boy of nine, he had suddenly become mysteriously ill. Then, while lying in his parent's tepee in a comatose state, he was summoned by two men who escorted him into the heavens.[14] There he was shown scenes wondrous and mysterious, images of lightning and thunder and four groupings of twelve horses.

He also describes the sacred tree and the hoop or circle, symbols of unity, well-being and harmony with all things created. I

---

[13]   De Mallie, *The Sixth Grandfather*, 16–17

[14]   Neihardt, *Black Elk Speaks*, 22

found myself especially captivated by the majesty and scope of the things he described and saddened by a vision that included a broken hoop—an apt depiction of the state of his people under duress brought by the U.S. government.[15] It seemed to me as if the God who had managed to communicate to me out of my culture and circumstances had spoken to Black Elk using imagery from his. I was especially intrigued by his depiction of the holy tree. It reminded me of the biblical imagery of the Tree of Life and the cross of Christ, symbols of life and hope and the restoration of all things created.

What fascinated me the most, however, was Black Elk's description of a man whose appearance was neither White nor Indian, arms spread wide and standing against the holy tree, whose form changed to reflect "all colors of light," and who told him that all things earthly and created belonged to him.[16] It called to mind the biblical image of Jesus in all of His glory, "the light of the world", the Creator and Sustainer of all things. Had he seen Jesus?

I didn't tell anyone that I considered this. At the time, drawing an inference like this from an obscure Native American prophet's visions would have been considered radical, and I am not sure how my seminary professors, ever so cautious about such things, would have reacted to something this foreign to their experience.

Missionary practice has improved today, thanks in no small part to a better understanding of the way God has very often foreshadowed His glory and power in and through aspects of the cultural traditions of people throughout the world. Knowing how and where to look to discover points of agreement with Scripture and how to relate biblical truth in the context of a

---

[15] Ibid., 38
[16] Ibid., 249

given people's culture and tradition is often a key to bridging the Gospel to them. It is what God the Father has done in sending His Son Jesus into our world. He reveals His love in the person and work of Jesus.

The more traditional academic setting made my adjustment easier. Once more, I was in America's heartland. That meant cornfields and miles of open spaces. Except for a few Black and Hispanic students on campus, there was little diversity in the seminary. I was, of course, the only Native American. Occasionally a classmate, recognizing how rare it was to have a Native American on campus, would ask me how I became a Christian. I purposely left out my fractured history through Lutheranism, explaining only that I had become a believer through Billy Graham's ministry. This would usually elicit comments like, "Really? That's interesting." Still feeling some of the pain of having been rejected by my former denomination over doctrinal issues, I was pleased I did not have to say more.

In some ways, I became something of a local celebrity because of my ethnicity. Occasionally, as word spread that there was a Native American on campus, I would be invited to speak at local churches. I got to meet many people this way and began to learn to tell the story of my tribe. Of course, fellow students would often ask, "How did you get a last name like Johnson?"

Near the end of the academic year, which was really my second year of seminary, I was asked if I would consider a one-year internship at a Lutheran Church Missouri Synod mission in southeastern Montana in the obscure little town called Colstrip I described earlier. It seemed like a fortuitous opportunity. Like a man without a tribe since my painful separation from my former pastor's denomination, I desperately needed a place to practice being a pastor. There was another incentive as well. The placement director for field education explained that Colstrip was near the Northern Cheyenne Indian Reservation. The assignment would provide a great opportunity to learn about Plains Indian culture. I did not take long to ponder the offer before I accepted.

In late August, I was on my way to "the Old West." I was assigned as an intern to longtime Lutheran pastor Leo Tormoehlen, who had a congregation in Forsyth, Montana. A tall man, probably in his mid-fifties, and blessed with an engaging smile and a friendly demeanor, Leo was a great guy to have as a mentor. I noticed almost immediately that he had a wonderful way with children that caused them to light up with smiles and laughter whenever he stooped to their level and engaged them in conversation. His passion for people and mission extended to the Northern Cheyenne who lived in Lame Deer. His church provided me the opportunity to serve as an intern and the Ford sedan I obsessed about in my encounter with the three Northern Cheyenne men and their car.

The town of Colstrip was set amid gentle hills with a sprinkling of Ponderosa pines and prairie grasses. Because it was still in the early development stages that would eventually lead to the construction of the large, coal-fed, electricity-producing power plants that would eventually provide jobs, there were few people living there when I first arrived. As a result, the town paled in comparison to bigger and better-known Montana towns like Miles City, Forsyth, and Billings. I noted, too, how many towns in the area like Custer, Miles City, Forsyth, and even places farther south like Sheridan, Wyoming, had been named after Civil War generals.

During my studies years later, I discovered that many Native Americans had fought on both sides during the Civil War. They were not even considered citizens of the United States and were thus impeded from being given appropriate recognition. (It was not until 1924 that American Indians were accorded U.S. citizenship) Some joined the military anyway, no doubt thinking that by serving in the army, they would get a better deal from whatever government came out on top.

One of the more famous of these Native Americans who fought in the Civil War on the Union's side was a highly educated Seneca man from Tuscarora, New York. His name was Ely S. Parker, a brilliant man who had been trained as an attorney and an architect. On temporary assignment to Galena, Illinois, to design a government building, he met and eventually befriended Ulysses S. Grant, who resided there. Impressed by the native man's skill as a writer, General Grant asked him to serve as his personal secretary when the war broke out. Tyler thus served alongside the man who would one day become president of the United States. He was rewarded for his service by eventually being made an adjutant general in the Union Army. (In those days a designation such as this denoted a position and not a rank).

As special secretary to Grant, it was Parker who copied the terms of the surrender agreement that General Robert E. Lee signed to end the conflict. Parker can be seen in the official photograph taken with others who were present at the Appomattox farmhouse where the document was signed.[17]

Following the end of the hostilities, Native American participation in the great conflict did nothing to advance favorable treatment. Once the war was over, some of the Civil War generals, including Custer, were sent west to deal with what some called the "Indian Problem." Hence the origin of the many western towns named for Civil War generals.

I was facing an Indian problem of my own. Maybe I should say I was an Indian with a problem. My predicament was this: I was a Native American Christian living in a mostly White community seeking to bring a message of peace and reconciliation

---

[17]   Armstrong, *Warrior in Two Camps*, 110

to a place of historic conflict. And some of the wounds were not that old. In 1877, a year after the Battle at Little Bighorn, the Cheyenne had been forcefully relocated from Montana to Indian Territory in Oklahoma. Under great duress that included disease and starvation, a courageous, albeit small, remnant led by Dull Knife and Little Wolf had managed to return to Montana.

I soon discovered the previously referenced long-standing resentments existing between Indian and Whites. Sometimes the festering tensions, like smoldering coal lying near the surface, would occasionally ignite at some athletic contest. A hotly contested basketball game between a high school with predominantly White kids versus one with Indians could take on more than the usual meaning.

In light of a multitude of broken treaties and all the injustices associated with them, the question underlying my dilemma as a young seminary student was a familiar one: how can a just and good God allow injustices like those the Northern Cheyenne had experienced? In theology, this age-old question falls under the term *theodicy,* from the Greek words for *God* (*theo*) and *justice* (*dico*).

While I was confident in my own faith relationship with God through Jesus and understood the origins of sin and injustice as a part of Satan's dark and sinister workings in the world, I found it very disconcerting that Satan rarely, if ever, got the blame he justly deserved for intensifying hostilities and magnifying radical evil. Unaware of the devious powers of darkness' ability to cloak its evil works behind the scenes of history, many Native Americans identified Jesus with the injustices they experienced. It had been that way since the early Spanish conquistadors, under the cloak of righteousness, ravaged the indigenous peoples of South America. It continued when Christianity was joined to U.S. government efforts to destroy Native American culture and identity in the name of civilization. Jesus had obviously been badly miscast in Indian/White relationships from the beginning, and that had affected their willingness to believe that He could be their Savior and friend.

As a young student, I was unable to grasp the depth of the deception or the magnitude of the offense to the Gospel these injustices incurred. Then, one day, a revelation occurred that provided me with a deeper insight. While reading about the horrific massacre at Wounded Knee, South Dakota, that took place on the Pine Ridge Reservation on December 29, 1890, I began to see a connection between Jesus and a lost dream that has since cast a long and dark shadow across generations of Native Americans in their relationship with Him.

Ironically, the path leading to Wounded Knee began with a dream of one Indian man that Jesus would serve as an advocate and champion of the Indian cause. This dream began to unfold on New Year's Day in 1889, when a Paiute man named Wovoka, or Jack Wilson to his White friends, reported that he had gone to heaven and conversed with God. There, he claimed to have met Jesus, who told him that He felt sorry for the way the Indian people had been treated. He further explained that He had been unjustly treated and was killed, but that He came back to life and then returned to heaven. He then taught Wovoka a dance that later became known as the Ghost Dance.

This new dance was a blending of Christian beliefs and tribal ritual, wrapped around a message of hope. The hope lay in this—if Indian people lived a good life and danced the new dance, the buffalo and wild horses would return, and the people would be restored to their former glory, never again to be troubled by the incursions of the Whiteman on their lands or way of life. Included was a promise that not only would the Whiteman be removed from the continent, their dead would be reunited with them along with all the vanished wildlife and their old ways would be restored.[18] In a way, it was reminiscent of the Jewish expectation of the Messiah who would restore the former glory of Israel and subdue their enemies.

Not all the Indians who heard of Wovoka's vision believed it. Some, like Black Elk, thought it had the appearance of fantasy and the feel of desperation.[19] Many however, were so fraught with grief and desperation over their mounting losses they were anxious for any kind of relief from the incessant pressure brought by the U.S. government. Soon, people began to learn the new dance, hoping that its promise was true.

Fearing that the spread of this new religion might lead to armed insurrection, nervous government officials in the Dakotas complained to the U.S. government. The government responded to the alleged threat by issuing an order to round up the perpetrators of this new faith, including the famous Sioux leader Sitting Bull and Minneconjou Sioux chief, Bigfoot. Sitting Bull, an aging leader by then, was arrested, and in the scuffle that broke out, was murdered by an Indian policeman working for the government. Bigfoot's band, made up of an estimated 300 or more men, women, and children, were rounded up and forced to march in the dead of winter under military escort to Wounded Knee on the Pine Ridge Reservation in South Dakota.

Ironically, the army unit in charge of their apprehension was none other than the U.S. Seventh Cavalry, the former command of Colonel George Armstrong Custer, whose demise at the Little Big Horn had taken place only fourteen years earlier. The newly reconstituted Seventh Cavalry was now under the command of Major Samuel Whiteside, a survivor of Major Reno's unit during the Little Big Horn battle. Whether revenge was on the minds of Whiteside and his men is not known, but

---

18   Di Silvestro, *In the Shadow of Wounded Knee*, 64
19   De Mallie, *The Sixth Grandfather*, 272

it is certainly easy to imagine. It is also likely the soldiers were jaded by the overall impression of the times that "the only good Indian is a dead one."

What is known is that during an apparent effort to disarm a native man in Bigfoot's encampment at Pine Ridge, a struggle ensued, resulting in the discharge of a firearm. It is said that the Indian man was deaf and did not understand the command to surrender his prized hunting rifle. The discharge of the firearm during the scuffle was enough to set off the soldiers surrounding the mostly unarmed band. The withering assault, including the use of a Hotchkiss rapid-fire canon, resulted in the deaths of virtually everyone in the camp, including U.S. soldiers caught in the crossfire.[20]

A few of the terrified band managed to escape and find safety in a nearby church. Mission staff worked feverishly to treat their wounds against the backdrop of the cross of Christ and Christmas decorations that had recently been put up. Most of these Sioux died from their wounds. Several mothers, their little children in their arms, managed to escape the initial melee but were eventually tracked down and shot while hiding in the bush. The soldiers involved later explained at an inquest that they could not tell whom they were shooting. For several days following the slaughter, bodies of men, women, and children lay partially exposed in the freshly fallen snow, frozen in grotesque poses. In a photograph taken at the scene, the arms of their chief's bullet-riddled body were extended upward in a seemingly futile gesture of supplication. A few days later, a burial crew was hired to dispose of the bodies at a cost of two dollars apiece. Most were placed in a mass grave six feet deep and sixty feet long.[21]

Today, the mass burial site, framed by a simple chain-link fence, sits on a hill above the ravine where the killing took place.

---

[20]   Marshall, *The Day The World Ended at Little Bighorn*, 131
[21]   Ibid., 162

In the distance lie a few scattered Sioux Indian home sites and a "rez" car or two rusting away in the front yard. Close by sits a burned-out and boarded-up church, and on the hill adjacent the grave site, a new church has been built over the site where American Indian Movement advocates held out during the Wounded Knee protest that began on February 27, 1973.

On some evenings, according to a Sioux woman I talked with who lived near the site, she could hear the poignant, haunting cries and pleadings of little children emanating from the killing field below. Perhaps the most telling evidence of America's inability to come to terms with its sad relationship with Native Americans was a commemorative inscription on a sign at the foot of the hill leading to the burial site, "The Massacre at Wounded Knee." It was placed over a much older, original designation that read, "The Battle at Wounded Knee."

Of course, it was never a battle; it was a dark and sinister massacre, enhanced by demonic forces that work behind the scenes of human prejudice and hatred to amplify human sin and its consequences. Little else remains of this once-grisly scene to remind the visitor of the evil that took so many innocent lives that day or to mark the time when the dream that Jesus, the Messiah of the Indians, seems to have died.

No one seemed better suited to place the horrific events of Wounded Knee in their proper context than Black Elk, the famed Lakota Sioux prophet. Surveying the deathly scene shortly after it occurred and looking out upon the frozen bodies of men, women, and children lying in the snow, he concluded, "A people's dream died there. It was a beautiful dream. The nation's hoop is broken and scattered . . . There is no center any longer and the sacred tree is dead."[22]

---

[22]   Brown, *Bury My Heart At Wounded Knee*, 419

As I read Black Elk's comment, referring to the broken and shattered hoop and the death of the sacred tree, I understood the significance of these images to the native peoples of North America, sacrificed for the sake of America's expansionist goals in the nineteenth century

Surely it had seemed as if Jesus the Savior of Indians had also died that day. In a way, He had.

Throughout the course of my life, God had been revealing to me a vital truth for a broken world. It is in the cross of Christ alone that we find hope in times of great darkness and inexplicable evil such as that which took the lives of so many innocent people at Wounded Knee.

In the moments when Jesus hung on that sacred tree nearly two thousand years earlier, He had reached across time and space to be present at Wounded Knee, just as He has done at every other place where manifest evil has wrought horrible suffering. And then, on that cross in a distant land and time, He took upon Himself punishment only He could assume for what happened there or at any other killing fields, death camps, or other places where horrific injustices have ever taken place. In that sense, He also died at Wounded Knee.

The wrath that God the Father poured upon Him was so terrible that Jesus, in His agony, cried out, "My God, my God, why have You forsaken me!" (Matthew 27:46) It was at that moment that He was taking upon Himself the punishment for all the evil ever committed.

It did not end there, of course. He was raised up from the grave. He had overcome "sin, death, and the devil." His death and resurrection accomplished our salvation. The wooden cross that had symbolized suffering, pain, and death has thus become a sign of life, restoration, and hope. Therefore, it stands alone in history as the key to finding hope to fix the broken and missing pieces of the world and ourselves. Its meaning goes even further than this. It means Jesus understands our tragedies. He has been there with us all the time. They happened to Him too. It is a simple truth, but one that is often ignored in a world of competing philosophies and discarded truths. In Colossians 2:13–14, we read these words of the Apostle Paul: "When you were dead in your sins and in the un-circumcision of your sinful nature, God made you alive with Christ. He forgave us all our sins, having canceled the written code, with its regulations, that was against us and that stood opposed to us; He took it away, nailing it to the cross."

The Cross of Christ is the Sacred Tree made alive once more through the risen Christ. And through what He accomplished on that tree by His suffering, death and resurrection, the hoop of all the people of the world is made whole once more.

CHAPTER 15

Big Sky, Bigger Ideas

—⟨◦⟩—

The only man who never makes a mistake is the man who never does anything.

—Theodore Roosevelt

On a cloudless day, the Montana sky really does stretch on forever in every direction, revealing an expansive landscape of buttes, gentle rolling hills, ponderosa pines, prairie grasses, and in the distance, majestic mountains. It is called Big Sky Country for good reason. The sky, on a clear day, is really big!

Along the lonely highway separating Colstrip and Lame Deer, I would occasionally see a deer or an antelope grazing in the distance. With a little imagination, I could even picture the large herds of buffalo that once roamed the region before they were eventually killed off. One of my more lasting memories is of a barely noticeable cement and stone historical marker erected along the roadside between Lame Deer and Colstrip. It describes the location a half-mile or so in the distance where Custer and his men had camped one last time on their way to their fateful destiny at Little Big Horn.

At the root of the conflict leading to the Battle of the Little Bighorn, which took place as previously referenced on June 25, 1876, was the supposed discovery of gold in the Black Hills. In 1874, two years before the Little Bighorn battle, Custer had been assigned to determine how much gold might be there.

His glowing report fueled the interest of prospectors, who then poured into the region. The ensuing resistance by the Indians at the encroachment on lands secured for them by the 1868 Fort Laramie Treaty led to increasing pressure to force Indians off their lands and onto reservations. Custer and the six hundred men that accompanied him were part of a larger contingent of soldiers sent to that part of Montana to subdue the Indians with force. His mistake was to divide his men into three battalions and then, without adequate support, to attack an encampment of twelve thousand Sioux and Cheyenne, including many women and children. Facing warriors determined to protect their families, Custer and the five companies accompanying him were quickly overcome and annihilated.[23] Today, a little more than one hundred and thirty-five years later, a museum located near the town of Crow Agency serves as an interpretive center. Adjacent to this is the famed battlefield with a fenced-off area called "Last Stand Hill," where Custer and a remnant of his men fought to their deaths. Custer was hastily buried near the place where he likely fell in battle. His body was later exhumed in 1877 and moved to West Point, New York.

My year of internship in Montana had been a time of many learning experiences not just about the history of Indian/U.S. Cavalry conflicts. Most were ministry related, and much of them were of internal conflicts I was experiencing. When I first arrived, I was quite naïve. I imagined things I was going to do for God. But my whole year in Montana seemed to focus on little lessons intended to help me understand I could not do anything for God that didn't meet at least five criteria: His person for the task, His purpose, His power, His timing, and for His honor and glory.

One important idea that I decided to accomplish for God incorporated none of the above. It was an idea born of my Billy

---

[23] Marshall, *The Day the World Ended at Little Bighorn*, 54–55

Graham experience. It began with a question: "Wouldn't it be great if I could organize a Christian crusade at Lame Deer, headquarters for the Northern Cheyenne?" Then I let my imagination run away with my naiveté. Together, these two wandered off to the land of unreality, fueled in part with misinformation.

I had heard somewhere that the famous country music singer Johnny Cash was part Indian. Where I got this notion I can no longer recall. Perhaps I thought that he had Indian blood because his hair was black and he appeared rough-hewn and, like so many native people I knew, a little battered by life. I had also recalled that he had recently declared his faith in Jesus and had appeared as a guest at one of Billy Graham's crusades, which was true. I decided it would be a good idea to write Johnny Cash a letter and invite him to consider performing on the reservation. Surely, his native heritage and newly acquired Christian faith would cause him to respond favorably. It was an idea conceived in ignorance. There was not the slightest chance it would happen. Nevertheless, I sat down and wrote a single-page letter of inquiry addressing the dire needs on the reservation and sent the letter to an address I copied off the back of one of his record jackets. It probably never got to him, most likely discarded by some bored-with-her-work secretary at the record company.

Even less plausible was my expectation that such an event would have been acceptable to the people I was trying to reach. I violated what would eventually become a cardinal rule of mine: I hadn't consulted with the local church or political leadership of the community to get their endorsement or support. Had I been successful in getting such a big-name artist to come, it would have failed miserably because there would have been little local involvement in the planning or the invitation, and hence no local ownership. More importantly, would the people even want it or believe it was something that could benefit them?

It is painful to think, even after all these years that I actually came up with this idea.

My thinking was reflective of the "shoot, ready, aim" mentality of a young Christian with much to learn. It was reminiscent of the earlier stages of Peter's ministry; he was so ready to do anything for Jesus but so unprepared to pay the price. Like Jesus' work in transforming Peter's zeal, my presumptive self-will reflected an aspect of my personality that God wanted to redeem.

Although there was far too much of me in my ideas and far too little experience, there was a redeeming quality to my personality that God could use: my imagination was beginning to manifest a willingness to think outside the box. Remember, I was the guy who hid under the table and given to fear. I was beginning to emerge into a visionary of sorts. Even though I could be impulsive and unrealistic, there was something to be said about my emerging readiness to attempt strategies to get the kind of ministry results traditional methods could not. I just needed to mature in my understanding and faith so that my ideas were God-inspired and in concert with His will and not my own. Anything less would be foolish and self-serving. Of course, this was not a lesson I would learn easily. Sometimes it takes a lifetime to quit making plans for God or believing that I was the one to carry them out. My story illustrates how necessary it is for God to purge us of self so our dreams for better things are the dreams He has inspired.

I did have some success, though. Eventually, I was able to organize and plan some events that involved the people I was serving and were a little less ambitious and more consistent with God's will.

During my time in Montana, I had gotten to know many excellent Northern Cheyenne Christian leaders in Lame Deer and the nearby community of Busby, people like tribal leader Ted Risingsun and Reverend Joe Walks Along and Willis Busenitz, a non-native Mennonite pastor serving in Busby. The Mennonite church, a denomination with which I had little previous experience, had served well in the area. They were among some of the best men I had ever met.

One day, just before the Christmas season, I got together with Mennonite pastors Joe Walks Along and Willis Busenitz from Lame Deer and Busby, respectively, to issue an invitation to their people to come to Colstrip for a time of singing, food, and fellowship.

The little community church in Colstrip had seldom been used through the years prior to my arrival, and like my house, was tired and in need of care. But it was functional. More importantly, most of my parishioners were mineworkers new to the area, and many of them were also genuinely friendly, kind, and hospitable. They had more than proved that when they welcomed me and put up with some poor sermons.

I remember the seasonably cold December evening we gathered together for the joint service. Some of my people wondered if the Northern Cheyenne Christians would show up. Rarely, if ever, had the two communities come together for anything except the hotly contested athletic matches.

Soon, however, cars began pulling up in front of the church. Thirty or more Cheyenne men, women, and children, bundled up against the evening cold, began piling out of pickups, cars, and a van or two for a time of praising God, fellowship, and food. It was a God-event held during the Christmas season. It was not about competition, divisiveness, or ancient wounds. It was about unity in Christ and peace with God.

I can still see the elder Cheyenne men and women walking slowly up the steps leading into the church—their black hair streaked with gray, their faces wrinkled by time and circumstances, and their dark brown eyes revealing a depth of character born of enduring much in life.

The members of my fellowship and the Cheyenne men and women greeted one another warmly, hands extended in friendship, as Indian and Caucasian reached beyond a painful past to embrace one another as brothers and sisters in Christ. We were one people, after all. It was a remarkable event, marking the first time the two groups had ever come together for worship, and more importantly, it demonstrated the power of God to bring reconciliation and unity where there had been such a painful history of distrust. Even if only for these few, God was fixing the broken and missing pieces of a sad history. Afterward, the church elders of the Lame Deer and Busby churches responded by inviting the Colstrip members to the reservation. My people gladly accepted, and once more renewed our newly formed friendships with these Mennonite Christians in their community; God was honored.

While I was struggling with many issues in my life, I barely perceived the important lesson of making sure my ideas for ministry were God-inspired and in concert with His will. From time to time and in later years, I would attempt things that were not His will with the same failed results as my efforts to have a famous entertainer come to the reservation. But God was patient with me and gentle in His rebuke, preserving in me creativity and a willingness to attempt new things to achieve different results. His larger purpose had been to preserve His will for my life when I felt increasingly doubtful about ever being useful in ministry.

There was one other vitally important lesson from my time in Montana that God was beginning to reveal to me as a result of a brief encounter with a man and his family that would eventually have a profound impact on my perception of what it meant to be a servant of God. Just as I was starting to make preparations to leave Montana and return to the seminary in Springfield, a remarkable college teacher, Dr. William Heinicke who served as a professor at one of our Lutheran colleges, had been invited by tribal officials to take college students to the Northern Cheyenne reservation. The students who were on interim break and who accompanied Dr. Heinicke were afforded a unique opportunity to do service projects in the community.

At the end of their several week period of volunteering, Dr. Heinicke was asked by tribal leaders if he would help transition a former government-run residential school into a tribally owned school with its own teachers and school board and administration. It reflected a new era on the part of the tribe in helping to shape its own direction through a school they owned and managed. They needed someone with an educational background to assist them in achieving this new initiative and they sensed Bill's passion for Native Americans.

It would however mean that Dr. Heinicke and his wife Pat and their five children would have to leave all that was familiar and safe and then to relocate to a reservation community where there was much poverty and could encounter prejudice since they would be a minority in a native community struggling with many issues. Dr. Heinicke agreed to do so and in a period of five years, acted as curriculum director while helping to devise policies, provide expertise on curriculum development and helping to train a native Cheyenne woman to take over as curriculum director of the school. It was a demonstration of what serving others really means: setting aside one's personal comforts and what is most familiar to help others achieve all that they can be---sometimes in spite of great personal risk and disadvantage. Later I would ask Dr. Heinicke to assist me with my ministry among my Quileute cousins in La Push, Washington, (one of the places I would one day serve) by assisting them to develop a tribally owned school. When I asked him to consider my proposal, I could not promise him a salary or even a place for him to live. All I had was an idea that if the people had their own school, they would develop a greater sense of community pride and self-determination. Once more, it was a reflection of my naiveté. Even with that Bill said he would be willing to take on the challenge if he got an invitation---not from me, but from the tribal leadership. He knew the importance of local investment in such an endeavor. One never came. Bill then prayed, "God, if you want me to go and serve the Quileute people, You will need to give me a sign." At literally the very last second, as he was about to sign a job offer he had received from a Lutheran college that included a deadline to sign on that very day, the phone rang. On the other end was then tribal chairman Chris Penn of the Quileute tribe requesting him to help them develop a tribally run school. Once more, God would ask Bill and his family to take on risk and inconvenience (We still had not arranged salary or moving costs) and assist the Quileute community in Washington State to build their own school. Great faith is required to assume a position without promise of salary, a place to live or any guarantee these would all be forthcoming. But God rewarded Bill's faith and his family's sacrifices. Financial support, much of it because of Bill's own efforts, was arranged. A tribally owned and operated school in the community of La Push is functioning well to this day thanks to his efforts and the efforts of those who came along afterward.

His example of servant leadership and faith had a profound impact on my life and eventually contributed to my commitment to recruiting and equipping native leaders to take responsibility for their lives. His example was a reminder to me of Jesus' words recorded in Mark 10:42, 43 and 44, "You know that those who are regarded as rulers of the Gentiles lord it over them, and their high officials exercise authority over them. Not so with you. Instead, whoever wants to become great among you must be your servant, and whoever wants to be first must be slave of all."

Nevertheless, even though I was learning vital lessons of faith and practice, a major crisis had gradually been looming during my internship in Montana. My expectations during my year of internship at Colstrip did not match my experiences, and that caused me to once more question my calling. Far from a willingness to serve others, I was ready to quit!

CHAPTER 16

My Conundrum

———≈≈≈———

A conundrum: A difficult and complicated problem.
—The American Heritage Dictionary

My year in Montana had ended. It had truly been a great experience in almost every way. I had even managed to survive rattlesnakes, my squeaky bed, my coal-fired furnace, and my cooking. More importantly, of course, the experience had afforded me more than the usual opportunities to preach regularly, conduct Bible classes, and counsel people struggling to make sense of their lives. But, instead of inspiring me to complete my last year of seminary, it exposed some of those parts of my life I had buried deep within my subconscious. I came away from my year of pastoral internship questioning my commitment to the ministry, especially to the Native American community. I was experiencing a conundrum, caught somewhere between uncertainty regarding my future and the riddle of my past. A more accurate way to describe my circumstances at the time is the Makah word *hayux'mis.* It has the sense of being caught in a difficult situation, something like the destabilizing effects of having nine people in a canoe built for eight.

Carrying this illustration a step further, ever since I had become a Christian, I had begun a life journey in a canoe that God had designed for me. But all of the hidden anxieties from my generational history as well as the unresolved issues of my present were like an extra man on board. It was destabilizing and threatened to capsize the canoe.

Witnessing the dark side of human grief and loss felt by a people who had endured extraordinary losses had contributed greatly to my self-doubt. The three alcoholic men and their broken car were only part of my exposure to things that discouraged me. The poverty, the broken families, the abuses, and the loss of hope I had observed over the course of my internship were the same kind of things I had witnessed in my own community and in my own family.

On a subconscious level, I had seen my reflection and that of my tribe in the lives of the people I sought to serve. Not in Colstrip, where I had served a white community church, but among the native peoples I knew I would someday be called to pastor. Some of the painful behaviors I witnessed in their world were still unresolved in my own. My inability to recognize my own dysfunction and deal with it had contributed to my discouragement and confusion. It was at the core of God's message to me: "You are just like those men and their broken car." This inner conflict surfaced several weeks after my internship ended in the form of a crude practical joke.

It was now late August. After a brief visit with family and friends back in Washington State, I was driving back to the Midwest through Idaho, Montana, and farther eastward toward Illinois. I was less than enthusiastic as I drove through the steep mountain passes characteristic of the mountainous west. In the several weeks between the end of my internship and my trip to visit family, I had plenty of time to think about my just-completed year. I contemplated ending my plans for the ministry. Lacking a clear alternative, however, I decided to return to the seminary anyway. I could figure things out from there.

Since the route I chose to drive back to Illinois took me through Montana, I decided to visit Colstrip one last time and say hello to my friends. I had also hoped to meet the new student intern who had replaced me.

Some very good friends of mine from the church I served were out on their driveway as I drove through the little town I had so recently called home. They were surprised to see me so soon. After some small talk, I asked about my replacement. He had only just arrived and was beginning to become acquainted with the community. Regrettably and without thinking, I decided to pull a foolish prank. I asked my friends to find the intern and tell him that an Indian man was in desperate need of help—his car had run out of gas just outside of town and he wanted to talk to a minister. Imagine that? Of course, it was a joke, and if they thought it inappropriate, they never said so. Instead, they quickly summoned him.

The young man soon arrived at the home of my friends. He was a seminary student like me but from Concordia Lutheran Seminary in St. Louis. He obviously did not know who I was. As he approached, I could see a look of concern mixed in with caution as he carefully eyed me up and down. Pausing for a moment to acknowledge his new parishioners, he introduced himself. I slouched to one side a little, doing my best to avoid direct eye contact while trying to cover up a hint of a smile. Then disguising my voice, I said in a barely discernible voice, "My name is Bobby. My car ran out of gas. Can you give me some money?"

Genuinely concerned but obviously cautious about handing out money to a stranger, especially one who might have a problem with alcohol, he began asking questions intended to determine my motives. Realizing he was not buying my act, I tried to appeal to his sense of guilt. I reminded him how badly Indians had been treated. I told him that Jesus would surely want him to try to help me. He deflected my appeal by assuring me of Jesus' love and stating that although he could not give me money, he could arrange for a ride. I could see his stress level escalate as he tried his best to relate to my desperate man in need persona. My ploy was obviously beyond any lessons he may have learned in classes on pastoral counseling. Meanwhile my friends who were witnessing this bizarre acting performance could hardly contain their amusement. Unable to carry on my ruse any longer, we all broke out in laughter.

The intern, with a look of consternation as well as relief, smiled broadly and then let out a sigh of relief. In the words of a popular television reality show, he had been "punk'd." I think we shook hands after it was all over. Many years later, our paths crossed once again. He was serving as a pastor of a congregation in Petersburg, Alaska, and I had become the Executive Director of the Lutheran Association of Missionaries and Pilots U.S. Reminding him of our first encounter, we enjoyed a good laugh. He had not forgotten it. Nevertheless, it was not something I was proud of, and I should not have carried out a deception like that at his expense or the native people, for that matter.

The truth was, my acting performance was a reflection of my increasing doubts about entering the ministry. My story about a broken car and needing help was a mirror image of the Native American experience. Broken and run-down cars were typical in the Native American community primarily because the Indian people, I knew, were poor and could not afford new ones. So, we had old cars, usually broken down and missing various parts. We often joked about cars like this. They are known as "rez" cars, automobiles that were barely running and probably not street legal, but somehow, due to the creative genius of some resourceful guy like Medaris Bad Horse, were still on the road. Similarly, broken cars reflected the whole of the native experience—down but not out and still on the road.

I was hesitant about returning to the seminary precisely because I feared the likelihood of facing the challenges of ministry to people caught in difficult circumstances like I had just encountered in my year of internship: people with broken and missing pieces, caught in addictions and poverty and in desperate need of help. I was one of them too.

When I arrived back on the seminary campus, I put some of this behind me in order to concentrate on my final year of school. In those final nine months, I would have to make a decision about my future.

Shortly after my return to the seminary campus, I received a note from the main office summoning me to meet with then seminary president, the late Richard J. Schultz. Wondering if he knew about my growing ambivalence about completing seminary, I walked into his office with trepidation. I managed to choke out a nervous greeting. Of average height, slim build, receding hairline and with a congenial sense of humor, the bespectacled President Schultz had always seemed approachable. He arose from his desk, smiled, shook my hand, and said, "Don, I have some good news. The seminary has received a gift from a benefactor for a Native American student. How would you like to use the funds?"

I was momentarily taken aback. This was not what I had expected him to say. After taking a few moments to gather my thoughts, I managed to thank him for notifying me of this. Then, without further hesitation, I announced I would like to see how other ministries were doing in a part of the Indian world I had never experienced, the Southwest: Oklahoma, New Mexico and Arizona. The funds would provide gas, food, and the occasional lodging I would need along the way. I could cut back on some of the expenses by depending on the people I visited to extend hospitality. This included staying with Lutheran pastors along the highway that might put me up for a few days. Then I suggested the information I gathered from visiting ministry sites and interviewing the people I met along the way would be used as a basis to write my Masters of Divinity paper that was a requirement for graduation. Since I would have to take off from school to drive to these states, commencement would have to be delayed for six months. I did not bother to mention that my journey to the Southwest would likely determine whether I would finish seminary.

In retrospect, I have no idea how I came up with this idea on the spur of the moment. It just seemed like the right plan at the right time, and I did not give its origin much thought. Nevertheless, whoever the donor was, the gift served to preserve God's call on my life.

Soon after my meeting with the seminary president, I began to plot my strategy. It was basic. My plan was to drive south though Missouri to Oklahoma and on to New Mexico and then Arizona and visit as many native communities, schools, pastors, and tribal leaders along the way as I could. Occasionally, I would have to journey off road to visit some of the more remote places. I bought some maps and began immediately to figure out the location of native communities and schools along the way. I was determined to see how God was at work in these places and record my observations.

Since I had sold the car I had used to drive to the Midwest following my year in Montana, I had to find another one. I eventually paid $200 for a 1960 manual-shift, six-cylinder Chevrolet from an Illinois farmer. It had good tires, a light blue paint job fading from long exposure to the sun, vinyl bench-type seats, an AM radio, and only 40,000 miles. I never gave much thought to the fact that it did not have air conditioning until I arrived in Phoenix in May when the temperatures soared into the high 90s and above.

In any case, my predominant feeling at the time that I began my trip was that I was on some kind of venture God had arranged. I was optimistic that I would learn something important. Soon, the cornfields of Illinois gave way to the interstate and the beginning of an important quest that took me south through Missouri to my first stop in Miami, Oklahoma. It was a place where there was a government-funded Indian residential school. The administration and teachers there were more than pleased to have a Native American student interview them for their insights and challenges. It would be the same everywhere that I went.

The three-month sabbatical turned out to be a critical turning point for me. Meetings with tribal leaders, native pastors, and teachers in government residential schools across Oklahoma, Arizona, and New Mexico provided me with just enough encouragement to sustain me through times of doubt. In every place I visited, I was afforded unique opportunities to meet people and visit places few outsiders get to see, places that were especially sacred to some of the people I visited. Naturally, since I was Native American, the people I met seemed more willing to share their thoughts and ideas. It was especially useful to converse with tribal people whose cultural expressions were far different from my own. Through all of my experiences, I could see that God was working in many settings to raise up native Christian pastors and tribal leaders strongly committed to faith in Jesus Christ.

As it turned out, no one experience or interview resolved my conundrum or ignited a renewed passion to finish seminary. Rather, it was the cumulative effect of all my contacts a little at a time that encouraged me to complete my education and move on with my ministry plans. It was God's way of patiently leading me to a greater confidence in His power to fix broken-and-missing-pieces people like me through seeing His power at work in other native Christians.

Before I returned to school for my final quarter, there was one other life changing experience. It had less to do with fixing my life and more to do with God building in me a message for later life. I was about to gain a completely new perspective on clock-time and how its invention helped to dramatically change everything.

Although I had never been outside the United States before, I had previously arranged to fly to Germany with several seminary classmates after my sabbatical ended. Learning about the people and the culture that had launched the Reformation and the Renaissance seemed like a good thing to do. I was able to apply for and receive a passport somewhere in Arizona.

Shortly after visiting various Native American tribes, I found myself boarding a flight with my classmates for Frankfurt, Germany. It was now the summer of 1973. When we arrived at the airport in Frankfurt, we were thoroughly screened by German security police. They were heavily armed and obviously on guard against any possible terrorist activity. The heightened level of security seemed odd to me at the time. Soon thereafter, we were walking the ancient thoroughfares of European cities like Frankfurt, Mainz, Koblenz, Luxembourg, Brussels, and Munich.

My European trip afforded a surreal contrast to the dusty back roads of isolated native communities in the semi-arid desert region of the Southwest. I devoured every smell, sound, and sight. It was in this place of ancient stone, brick-and-mortar buildings that the Reformation and the Renaissance had been birthed. I was able to visit ancient castles, marvelous old-world churches, and museums housing famous examples of art and industry. I even gazed upon the Gutenberg Bible (published about 1455) and the moveable type printing press that made mass production of writing possible. It was an innovation that greatly enhanced the spread of new ideas. None was more important or history-changing than the Bible. Available for the first time to the average man in the street, the ideas it contained quickly spread throughout Europe. Eventually, the Bible in the hands of ordinary men changed the course of world history and helped to facilitate individual growth in faith.

While I was in Germany, I came across something else that made an indelible impact on me. I saw evidence of the terrible consequences of war. Even though World War II was nearly thirty years past, there were still signs of destruction wrought by Allied bombers in some of the great cities. The horrible consequences of evil incarnate in the person of Hitler and in the Nazis had left Europeans with a horrific legacy of lost loved ones, death camps, and senseless destruction. It was evidence once more that mankind in defiance of God is capable of incredible evil. And like the tragedy that had occurred at Wounded Knee some fifty years earlier, demonic forces, cloaked behind people's ignorance of their existence, had worked once more behind the scenes to intensify evil and magnify the consequences of human prejudice.

Sadly, I saw evidence of another dark storm brewing, a foreshadowing of our present age. In Munich, my fellow classmates and I toured the Olympic Games complex where during the 1972 Summer Olympics, eleven Israeli coaches and athletes had been seized and killed by an Islamic terrorist organization known as *Black September*. It marked the beginning of a new and frightening way of conducting warfare that has since become a regular part of our present reality. This explained the heightened security at the Frankfurt airport.

For someone like me with an intense interest in international affairs going back to my childhood on the reservation and who had now become a believer in Jesus, this experience reinforced my emerging global perspective on evil and injustice in the world. The whole world was broken and missing pieces. To paraphrase the words of the prophet Black Elk, who saw the broken pieces of his people, the world's hoop is broken and shattered. There is no center any longer and the Sacred Tree is dead.

Something else of note caught my attention. In the great European cities, town squares with ornate turret clocks atop ancient buildings featured clever mechanical figurines that popped out from behind closed doors on the hour. Tick-tock time had been invented here too. Moreover, like the invention of moveable type, it had helped to transform European culture for more than 500 years. In addition, some aspects of the transformation to this new way of marking time would have an amazing impact on the speed of innovation and cultural change everywhere else. And something about this would contribute to mankind's propensity for doing evil things. I would also discover Native Americans possessed a unique perspective on all of this. This would only become apparent to me later.

Following my sabbatical and trip to Germany, I returned to the seminary to complete my final quarter. It had been six months since I began my tour of the Southwest and a year since my internship in Montana had ended. Now that I was finally back on campus in Springfield, I recalled something Abraham Lincoln reportedly said upon being invited to hear an evangelist preach about the Second Coming of Christ: "If Christ has ever been to Springfield before, I doubt if he will want to come back." I had not been sure I wanted to come back either, but now I was anxious to complete my final quarter and receive my first call. In spite of almost bailing out on His plan, God had once again provided me the experiences and opportunities I needed to keep me in the canoe of His purpose for my life.

All along the way, He was fixing the broken and missing pieces of my life and quietly forging in me a message to share with others.

CHAPTER 17

The Crab Story

But Jesus said to them, "Only in his hometown and in his own house is a prophet without honor."

Matthew 13:58

After my trip to Germany, I returned in the fall to Springfield to complete my training. My final quarter of seminary went by quickly. I managed to complete my Master's of Divinity thesis based on some of my research in the Southwest. The next thing I knew, I was sitting in the front row of the campus chapel on a crisp, December morning next to four other guys. All of us, for different reasons, were out of sync with the usual call service normally held in May. A call service is for new candidates for the ministry to receive their first assignment. Recalling the twists and turns that brought me to this moment, I barely comprehended the words of the chapel speaker preaching on the sacred task that was ours as God's messengers to a broken world. As the sound of his voice faded into the background, my mind began to drift off into a myriad of circumstances that led me to this point.

The last few years had been anything but predictable. I had broken and missing pieces too. Nevertheless, I had experienced God's gracious leading in unusual ways. If not for last-minute interventions, I might have abandoned all hope for ministry. But here I was, a Native American from a small tribe located two thousand miles away awaiting assignment to my first ministry location. From the beginning, it seemed an improbable outcome and me an unlikely candidate. For me, the Christian walk of faith was often full of surprising twists and turns. Ever so slowly, I was forming a picture of the person God was fixing and beginning to develop the skills I needed to be of use to Him. My mind's wanderings abruptly ended when the chapel speaker indicated it was time for the placement of the candidates.

A pastoral candidate's first call was sometimes a surprise. Not so for me, though. During placement interviews, I had been informed that there was interest from my home district in beginning a new mission to Native Americans in the Pacific Northwest among my own tribal people. Was I willing to accept their assignment?

My denomination's record of mission to Indians was spotty at best except for a brief moment early in its history. In the 1840s, during its early formation, the denomination had some history of mission to native peoples in Michigan, inspired by a German visionary living in Bavaria named Wilhelm Loehe. But as often happened in the history of missions to Native Americans, the efforts to evangelize the Indians came to an end when they were driven off their lands to make room for the rising tide of immigrants. The missionaries then turned from their failing efforts among the Indians to ministering to the increasing number of German families coming to America, most of them also un-churched. The popular tourist town of Frankenmuth, Michigan, is part of this legacy. A large Lutheran church there retains a small museum nearby containing a few relics of this short-lived first effort. One hundred and twenty years later, I represented an opportunity for my denomination to begin anew.

Surprised by this opportunity to work among my own tribe, I tentatively agreed to accept their offer to return to my hometown to found a new ministry. But establishing a congregation among my own tribal people? And introducing a totally new denomination to them? How wise was that? And what about *me* for considering the possibility? Was I insane? How could I expect to be successful among my own people? On the other hand, as someone familiar with the community, why wouldn't I be successful? Nevertheless, when my interview was concluded, I agreed in principle to accept a call to my hometown.

You can imagine my reaction then when I heard the seminary official say with muffled voice, "Candidate Donald W. Johnson is called to serve the May-caah Tribe, Neenah Bay, Michigan." Or was it "Washington"? I panicked. "That's not my tribe! That's not my state! Please God, not another off-road experience!" Had the person making the announcements mispronounced the names? Or, had my anxiety caused me to scramble his words? In any case, I quickly realized he had meant to say "Makah" in the community of "Neah Bay, Washington." Palms sweaty and my heart racing, I reached out and grasped my diploma. I was going home!

Soon, I was shopping for a reliable car. Cars, as you know, have an important place in my story. I went to a local Chevrolet dealership near Springfield to look over the possibilities. The owner of the car dealership, a man known for providing seminary grads with a good deal, was there to welcome me. He was your typical car dealer, personable, extroverted, high-energy, and in-your-face type. The first time he saw me, he presumed to know exactly what I needed. He walked me over to a lineup of brand new Chevrolets and said, "Young man, which of these new cars would you like? I recommend this one over here. I know how much you pastors drive. You have to have a reliable car."

Momentarily taken aback by his forthrightness in telling me what I needed, I took a step back from him. Recovering enough to look him square in the eye, I said, "Do you have any idea what it would be like for me to drive a brand new Chevy like one of these onto the reservation? The roads are full of potholes, and people are living in poverty. What do you think will be their impression of me if I come driving onto the rez looking like some rich guy in a brand new car like one of these? How would that reflect on Jesus?"

I was exaggerating a little. Well, maybe a lot. People in my hometown weren't rich by any stretch of the imagination, and lots of people were on the edge of poverty, but some could and did afford nice cars. And the roads were probably a little better than I described, but not by much. The owner of the auto dealership was surprised by my frankness. Obviously, he was used to selling brand new cars to seminary grads eager to drive to their pastoral assignments in new cars.

For a moment, we just stood there looking at one another. Finally I continued, "What do you have in used?" "Well," he said, the tone of his voice reflecting his obvious disappointment, "I got this old car out back on a trade. It's not much but at least it has low mileage." His demeanor suggested I was about to see the duplicate of Medaris Bad Horse's car. He escorted me around to the back lot, and there it sat—a shiny, two-year-old, sky blue, four-door Delta 88 Oldsmobile with Landau top, low mileage, and in mint condition. At half the cost of a new Chevy, it was larger, better looking, and came equipped with every amenity—including a tape player, which was the latest innovation of the time.

Seeing the nearly new Olds sitting on the back lot was sort of like a love-struck guy spying the girl of his dreams for the first time. I was giddy with excitement. Forgetting everything I had just told him about driving onto the reservation in a shiny new car and the image I might project, I said, "I'll take it." Sitting in his office filling out the sale documents, I could not believe my good fortune. It felt as if I had made the deal of the century.

As I slowly drove my Olds Delta 88 off the lot and onto the highway, I remember the deep sense of pride of ownership I felt as I maneuvered it down the road to the rest of my life. It was the best car I had ever owned. Within a few days, I was heading to the west coast through Nebraska, Wyoming, and beyond, with songs from John Denver's *Rocky Mountain High* album playing in the background. There was much to think about. I was going back to my hometown—the same community I had left under duress thirteen years earlier! Now driving west through the mountains, I felt ambivalent. What awaited me in the place once so familiar to me that I did everything I could not to leave? Then, there was the usual question: what kind of wolves might be lurking there, and would any of them come knocking on my door? I still didn't like wolves coming around or fully appreciate why they might be useful as part of God's purpose for my life.

Then there was this additional, slightly discomfiting thought. Familiar with the story of Jesus' return to his hometown of Nazareth, I knew there would be some challenges. His homecoming did not go as well as well as we might have expected. People who should have known better and welcomed His return said, "Who does He think He is?" Like disgruntled shoppers, the people in Nazareth wanted Him at the old price—the way they remembered Him—not the radically different person He had become, the Messiah with a life-changing message demanding a commitment.

This phenomenon occurs in many contexts. In many Native American communities throughout North America, there is a story that illustrates this. Among my people, it is known as "The Story of the Crabs." It goes like this. One day, an Indian and a White man decided to go together to the bay in front of the village to catch crabs for the evening meal. They were successful in their endeavor and filled their respective buckets. On the way up the beach and to their houses, the White man's crabs kept climbing out of his bucket. He had to stop every few steps along the way to put them back. But the same problem did not seem to be occurring to the Indian man and his crabs. Finally, out of frustration, the White man asked the Indian, "Why is it that your crabs stay in the bucket while mine keep crawling out?" The Indian responded that his were Indian crabs. "Once one starts climbing to the top, the others reach up and pull him back down." It is a sad comment on the self-limiting dynamic that can occur in various settings, not just among Native American communities.

Through the years, I have learned that an adverse reaction to a native son rising above the expectations of his peers is more likely to occur in communities with a history of deeply rooted traditions coupled with a pattern of subjection to a more dominant culture. This would seem to be applicable to virtually every people group at one time or another. The Nazarenes, for example, were Jews under the rule of Rome. New ideas and teachings that might go against their understanding were often perceived as a threat to their already-threatened cohesion and identity. Further, Nazareth, like my hometown, existed on the geographical fringes of the nation. Isolated farmers eking out a living on the edge of their country, they were little regarded by the rest of Jewish society. Recall Nathaniel's prejudicial assessment of Jesus upon hearing of His hometown, as recorded in John 1:46: "Nazareth! Can anything good come from there?" The apparent marginalization and isolation of the Nazarenes seems to have reinforced feelings of unworthiness, contributing to their lowered sense of expectation for themselves and their children. These hidden anxieties would surely be passed on from one generation to the next, contributing to self-imposed limits on their potential. It would likely have the additional affect of creating a community resistant to change.

One obvious evidence that this had occurred is that it appears the small village of Nazareth had gradually began to adopt a subtle presumption that no one in their community should think to rise above the expectations of the community. Thus when Jesus broke the mold by leaving the community to assume His Messianic role and then returned to His hometown to offer them a truth that could set them free, instead of honoring Him, the people tried to pull Him down to their expectations. The Nazarenes had unintentionally put themselves in a box shaped by rigid tradition, the remoteness of their geography, and an attitude forged by their response to a dominant culture. Together, these acted to hinder the power of the Gospel in their community. Because of these things, they never got to know how much God loved them. The story of Jesus' return ends with this assessment in Matthew 13:58: "And He did not do many miracles there because of their lack of faith." It is a vivid picture of how our generational history can limit our creative responses to God's love and the new opportunities He affords.

Had I better understood this, I might have had further doubts about embarking on a ministry in my hometown. Fortunately, God had other plans and blessings that would far outweigh the risks of ministering to my own people.

When I finished seminary, I was single with no prospects. Within a few weeks of returning to the Pacific Northwest, however, I had met and began a courtship with my wife-to-be, Mary. At the time she was nineteen—an attractive, deeply committed Christian woman who was working in a Bible bookstore in Tacoma. She was predominantly of English/Irish ancestry.

Our first meeting was anything but promising. I first met this petite young woman, with a pleasant smile, a pretty face, and a friendly demeanor, while browsing through the store for Bible materials in preparation for my ministry. She was polite and helpful, and I was attracted to her the first time I saw her.

But from what I could determine, she was not particularly interested in me. Nor was I the most charming person with women. I might have walked out of her life the same day I met her if we hadn't gotten into a conversation initiated by her curiosity. She had seen an article in the religious section of the local paper describing my upcoming ordination and my return to Neah Bay. She asked if I was the person in the article. This began a dialogue that led to a date that became a commitment to more dialogue and eventually to more dates. Some of my awkwardness disappeared as together we discovered a common bond in our faith. There were two immediate obstacles, however, that lay just under the surface of our conversation. The first was my native heritage and her English ethnicity. I wondered how I would be accepted by her family. Or how the people in my community might accept her. Thankfully, it turned out not to be a problem. Our families seemed to embrace our relationship, even though I found her father somewhat intimidating at first. His bark turned out to be more of a father's natural concern that his daughter be well taken care of.

Then, there was this additional, potentially relationship-killing issue: she was from a different denominational tradition than mine and would soon be departing for a Bible school in Oregon. She had been an active Christian and church member since she was a young teen and had a very evident desire for spiritual growth. I had sensed this about her almost immediately, and that was one of the things that I admired about her. But then there was this question: could she leave her denomination and embrace mine? And then there was the timing. She was about to leave for school. Out of touch could mean out of mind. Over a period of a year, we began a long-distance, sometimes frantic courtship while she attended Bible school and I began to establish my ministry. I would drive the nearly three hundred miles from my community to Portland, Oregon, to spend part of a day and have dinner with her. There were some awkward and tenuous moments as we worked through our differences, but eventually both of us felt God intended for us to marry. One day, she came to my community, and we took a long walk on the beach, talking about our relationship. It was a critical moment. Should we end our relationship or continue it, knowing it likely meant marriage? We decided on the latter. Soon, we were engaged, and a year later we were married. She joined me in ministry at Neah Bay, becoming a tremendous asset to my life and my ministry, and together we began raising a family and had three children, two sons and a daughter, of whom we are very proud.

Initially, I wondered how people in the community would accept her. Thankfully, her graces and friendliness won over many, and she was well accepted by the people there. More importantly for me, she filled the emptiness of my life. One of the more outstanding attributes of her faith was the ability to see positive possibilities when darkness seemed to enclose around me. Whenever I felt I was being pulled back into the bucket by my own self-limiting mindset or that of others, she encouraged me to crawl back up to the top. And when wolves began pounding on my door and started to huff and puff, she reminded me to trust God. She became light for my tendencies toward negative thinking.

But that first year at Neah Bay, I was alone. It was a difficult adjustment. Things did not go as I well as I had expected or hoped.

People in Neah Bay were genuinely pleased when I returned. I remember driving into town for the first time in my impressive car. The town seemed smaller than I remembered it. Some of the businesses, mostly seasonal salmon fishing resorts, were closed or being run by new owners, and the hillsides had been logged extensively, leaving areas looking barren in places.

Logging had evidently become a larger part of the tribe's economy. I noticed more than a few junky rez cars typical of every native community I had visited. As I steered my Delta 88 slowly along the front street next to the bay, no one seemed to notice it. People were just glad to see "Donny" had returned. That is what they called me as a kid, and for many, that is who I would always be.

Not long after my return, family members held a welcome home party for me in traditional Makah fashion. The entire community was invited to the hall for a dinner. The community hall was a rectangular wood structure, maybe 200 feet long by 150 feet wide, that seemed to have been there forever. Its one purpose was to serve as a gathering place for all official community functions, which included potlatch feasts in honor of some special occasion such as name-giving parties, or for memorial dinners and welcome-home ceremonies like mine. A potlatch feast, perhaps the most well known of tribal ceremonies, is common among all of the tribes throughout the Pacific Northwest, all the way to Southeast Alaska. Usually relatives and dignitaries of neighboring tribes are invited and gifts are bestowed to honor the guests. Traditional native dancing, welcome speeches, and protocols appropriate to each occasion are a part of every ceremony. Dinner usually consisting of beef, mashed potatoes, baked salmon, and coleslaw are served first to the elders and then to everyone else. These events could last long into the evening and into the next day. Clock time was never a determining factor.

My welcome home party concluded with a "love circle." As I sat in a chair in the front of the hall with members of my family, tribal members filed by to the rhythms of Makah traditional drummers and singers and dropped money into a basket in front of me—a traditional way of saying, "Welcome home!"

Soon after the celebration, it was time to begin ministry. I announced a get-acquainted meeting to discuss my ministry at the same community hall where, just days earlier, hundreds had come to welcome me home. I wanted to take advantage of my celebrity. The resounding welcome held promise for a great turnout. However, only nine people came, mostly out of curiosity or simply to wish me well. To the community, I was still "Donny," the young boy they knew who left thirteen years before. Like Jesus' experience among His own people, I was too familiar. It would take time for me to earn their trust.

An old, dilapidated building called the American Legion Hall served as my first church. Its roof leaked like a sieve, the wood floor creaked, it smelled of mildew, sand from the nearby beach seemed everywhere, and there was no heat. Average attendance, including my wife Mary when she eventually joined me, was probably nine, six of them being children. On a really good Sunday, it might mushroom to fifteen. Usually, most who attended were not originally from the community. None of my family or relatives attended.

Returning home once again surfaced some of my negative, familiar thought patterns. Unlike Jesus, the perfect Son of God who had returned home confident of His purpose and His ministry, it was hard for me not to revert back to my old pattern of thinking of myself as "less than"—lacking in ability and confidence. Feelings of insecurity and uncertainty resurfaced. This was a great environment for God to begin to help me understand that I, too, was like a crab in a bucket struggling to make it to the top. Each time I neared the top, if others did not pull me back down, I found a way to fall back down on my own. There was something important about returning home to serve my own community that I would only begin to appreciate years later.

Returning home to my people was thus a great place for God to begin teaching me about the history of my broken and missing pieces and that of my tribe. Additionally, through all the experiences I would have there, I would learn key aspects of servant leadership and, perhaps just as importantly, something of the broken relationship we all have with God's creation and how that is affecting all of us. Not only was God helping me learn the roots of my own dysfunction, He was preparing in me an important message to share with others. That message would have something to do with how we perceive time and how that affects our relationship with the natural world and with God as well.

CHAPTER 18

Once There Was Time

———————=∾∾∾=———————

> *"This is what the Lord says. Stand at the crossroads and look;*
> *ask for the ancient paths, ask where the good way is, and walk*
> *in it and you will find rest for your souls . . . ."*
>
> Jeremiah 6:16

Long exposure to the culture outside of my community, especially to the educational system, oriented me to the tick-
tock rhythms of the clock. I carried that mindset with me as I
began ministry in my hometown. Initially I did my best to ensure
church services began at 11:00 A.M. and ended at noon. That
had been the way I was taught in seminary. Many people in my
community, however, were not as scrupulously tied to the clock
and often joked about showing up for functions of one sort or
another on "Indian time." Interpreted, that meant whenever they
were done with something else of importance. It was often an
irritant to those who, like me, expected people to show up for a
given event at a specific time. I had to learn to adapt or face constant irritation. Nevertheless, the contrast of the two ways of telling time eventually helped me to understand that the way people
mark time often plays a significant role in determining how they
relate to family, tribe, money, the earth and even God. This insight began to unfold as I learned more about my tribe's history.

For thousands of years, my ancestors had adapted their
lives to the seemingly endless cycles and seasons of the natural

world. The seasonal rhythms of nature provided an abundant harvest for my people. And these, in turn, shaped how they patterned their activities. For Makahs, this typically meant the hunt for whales and fishing for halibut in the spring, the gathering of berries and the harvest of salmon in the summer and fall. This pattern, repeated again and again over eons of time, had shaped not only a way of life but it's meaning as well. As you might imagine, when my people were first introduced to clock time, it was not an easy transition.

It did not take long, however, to learn that arriving at work late or not showing up for school on time could cost you dearly. It was, of course, a goal of government to force Native Americans to adapt their culture to the new kind of time.

Nevertheless, like Midwest farmers ever dependent on the seasons for their crops, my people continued to rely on the age-old cycle of the seasons, especially those fishermen who continued to rely on the harvest of halibut and salmon. Most understood, however, that in order to survive in a modern world, one had to accommodate the demands of either time accordingly, to live, as it were, in two worlds of time.

Even though I had learned to accommodate the two kinds of time, I was aware that something about clock time was inherently antithetical to native ways of thinking and had contributed to our loss of tribe and the values that had once informed our way of life. The more I thought about it, I could see that there was something about it that was increasingly affecting everyone else too. Or so it seemed. But was this true? And if so, how could this be and what were the reasons?

My interest in the answer to these questions was initially stimulated by events taking place in my community at the time of my return home. When I arrived to begin my ministry, my tribe was actively engaged in excavating the ancient village of

Ozette, near the place where the *Hojun-Maru* had broken apart many years earlier.

Several centuries before the Japanese sailors had crashed on the shores of Cape Alava, an older village in the same area had been buried by a sudden landslide, likely catching the people living there at the time off guard. Heavy rains had apparently weakened the hillside above, triggering the disaster. In any case, the mud and clay that had buried the village preserved a treasure trove of valued possessions from another era, an age when our people lived in sync with the natural world. A world when there was time for family, relationships, and story. And, an age far less complicated than our present one. An age when, once there was time.

The world being excavated by the archeologists assisting the tribe to recover the valued treasures from another age was obviously a much slower-paced world than our present one. In my mind's eye, I can visualize an Ozette family sitting around a crackling log fire in a cedar longhouse in the dead of winter, listening to the stories of elders describing a successful whale hunt or recounting the wisdom of the past.

Wealth to the people then was associated with the passing on of ancient wisdom, genealogies, and oral traditions and the songs and dances preserved through thousands of years. It did not come from owning property, accumulating money, or attaining mastery over nature.

This last point is especially significant.

My people and many other tribal peoples I have met through the years have had a long and abiding sense of oneness with the natural world. It has contributed to a generally held belief among all tribes that the earth and all things created are sacred. Attempts to exploit its resources without considering its delicate symmetry or its connection with us were considered a violation of the design of the Creator and a threat to human existence. An important insight grew out of this perspective: the fate of humankind is linked to our stewardship of the Creation. Said another way, if mankind is dysfunctional in carelessly exploiting the natural world, the natural world manifests disorder and chaos. Biblical revelation seems to take this a step further by linking humankind's rebellion against God with disruptions in the natural world. I'll say more about this later.

Tribal elders assisting the archeologists to interpret what they were recovering from Ozette helped contribute much to our understanding of this ancient worldview. For these vitally important people in our community, memories of a world that they were familiar with as children were stirred by the recovery of hand-carved bowls with the smell of seal oil still evident, skillfully designed furniture, spear points made of mussel shell and bone, whaling harpoons, artistically carved fish clubs (the face of an owl forming the handle of one of them), and matting to sleep on, as well as fish hooks, hair combs, cooking boxes made of cedar, and even cleverly designed toys for children such as game paddles (they resembled ping pong paddles) and a top spinner.

Along with the excitement these elders experienced as they examined these valued treasures from another era was a hint of sadness too. They knew too well that something vitally important to the tribe had been lost in the transition from the world of their ancestors to the present one. And for them, it seemed to coincide with the introduction of the new way of telling time and the loss of their sacred lands and the old ways that once helped preserve family and tribe.

Born near the end of the nineteenth century, when many of the old ways were still practiced, the Makah elders possessed an intimate familiarity with the time-honored ways of our ancient heritage. However, throughout much of their growing up years, they had withstood the worst of the increasing government interventions that were intended to force change. Having to attend residential school far from home while also enduring the efforts of the government to prohibit the practice of ancient tribal traditions, including the speaking of the Makah language, were grievous, contributing greatly to the generational dysfunction I have already described.

However, this was not the only catalyst for change affecting their world. Like every other place in America, they had also experienced the inevitable consequences of a modern world in a rush to innovate new technologies such as automobiles, televisions, telephones, and more recently, cell phones, iPods, flat screen TVs, computers, and of course, clock time. These, like many other technological advancements intended to save time, improve communication, order productivity, and make life easier, had certainly improved life in the community.

Nonetheless, there had been unintended consequences; the introduction of things new and innovative and the accrual of information at ever more frequent (exponential) rates tend to make past experience and wisdom seem irrelevant, and they often require an abundance of natural resources that, as we have witnessed, can have serious consequences for the environment.

One of the more well-known and respected elders in my community was the late Isabel Ides. She was a relative of mine and through all the years of her life had been a wonderful resource to our tribe. She along with her husband, Harold, knew our tribal history and traditions better than almost anyone else. They were also among the most innovative; they purchased the first television in our community. As a young boy, I remember how excited I was to go over to their house to watch it. They were also the first to buy a car after a road was finally constructed connecting our community with the outside world.

These were certainly useful innovations and brought much satisfaction and ease of transportation. At the same time, the new entertainments, especially as technology expanded their capacity, could become addictive. In addition, new transportation afforded more mobility, allowing people to readily leave the community, maybe for good. The challenge of preserving family and tribe became more difficult with every decade of innovation, educational opportunity, and increased ease of travel. It raises an important issue.

There has always been a tension between the new and innovative and preserving the continuity of the tribe and the old ways that held it together. In fact, in all of my years serving as a pastor and later as an elected tribal leader, our tribe was engaged in a conscientious effort to recover and preserve the wisdom of the elders, including the restoration of the language and customs. At the same time, our tribe was being introduced to more and more information and new innovations happening at ever-shorter intervals that challenged the relevancy of our traditions and the cohesion of the tribe.

Tribal elders who had witnessed these rapid changes first-hand could see that in the years during which these advances in technology had taken place, there had also been an increase in alcoholism, hard drugs, car accidents, health problems, and behaviors that would have been unacceptable to previous generations. The interface of our tribal traditions with rapid changes driven by modern world innovations was not always compatible.

We are not, of course, the only culture to experience this phenomenon of the human experience. Ever since the Fall into sin and the loss of Eden, people everywhere have struggled to strike a healthy balance between adapting to innovations that change their lives while also seeking to preserve the core values that helped to guide and shape their heritage.

There appears to be, as many in our age can attest, an of-ten-repeated pattern in humankind's interaction with too-rapid change wrought by innovation. The things man invents to make life more efficient and save time, when joined to our fallen nature and a similarly broken world, can take on a dark side. When this occurs, as author Nigel Goring Wright observes in his book, *A Theology of the Dark Side*, we become "prisoners of created forces that have become disorderly."[24]

The disorderly, dark side aspect of mankind's progress, and its impact on our wellbeing, has most recently surfaced in our present age of international commerce. Consider how the global market, driven by profit and facilitated by technologies that make for shorter time and distance and greater speed in communications, has also been accompanied by increasing interdependencies and hence, vulnerabilities. Loss of confidence in the market in one part of the world can instantaneously trigger economic downfall everywhere else. Then there are problems with trading partnerships.

Our reliance on the Middle East for oil to fuel our quest for progress has not only destabilized our economy, especially when turmoil in that part of the world threatens supply, but the increasing tensions over fundamentally different values and beliefs introduce the possibility of conflict as well. It doesn't end there, of course.

In order to escape our dependence on foreign oil and give stability to our own economy, we consider alternate sources of energy, such as wind generation or nuclear power. Abundant and environmentally clean if contained properly, these promise to free us from environmental degradation and dependency on foreign energy. But at what price? Each is expensive and, like many innovations, come with the potential to adversely impact the environment or even us, especially when safety-insuring measures are breached, such as when the nuclear power plant in

---

[24] Wright, *A Theology of the Dark Side*, 57

Japan lost its cooling capacity during the March 2011 tsunami. Then, of course, spent fuel from nuclear power plants has a long shelf life. What to do with the highly radioactive fuel rods are a major concern and an ongoing source of debate.

The capacity for the things we invent for a good purpose to take on a dark side consequence has never been more evident than in the world of electronic innovation. Consider the Internet.

Ever since micro-technology began to explode upon the world scene in the 1970s, the Internet revolution it enabled, has afforded an amazing new way of communicating, all the while seemingly affecting the brains' chemistry and people's behavior. As a result, many of us experience expanded frequency of communication with friends and relatives. But quite unintentionally, it has also introduced a whole new way of isolating ourselves from the people around us we love, especially our families. Many people, for example, spend so much time surfing the Internet or engaging in cyber games with anonymous individuals that it becomes not only addictive but also a substitute for face to face relationships. Worse, we have seen how a single picture placed on YouTube can spread malicious gossip around the world and destroy someone's reputation overnight; and observe how criminals have used the Internet to increase drug trafficking, engage in fraud, promote pornography, commit identity theft, or even to lure children into dangerous situations. Perhaps more ominously, some nations have taken its dark-side applications a step further and are even devising programs to conduct cyber warfare that threaten things like the nation's power grid system or communications capabilities.

Then, there have been the human quality of life consequences felt by society as a whole reflected in growing unemployment due, in part, to growing trade imbalances and innovations in communication and manufacturing technology that enable corporate decision makers to increase their profitability while decreasing their work force. Usually this translates into letting go of older workers who are deemed less valuable. This often means that the survivors of a reduction in force are required to assume a heavier workload to compensate for lost staff and to accommodate the new capacities afforded by technology. The loss of jobs due to innovation and outsourcing work to other nations where labor is cheaper has dramatically impacted our economy, as evidenced by recently released government statistics (Bureau of Labor Statistics U.S. Department of Labor News Release, November 2011) revealing that the proportion of our total population that is working has fallen to 58.4%. It reflects, too, why America has increasingly become a debtor nation and why we produce less, import more, and borrow to pay for the promises the government has made to its citizens.

In all of this, we learn a brutal truth. In a clock-driven, technological world, time is equal to money, and when it is joined to corporate profit margins and, sometimes, outright greed, people and relationships are diminished in the exchange and, perhaps more tragic, the older wisdom is deemed less valuable. The bottom line for much of corporate America becomes not the general good but how to increase profits and the value of dividends paid to stockholders.

Then, there is perhaps the cruelest irony of all. In a world of rapidly increasing technologies intended to increase productivity and save time, we not only feel as if we have less time to accomplish all that we have to do, but time seems to be going by faster. As a result, half of all Americans tell pollsters that they don't have enough time to do what they want. This sense we have that we don't have enough time and that things are happening in compressed time periods is reinforced in part, by technologies that enable us, in the privacy of our living rooms, to witness major traumatic events across the world as they occur. Thus events, including natural disasters and political upheavals, have the sense of occurring in ever-shorter time intervals. Consider the following.

In a little more than a decade since the beginning of the new millennium, we have witnessed up close 9/11, the war on terrorism, a massive hurricane called Katrina, a huge tsunami in the Indian Ocean, a deadly earthquake in Haiti killing over 200,000 people, the largest oil spill in U.S. history along the Gulf Coast, huge flooding in Pakistan killing thousands, a dam bursting in Hungary, the collapse of many of the world's financial systems, a major recession, a category five tornado in Joplin, Missouri, and increasing political upheaval in the Middle East. Even as I was writing this, a magnitude 9.0 earthquake, the fourth largest in recorded history and an estimated 1,000 times more powerful than the one that leveled much of Haiti, struck Japan, resulting in a large tsunami, damage to a nuclear power plant, and many thousands of deaths. The quake even rocked the earth slightly off its axis. "Things are happening so fast," said an acquaintance of mine, "that you don't even get a chance to absorb the last one before something else happens."

With all of these events happening in the world on an almost-daily basis and the introduction of new knowledge and technologies being introduced at ever-increasing frequency, we begin to see a pattern familiar to Native Americans. Too rapid of change coupled with insufficient resources to effectively process all that we experience results in heightened anxieties, societal confusion, and eventual loss of core values that once held the tribe together. It leaves us feeling as if our ship on the sea of life has been disabled and we are adrift in a storm of chaos. How is this possible? It begins with our human frailty and susceptibility to disorder.

Human nature does not handle rapid change very well, especially those we see occurring all around us today. The seemingly endless assault on our senses caused by upheavals in politics, our recession-ravaged economy, major disturbances in nature, and the onslaught of innovations and information is overwhelming. This often leads to questioning, maybe even abandoning past beliefs and adapting new patterns of behavior to fit the ever-changing new conditions. It is as if the rudder of our lives has broken off and our sail shredded by life's storms. The loss of personal freedom is one consequence. Bad behaviors are another.

Consider, for example, how America's fear-based response to 9/11 has changed the way we enforce security at airports and the impact that has had on individuals. We now have to adapt to long check-in lines, taking off our shoes, coats, sweaters, etc., and submitting to embarrassing pat downs and full-body screening devices. Even elderly people barely able to manage with walkers or wheelchairs are made to submit to these kinds of indelicate procedures. It may be necessary to ensure our security, but in the exchange, we lose something of our dignity and individual freedom. This amounts to a cultural change rooted in fear.

The cumulative effect of the daily stresses like those I have described surfaces another challenge: they amplify generational differences within society. The reason for this is that older generations tend to react to the stresses of today's rapidly changing world by clinging to the cultural values forged in their youth. Meanwhile, younger generations, their emerging beliefs shaped by the present events around them and the incredible amount of new information, often discard as irrelevant some of the values of their parents' and grandparents' generation.

As a result of the rapidly changing culture of our present age, there are an estimated five generations and sub groups within each living side by side in America today, each one with its own set of beliefs and values shaped, in part, by the major events occurring in their own era.[25] You can see the possibilities

---

[25] Underwood, *The Generational Imperative*, 30

for inter-generational conflict. Since the things that influence values-formation like recessions, war, or major disturbances in nature are occurring at shorter time intervals, generational differences are being defined more rapidly. The values that once may have been rock-solid principles for one generation are considered irrelevant for another. Society attempts to adapt to these different values by accommodating the new reality. Behaviors that were unacceptable in one generation become the new normal in the next. This results in increasing political stresses as society becomes divided over the meaning of past core values.

It is, of course, difficult to raise a family, sustain a congregation or tribe, or maintain the unity of a nation in a world like this. The confusion over beliefs and core values, coupled with increasing anxieties and pressures from a declining economy, the threat of conflict, or some new natural disaster places overwhelming stresses on marriage, the family, and people's relationship with God. Statistics tend to bear this out.

The increasing number of failed marriages, along with the recession, has resulted in fewer people wanting to marry and many couples simply agreeing to live together. This phenomenon was born out by a recent government report issued in September of 2010, revealing that the number of married women eighteen and above in the United States fell below 50% for the first time since such statistics have been kept. A more recent study released in November 2010 by the Pew Research Center indicated that four out of ten people now believe marriage is becoming obsolete. This is compared to 28% in 1978.

These modern forces for change, like the government-driven changes that had so dramatically impacted my people, now seem to be having the same affects across all cultures. The stresses of our fast-paced world are pushing everybody and everything faster and faster toward change, and we are not handling it very well. Worse, events seem more out of control than ever and heading toward oblivion. Clock time and the progress it has ordered do not seem to be our friend in all of this. In fact, it is having the effect of accelerating the consequences of human nature's dark side. And that has, in turn, served as an invitation to the dark spirits to enter the vacuums created by the confusion over lost truths and values.

So back to the question I began with: what role if any did clock time have to do with this? And why is it that it was antithetical to traditional Native American thought?

The relationship between clock time and its connection to the stressful events of our present age may come as a surprise to some of my readers. It was to me, especially when I began to uncover its vital relationship to mankind's progress and the natural world. My interest in this first was piqued when I discovered two opposing ideas that have been advanced by its invention. One had to do with devotion to God; the other had to do with mastery of nature and the glorification of man—two diametrically opposite ideas. One can better understand this by reviewing the events leading to clock time.

Before the invention of clock time, the natural world was viewed with ignorance and suspicion and hence acted as a barrier to discovery and invention. Sometimes myths were associated with it, like goblins and witches inhabiting the forests, or beliefs that the world was flat and that the earth was the center of the universe. Together with the reality that people were forced to live their daily lives by the availability of sunlight and the seasons of the year, ignorance of the world of nature and forced dependence on its seasonal cycles acted as a hindrance to scientific innovation.

Some kind of breakthrough was needed to set mankind free from its cycles and seasons that could then inspire a new freedom to think about the natural world and to provide order for progress. What was required was some kind of innovation that would accurately segment time on a consistent, daily basis that would then allow people to order their lives more deliberately.

Through the centuries, efforts to achieve this goal were reflected in innovations like sundials, water clocks, hourglasses, etc. None of these, however, was very effective in achieving this goal. Each was flawed. But then came an invention that would forever transform the speed of progress and hence the way people experience life in the world. It was a simple device that would eventually result in the development of the mechanical clock and the familiar tick tock of time.

Much to my surprise, I learned that this innovative mechanism had its origins not in the minds of secular scientists but in the sanctuary of the church. In the fourteenth century, an obscure person connected with the church, probably a devoted monk, invented a contrivance that has come to be known as "the verge escapement." This simple apparatus permitted the free-fall check and release of a weight connected to a rope that was used to call people to worship. This was accomplished by connecting a weight by intersecting cogged wheels to a vertical axle that carried a horizontal verge. This device controlled the wheel's rotation.[26]

What was so amazing about this invention is that the check and release was accomplished at precise intervals, eventually giving us with each check and release the "tick tock" sound of the passage of time. This new machine was called the "clock" or bell because that is what it did. It timed the ringing of the bell for worship at precise intervals. The connection of clock time development with the church was such a surprise when I first read about it that I remember thinking, "No wonder my denomination and others like it are so time conscious and precise in their liturgical forms. It is part of their heritage."

---

[26] Andrews William J.H. *Scientific America Special Edition on Time, June 2006*, 48

The clock's application as a means of ordering worship was only part of its meaning. It had another, less praiseworthy application as well. It helped to facilitate the long-held quest of mankind to break free from the limitations imposed by nature and, by extension, God as well. This was possible because at about the same time of its invention, a powerful idea was gaining ground in Europe known today as Humanism. It had many good aspects to it. However, part of its focus was the exaltation of man's capacity to shape his own destiny apart from the dictates of nature or even God the Creator. The thought went something like this. If one could master time, one could, by extension, gain mastery over the natural world. Historian Daniel Boorstin captured this application of the clock's meaning when he concluded, "Here was man's declaration of independence from the sun, new proof of his mastery over himself and his surroundings."[27] The invention of the clock thus had two components: one was directed toward worship of God, the other of mastery over the natural world. One need only review the history of its evolution to see its impacts on mankind's progress.

The first clock was a simple mechanical device to begin with but in its simplicity was a key to unlocking the door to greater technological accomplishments. Over the next five centuries, the clock would evolve to give order to progress. In that time, the clock was modified by being made more portable (spring technology), more accurate (the pendulum), and more available (mass production), enabling people everywhere in the world to begin to order their lives in accord with its rhythms. It was becoming something akin to a new common language of Babel, a key to opening up the door to technological advancements.

By the nineteenth century, pocket-watches were common. By the early twentieth century, wrist watches. Over the course

---

[27] Boorstin, *The Discoverers*, 39

of its evolution, the clock contributed to navigation and thus discovery, trained a world of people to live by its order, and greatly facilitated innovation and mass production. In fact, the invention of the clock was the beginning of miniaturization of technology and the first phase of computer development. And during all of this, the productivity it helped order required ever more natural resources. Thus, the earth was being increasingly subdued and exploited since progress required more and more of everything.

Realizing how much the clock had evolved and how its invention had influenced progress was surprising. It brought back memories of my visit to Europe and the marvelous clock towers I had seen in the market squares of the great cities. It turns out that these were not only testimony to mankind's devotion to God. Perhaps more significantly, they were a reflection of mankind's genius in his efforts to attain mastery over the natural world and, by extension, as some Humanists interpreted the new age of discovery—asserting independence from God as well. Humanism had many good benefits that have unquestionably blessed all of mankind. But unfortunately, the elimination of God from the equation in humankind's progress has served to undermine truth and accelerate chaos and disorder in our present age. That is because when we turn away from God by asserting our own authority, it is easier to ignore morality and the principles He has established to guide all of our relationships. Hence we invite darkness and chaos into our lives and culture.

This last suggestion reminds me of what a friend termed "the foundational, malignant narcissism" underlying mankind's relationship with our Creator going back to Eden and Satan's temptation of our first parents to "be like God." It has been our natural tendency to desire to master our fates, to take control and be in charge. And of course, it has resulted in the serious consequences I have related including man-kinds pro-clivity for taking technology and using it for self-serving and even evil purposes.

Ironically, America was born of these two: its religious side on the one hand and its Secular Humanism side on the other. The two divergent values have long been at odds with each other in America and frames some of the current political debate in our country. Some people would like to think you can dismiss the religious heritage of America and its values as irrelevant in a modern world. Humankind, by the power of his intellect, can solve all of his problems.

The promise of a brighter future because of man's genius was the theme of the Seattle World's Fair in 1962. It certainly seemed hopeful, but as we have all observed during the years since, while innovations can and do make life better and easier, they have the potential in their interaction with human nature to unleash a dark side and accelerate and amplify evil. And when this occurs, nations, tribes, families, and communities increas-ingly become dysfunctional and less secure. In a tragic kind of irony, just when we need God most, people's faith in Him is blurred by skepticism and unbelief.

In spite of all that we experience in our increasingly com-plicated world, there is reason to hope for a better future. That hope for a better future began for me when Jesus entered into my life that July day in the shadow of the Space Needle. He not only declared me forgiven; Jesus made me a son and a part of His eternal kingdom, thus securing my life for all eternity.

It is great comfort to know that in the midst of rapid chang-es, God continues to maintain control of all of history and offers us peace in times of tumultuous events. Jesus Christ is as relevant as He has always been: "the same yesterday, today and forever." (Hebrews 13:8) This was the assurance that first caused me to attend the Billy Graham meeting so many years ago. Furthermore, it is a message that is still relevant for our present age.

Dietrich Bonhoeffer offered some practical advice in a message titled "Making the Most of Your Time." In that message, he said, "Time belongs to death, or still more so, to the devil . . . We must return it to God."[28]

A simple message, to be sure, but ironically consistent with the original intent of the clock's inventor—to encourage an orderly, regular worship of God, coordinated by the tick tock of the clock. Thus, the proper response to all the stresses we see unfolding on a daily basis is to take each day and willingly give it over to God. What better way to do that than to begin each day with prayer and worship? It is the only way for us to cope with the present age.

Time, whether it is marked by the seasonal cycles of nature or by the mechanical clock, is a gift from God. However, we do need to avoid its dark sides. The Apostle Paul, in Ephesians 5:16, wrote, "Be very careful, then, how you live—not as unwise but as wise, making the most of every opportunity, because the days are evil."

---

[28] Metaxas, *Bonhoeffer: Pastor, Mentor, Prophet, Spy*, 260

CHAPTER 19

My Time, God's Providence

What then is time? If no one asks me, I know. If I want to explain it to someone who asks me, I do not know.
—Saint Augustine, Confessions

B orn to the world of Indian time while having been educated in a clock-time world provided me with some insights relative to their strengths and liabilities. Clock-time-driven technology, as previously noted, has inspired innovation and productivity. However, when joined to man's worst tendencies, it has demonstrated the capacity to greatly accelerate, if not magnify, the consequences of evil, and in that sense, may even be serving to expedite the day when Jesus returns to intervene in world history.

Indian time, also known as circadian time, is relational and coordinated with the natural world and is less likely to act as a high-powered propellant in driving world events. As a result, circadian time-tellers like the people I came from have not generally been at the forefront of industrial development and technological innovation. On the other hand, Native Americans have long been careful observers of nature and are generally credited with agricultural innovation as well as the discovery of cures for many kinds of diseases. For example, the cure for malaria, a disease that had long been the scourge of much of Europe and Africa, was first utilized by tribes in South America.[29]

When either of these types of "time" is given a value it should not have, such as when the time-is-money philosophy becomes our chief purpose in life or when nature is elevated above the Creator as in nature worship, it becomes idolatrous. The two kinds of time, therefore, need to be placed in a God-pleasing context and balanced to offset their worst tendencies. This means that whatever way we experience time, we need to yield it to God's eternal purposes, otherwise either time becomes a pathway to darkness, and life's meaning is reduced to the here and now, finite and increasingly fearful in a world with broken and missing pieces. It was this realization that caused me to be open to the prompting of the Holy Spirit to receive Jesus as my Savior at the Seattle World's Fair.

However, when Jesus entered my life, He did not only grant me salvation; He provided me with a new kind of perspective on reality that included life and purpose beyond the grave. It was ever-lasting life, and it occurred in what seemed a timeless place where God was present. Words like *eternal life* and *forever* were the words frequently used to describe this new reality. At the same time, I was living in the two kinds of time I have already discussed. It was time within eternity and included the past, the present, and the future. These seemed to happen inside eternity but were not eternity. Sound confusing and beyond our understanding? It should. Even no less a brilliant mind than Einstein was baffled by the concept of time as we experience it. He wrote to a friend, "The past, present and future are only illusions, even if stubborn ones."[30] In other words, even though we live inside time and space and mark our existence by it, no one understands what it is.

---

[29] Hobhouse, *Seeds of Change*, 1
[30] Davies, Paul *That Mysterious Flow, As Quoted in Scientific American*, 7

What is more, along with the gift of eternal life, God had bestowed upon me the promise of blessing for my present. It did not, however, exclude any trials or tribulations in my life. Rather, it meant that in all of my circumstances, however they would unfold throughout my life, good would come of them. Life lived inside eternity in time and space was a great place for me to learn spiritual self-discipline and faithfulness in all of my circumstances. What is more, the Holy Spirit of God would transform the worst things in my life into the best things. There was this condition, however; while the omniscient God knew perfectly well my past, present, and future, He was not about to share this information with me. I would have to trust Him from day to day, even when things seemed not to make sense. Faith was critical in my relationship to God; it is the one attribute of life in time and space that connects all of us to God's eternity.

Obviously, as some of my story illustrates, my time and expectations were out of sync with God's timing and purposes for my life. Nevertheless, my disappointments afforded an excellent opportunity to think of my life in terms of God's time and His purposes as they began to unfold in my life. What kind of time was this? What kind of purposes did He have?

With these things in mind, I began to imagine my life as spread out from all eternity before God, something like a tapestry that He has created and is carefully weaving on His eternal schedule, not mine. In Ephesians 2:10, we read, "For we are God's workmanship created in Christ Jesus to do good works which God prepared in advance for us to do." Then in Psalms 139:15–16 we read, "My frame was not hidden from you when I was made in the secret place. When I was woven together in the depths of the earth, your eyes saw my unformed body." These and many other verses like them reveal that our lives have a God-intended purpose from before all time as we experience it.

On the other hand, we experience God's purpose for our lives within increments of this time and space that God created inside eternity. Our existence in time and space is something like an arrow shot through the air, with a beginning and an end and all the time in between. During our individual journeys in time through space, which is ever so brief as we experience it, we would like to have everything in between our beginning and end be as painless and stress free as possible. We want all things to work out well and with as little pain as possible, and we do not want wolves pounding on our doors.

However, life is not that way. There are uncertainties and random tragedies that seem to make no sense at all, not unlike the kind my family had experienced. Some of these occur, as my story reveals, long before we were born and affect us in our generation. These are the things, the good, the bad, and the ugly, that God in His foreknowledge has known about us from before the creation of the universe and graciously works to weave into a beautiful design according to His time and for His purposes. And since God is God, He can take even the most dark and tragic parts of our lives and weave them into something wonderful.

At the same time, we are not automatons whose lives are manipulated from above by God randomly pushing buttons at every whim. In the context of life in the time God has allotted to us, we have been given what my theological professors referred to as "free will." It means we have the freedom to accept our circumstances, regardless of what they may have been, and allow God in His gracious work in our lives to transform them for His glory. Or we are free to reject them as unfriendly intrusions into our lives, in which case they become a curse. Living with feelings of failure, doubting God's goodness, or harboring anger or bitterness because of our circumstances is a choice we can make. But when we do so, we short-circuit our connection with God's eternal purposes and frustrate His grace in our lives, which causes us to feel as if our lives are purposeless. It is evidence of a lack of faith.

Obviously, struggling with my little faith in times of disappointment, I would find myself once again under pressure to find His purposes in my disappointment. Caught in the limited understanding of my present, I would lose sight of my eternity in God's plan. Inwardly, I would begin to doubt God's good intent, much as I had when Medaris died in that senseless car accident. My disappointment over his death had nearly kept me from the ministry and thus short-circuited my role in God's plan for my life. God, however, was patient with me and nurtured my disillusionment with positive experiences at just the right time to renew my confidence and faith and to reconnect me with His eternal purpose for my life.

One day, however, I was provided a unique opportunity to begin to appreciate how faith and His providence combine to prepare us for His eternal plan. It was a lesson learned as a result of a harrowing experience that took place on the sea. Ironically, it occurred while I was doing something I really enjoyed, an activity that took me away from the stress of work.

The occasion was a salmon-fishing excursion with a friend. It was a near-perfect day; the weather was clear, the ocean flat, the scenery breathtaking—and the fish were biting! We were fishing off Tatoosh Island, near the entrance to the Strait of Juan de Fuca. It is one of my favorite fishing places. Located at the place where the ocean meets the waters between Vancouver Island and the Washington coast, it is an ideal gathering place for salmon during the late summer. Sometimes, when the salmon are schooled in large numbers and the water is clear, you can look down twenty or thirty feet into the depths and see large fish darting here and there, chasing herring or some other food fish. This day was no exception, and my friend and I were catching salmon almost as quickly as we could get our lines into the water.

Wrapped up in the excitement of each catch, we hardly noticed the tide change and did not see that other boats had departed. Suddenly, the seas around us had become disruptive and angry as crossing currents collided, producing turmoil and chaos in what had just moments before been a placid sea. Buffeted by the short, quick chop, we found ourselves being sucked by the now-angry currents into shallower waters near rocks rising out of the sea by the island.

In normal weather, my eighteen-foot boat with its deep V-hull was seaworthy and could handle the short, three-to-four-foot chop easily, and we could have simply motored out of this area to calmer waters in the strait. However, at about the time the tide changed, the wind kicked up and began blowing a steady twenty miles per hour or more from the southwest, accompanied by large swells coming from farther out on the ocean—a perfect storm of events. The fifteen- to twenty-foot or more rollers, as we called the large ocean waves, were at times breaking at their peaks.

The combination of the tide change and the strong, wind-driven ocean swells in this area off the island was alarming. We were caught in a bad place, with no one in sight to come to our aid if we were swamped by a breaking wave. I had another problem too. If I tried to turn the boat around to go with the breaking swells and run east toward safer waters in the strait, a following breaker might submerge the transom, (back of the boat) likely killing the engine and causing the boat to flounder and sink. As we quickly pulled in our fishing gear, I fought off panic and considered the best course of action.

Then I remembered the counsel my father had given some years before: "If you ever get caught up in a tide change with wind and big waves near this area off Tatoosh, the best thing to do is point your bow straight into the wind and waves toward the southwest side of the island until you reach the far end. There, you can maneuver around to the leeward side where the wind will be less and the waves smaller, and you can work your way around through the inside passage way between the island and the mainland to safety."

Heading directly into the swells further out into the ocean seemed just the opposite of my intuitive impulse to turn the other way and run with the waves. Why head straight into the teeth of the wind and waves, farther out into the ocean? I trusted my father's advice. In the process, my small boat took a few waves directly on and shook and shimmied as it did. However, as I made my way carefully toward the southwest tip of the island and around to a place where, just as my father had predicted, the waves were smaller, I was able to work my way around the island to the safety of the strait. I breathed a sigh of relief. It was one of those times where a different decision might easily have had a tragic end.

Through the many years since this experience, I have come to understand how closely it resembles my life with God and maybe yours as well. The sage advice my father had given was prophetic. The unexpected collusion of tide and wind very much resemble life as we experience it: chaos and randomness intruding just when seas seem calm. My father's knowledge, based on years of his own experience, provided him a prophetic understanding of my future, enabling him to picture me in that place someday under these very conditions. And although it is a dim and imperfect comparison, his foresight was something like God's perfect foreknowledge of events; whereas my father knew me and the likelihood of the weather taking a sudden turn for the worse, God knows these things for certain. And, just as my father did not cause the storm, God our Father does not cause storms that come our way. But as God, He does know from all eternity the many circumstances of life, some tragic, that will likely arise unexpectedly to disturb the harmony of our families, our communities, and our world. He knows our tendency to resent our trials and to rely on our own resources—to run from the storm. Therefore, God calls us to reliance on Him.

Very often, His counsel is exactly opposite our natural tendencies. Instead of running from our problems, He calls us to point our bow straight into the teeth of the storm as in James 1:2–4: "Consider it pure joy my brothers whenever you face trials of many kinds because you know that the testing of your faith develops perseverance. Perseverance must finish its work so that you may be mature and complete, not lacking anything."

Through His grace working through all of our circumstances, God has assured us that the trials are meant to strengthen our faith and our character so that we will be made more like Christ, and in time (His time), we will find calm for the troubled waters of our souls. Thus, the God-purposes in our lives are most often forged and worked out through the testing of our faith. Malcom Muggeridge, a famed writer, BBC broadcaster, and often-quoted theologian said, "Contrary to what might be expected, I look back on experiences that at the time seemed especially desolating and painful, I now look back upon them with particular satisfaction. Indeed, I can say with complete truthfulness that everything I have learned in my seventy five years in this world, everything that has truly enhanced and enlightened my existence, has been through affliction and not through happiness, whether pursued or attained" (A Twentieth Century Testimony).

Our lives, connected by faith in Jesus for salvation, are under eternal warranty to God our Father, who assured us in Romans 8:28 that "all things work together for good." We simply need to place our confidence in His gracious love and have faith that He will take us through the difficult times. Faith enables us to grasp

220

this promise and to see beyond our present moment-by-moment circumstances to the eternal plan God has been weaving, to see, however dimly, a bigger picture of ourselves on the tapestry He is weaving.

More often than not, the walk of faith is just that—a walk into the unfamiliar accompanied by the confident assurance that things have an eternal purpose, even if we do not see the outcome during our earthly existence. In Hebrews 11:1, we have this assurance: "Now faith is being sure of what we hope for and certain of what we do not see." According to His eternal perspective of our history, God has seen our past, our present, our future, and the outcome of all that He has allowed in our lives. Moreover, as God who exists outside of time and space and whose Divine presence encompasses all that He has created, we can be assured that He is always with us to take us through the storms to safety. We read in Jeremiah 29:11, "For I know the plans I have for you declares the Lord, plans to prosper you and not to harm you, plans to give you hope and a future."

CHAPTER 20

The *Tenyu Maru*

=◦◦◦=

"We know that the whole creation has been groaning as in the pains of childbirth right up to the present time."

Romans 8:22

God's time, clock time, and circadian time all seemed to come together for me in a most unusual set of experiences. It began to unfold when a local man came to persuade me to run for election to the Makah Tribal Council. How could this be part of God's timing for my life? A pastor serving as an elected tribal leader? Was this a good idea? Would it impact my ability to serve my congregation? While I was full of opinions about effective leadership, especially servant leadership, it was this concern that kept me from running for office.

Then there was this: tribal leadership can be an especially risky business. Jealousies and petty arguments between clans often trigger controversy and upheaval leading to political instability. Sometimes contemporary clock-driven economic goals intended to create employment clash with traditional cultural and religious values related to tribal cohesion and reverence for the natural world. I have known of tribal governments that prohibited natural resource developments even though it would provide badly needed employment because to tear up the land or open areas up for tourism violated their beliefs about the sacredness of the earth. For this reason, tribes that retained the greatest part of their traditions were often least able to pursue economic development.

If these were not challenge enough, at times our tribal government was under intense pressures from certain community members to resolve long-standing grievances or do something about problems related to drug and alcohol abuse that, with the passing of the years, were becoming increasingly prevalent. Since many of our problems were systemic and, as evidenced by my experience, rooted in hidden anxieties going back several generations, they defied government solution. It meant that a leader caught up in dispute might have a short shelf life. Why place myself in this situation?

However, after prayerful soul-searching and consultation with family and church members, I decided to run for a three-year term. In spite of the risks involved, it seemed to me an opportunity to take my Christian witness into the government where I could possibly make a difference. Naturally, I felt my years of education would serve me well in leading my people since I was used to the way things worked in the education and business world. What I would later discover is that God would use my time as an elected leader to teach me valuable leadership lessons for service in His Kingdom. And perhaps more surprising, something about a God-message the natural world has for all of us.

The tribal election pitted me against an older native man who had lived most of his life in the community and understood well the traditions of the tribe. Having been away from my community for so many years, I was ignorant of much of my tribe's history and had missed out on some of the cultural traditions that had been handed down by the elders. I did, however, know how to get things done due in part to my clock-time orientation, which lends to business management. Perhaps this was one of the reasons people seemed willing to allow me to serve on the council. As it turned out, I won a close election—less than ten votes separated us. My election meant that I was now wearing two hats: that of pastor and tribal leader. It also meant I was walking in two worlds of time: the one of my tribal heritage and the other driven by the clock. Sometimes both would come into conflict.

At our first meeting, through a simple election among council members, I was appointed chairman. I had, in effect, been made the leader of my tribe and official spokesperson to the U.S. government and state agencies. I had taken on a lot of responsibility while also serving my congregation. It meant I would have to use my time wisely.

The challenge of leadership and the demands on my time turned out to be far greater than I imagined. Unemployment was high, our water quality was at risk, roads throughout the community were in bad repair, and the sewer system needed re-placement. We also had horses and cows running loose around the town and abandoned junk cars were scattered about. These constituted a very real health hazard. What's more, the tribe had just assumed responsibility for managing its own forest resources as well as several salmon fishing resorts previously run by outside interests. Managing all of this required a type of accountability and entrepreneurial thinking new to my experi-ence. Nevertheless, I was convinced that this was part of God's plan for my life.

In retrospect, the challenges of tribal leadership seem to have been God's way of preparing me for the complex challeng-es and the occasional difficult people I would encounter in later years as head of the Lutheran Association of Missionaries and Pilots U.S. I would also discover a unique opportunity to learn something about our broken relationship with God's creation and how it not only was affected by our industrial activities, but perhaps even more importantly, how the natural world mirrors our social dysfunction. It was a profound insight derived in part from my studies related to time management and its relationship to subduing the natural world. Of course, not aware of this at the time, I found the adjustment to my new responsibilities difficult and, initially at least, very much unrelated to my theological training.

Travel, and lots of it, was part of my new job. On more than a few occasions, I was required to journey to Washington, D.C., where I solicited help from government representatives in acquiring appropriations to repair the commonplace things of life such as roads, bridges, sewer lines—necessary aspects of infrastructure. As part of this, I even had occasion to meet then-Senator Bob Dole from Kansas and Senator Daniel Inouye from Hawaii, who at the time had taken on the assignment of serving as the representative of Indian concerns to the Senate.

However, most of my responsibilities were related to the restoration of our increasingly depleted salmon runs and working to solicit help to accomplish this from appropriate government agencies such as the U.S. Fish and Wildlife Service, the U.S. Forest Service, and the U.S. Department of the Interior. My involvement with salmon management taught me a lot about salmon and why their numbers were decreasing. But more importantly, my investment in this vital resource was the beginning of a new understanding of what God has been saying to us through His Creation.

Sadly, wild salmon throughout the Pacific Northwest (fish natural to their river of origin) have been decimated through the years by over-harvesting by commercial and recreational users, hydroelectric dams that blocked spawning areas, poor logging practices that destroyed habitat, and industrial pollution that poisoned rivers. These were the very kinds of masculine activities (industry, building, and expansion, etc.) that reflect the tensions between man's efforts in pursuit of progress and nature's sensitivity (Mother Earth) to those activities. My tribe especially felt the consequences. Losing the salmon meant we were at risk of losing our historic dependence on the sea, likely resulting in even more damaging impacts on our traditional way of life.

The Makah people, as you may infer from my writings, have had a long, if not storied, history of reliance on the sea and had been especially known for their prowess as hunters of the great whales that annually migrated along the coast.

Typically carried out in the spring or fall of the year when whales were migrating between the Gulf of Mexico and Alaska, whale hunting had long been an integral part of the life of the community. It was also quite dangerous, requiring a highly trained crew. Imagine eight strong men specifically selected for this purpose paddling (locals call it "pulling)" far out onto the ocean in a forty-foot cedar dugout canoe with a harpoon connected to a rope with air-filled fur seal bladders attached intended to impede a wounded whale.

Spearing a large sixty-foot animal weighing anywhere from twenty to fifty tons was surely an exciting adventure but not one for the timid or those who wanted an easy meal. You had to be able to come alongside the behemoth at the right angle of attack. If not, one blow from the tail of an angry whale could easily break a canoe in half, leaving the crew at the mercy of the cold seas. For this reason, the man charged with the responsibility to thrust the harpoon had to know exactly when and where to place the hard wood lance and needed the strength to insure that its business-end, tipped with a sharp blade made of mussel shell and barbs of elk bone, entered deep within. Sometimes the speared whale, with canoe in tow at better than twenty miles per hour, would pull the men far out to sea before finally tiring and then succumbing to a final deathblow from another harpoon. Once the dead whale lay there on the surface, some brave individual then had to jump into the brutally cold ocean and then, using a sharp needle threaded with a specially designed cord, sew the whale's mouth shut so it would not fill with water and sink to the bottom of the sea.

The paddle back to the beach with whale in tow was a proud moment for captain and crew. It was worth the effort too. A large whale could feed an entire village, and its skeleton could serve a variety of useful purposes. No part of the whale went to waste. You can imagine the excitement generated throughout the village whenever the whalers beached their canoe with their prey in tow.

Although whaling and scenes like I described above had long held a special place in the life and culture of the Makah and had been protected by the treaty of 1855, it came to an abrupt end after a large number of whales taken by commercial whaling fleets threatened their extinction. Before this time, however, commercial whaling in general had enjoyed a long, if not illustrious, history in American lore. One need only visit the display of New England whaling techniques and whaling ships on display such as the *Charles W. Morgan* being restored and available for a walk-through tour in Mystic, Connecticut.

Oil rendered on magnificent New England whaling ships like the one being restored there played a vital role in America's rush to industrial development, providing fuel for street lamps, additives for cosmetics, and lubricants that helped to grease the machinery of the Industrial Revolution before petroleum became readily available. By the 1880s, however, a commercial whaling fleet that extended from the Atlantic to the Hawaiian Islands and from there all the way to Alaska took thousands of whales each year.

Unfortunately, the expansive whaling fleet destroyed too many whales, threatening their extinction. Eventually, the government stepped in and forbade all commercial whaling as well as Makah subsistence whale hunts. However, in 1999, with permission from the International Whaling Commission, the Makah were allowed to take a whale. Not without controversy, of course, as animal rights groups vigorously protested the Makah efforts. Nevertheless, the taking of a whale in the traditional manner utilizing canoe and harpoon for cultural and subsistence purposes inspired tribal people from around the country and even Africa (an African chief came to the Makah tribe to pay tribute to the event) to acclaim the event as a great moment for tribal people everywhere. Traditional tribal people from around the world knew something of importance was symbolized in the recovery of something from the past.

The event also illustrated a challenge for our world today. The loss of the Makah whaling tradition due to overharvest in previous generations was one more example of how the natural world can be disturbed by man's efforts to achieve progress and its impact on a way of life. Its affects on my people, like the growing litany of man-caused disturbances of God's creation, precipitated a change in culture, not to mention the denial of a treaty right. Fortunately, this loss was not as destructive to my tribe as the slaughter of the buffalo had been to the Plains Tribes. The Makah had an alternative.

In the face of this new challenge, Makah fishermen turned to commercial halibut and salmon fishing as a means of supporting their families. Like my father had done, many of the Makah men gradually evolved from fishing from thirty- and forty-foot cedar dugout canoes utilizing hand held fishing lines and rod and reels to forty-foot or more diesel-powered trollers (fishing boats) capable of fishing many lines at once. Even with the introduction of modern technology, it was not an easy living. The waters surrounding our area could be rough, and fog, wind, and rain were common. And whereas the ocean had once been teeming with salmon of all kinds, now their numbers were declining.

As the leader of my tribe, it was my job to negotiate annual fishing regulations that would permit my tribe to take a portion of the allowable harvest of salmon passing through our area. At my first meeting with the Pacific Fisheries Management Council (PFMC), the federal agency under the U.S. Department of Commerce responsible for the establishment and regulation of annual salmon harvests, I began to understand the growing conflict between disparate interests competing for a resource that was showing signs of stress. The prognosis for recovery was often complicated by multiple jurisdictions, each wanting a piece of a smaller pie. These included recreational users, commercial fishermen, fish processors, various states, Indian tribes, etc. It was particularly distasteful to see the manipulations that sometimes favored one group over another. The saying, "They never taught me this in school" suddenly had relevance for me. Standing before the regulators of the salmon management council and pleading my case or trying to explain the restricted quota assigned to my fishermen back at home were no-win tasks. I was obviously far afield from my seminary training. Or was I?

I soon discovered that there was something in this experience that struck a barely recognizable theological chord. I was beginning to understand firsthand how the oceans and the creatures living in them are becoming increasingly affected by the exponential growth of human populations, the industry required to support them, and the resulting pollution of God's creation.

Watching the decline of salmon species and the contamination of the ocean reminded me of biblical references in Romans 8 referring to creation "groaning in travail" and other images of God's creation increasingly in distress. The natural world was obviously subject to human exploitation and often reacted with chaos and unpredictability to the careless disregard for its delicate balance and symmetry. It also reminded me that man and nature are mysteriously connected in a way that joins our fates. This was, as I related previously, a belief held by most tribes. I have never forgotten the words of a tribal leader who, at one of the salmon management meetings I attended, warned the participants, "If we profane the earth, we corrupt ourselves. What we do to Mother Earth, we do to ourselves." The truth of this became especially evident in several significant events that occurred during my tenure as leader of my tribe.

Every year in the Strait of Juan de Fuca, as many as twenty thousand ocean freighters carrying the products of many nations pass by my hometown on their way to Seattle or Vancouver or some other port in Puget Sound. Against federal regulations, they would occasionally dump garbage or pump their bilges along the way. The accumulation of years of this practice has resulted in the pollution of some areas of the ocean and has even introduced exotic bacteria or foreign viruses into once-pristine waters. Salmon casually swimming through polluted waters are subject to the possibility of being infected, leading to the likelihood of passing a virus it has contracted on to others. This, in fact, did happen one year during my tenure on the council.

One day, the U.S. Fish and Wildlife Service, while conducting a routine sampling of salmon returning to a fish hatchery located on the Makah Reservation, discovered one salmon infected with a virus that was previously confined only to fish found in European rivers. The virus had apparently been transported to U.S. waters by a passing freighter that likely pumped its bilge into the Pacific off our coast.

Fearing the infected salmon might pass the disease it had contracted to other stocks of fish along the west coast, further devastating their numbers, the U.S Fish and Wildlife Service biologists poisoned the entire river, effectively killing all of the returning salmon.

There were other obvious signs of distress in the natural world as well. Our beaches were often littered with discarded waste such as plastic and styrofoam cups, bags, nylon rope, fish netting, bottles, and other trash. Sometimes you would see a sea gull or some other ocean bird with the plastic coupling from a six-pack wrapped around its neck or rusty fish hooks in their bills. It was sad to see but by no means the worst of it.

One bright summer morning in July of 1991, while convening a regularly scheduled council meeting, our deliberations were interrupted by an abrupt knock on the door. Standing in the hallway awaiting an audience with us were representatives of law enforcement, the local health clinic, and the U.S. Coast Guard. There was a disaster unfolding.

Within the hour, a large Japanese fish-processing vessel, the *Tenyu Maru,* with seventy men aboard, had been rammed in dense fog by an outbound Chinese freighter twenty miles west of Cape Flattery. Damage to the bow of the larger Chinese cargo ship was minimal, but the *Tenyu Maru* had been so severely impacted that the vessel was sinking, and its crew was in immediate jeopardy. I had difficulty believing that with modern radar and other navigational aids this could still happen, but it had. Men were in the water and a rescue was underway. Could we serve as a staging area for temporary care of survivors? We, of course, offered our full cooperation.

I never thought about it then but in retrospect, it was somewhat ironic that 159 years after the *Hojun-Maru* broke apart off Cape Alava, our community was once more a place of refuge for Japanese sailors in distress. Only one sailor was lost, and most were transported to larger care facilities instead of our community. That was the good news.

The vessel, however, sank quickly in over five hundred feet of water, spilling thousands of gallons of diesel fuel and chemicals used in fish processing into the ocean. It made for a deadly toxic mix. Within hours, the air along the beaches I loved to walk was thick with the acrid smell of diesel fuel. Birds and other marine animals soon began washing ashore, covered in oil; many quickly succumbed to the tarry mess that coated their feathers with thick, black, sticky goo. As many as 3,000 perished. Soon, the unpleasant smell of bunker fuel was accompanied by the oil washing ashore in clumps. Farther out on the ocean, oil slicks driven by the whim of currents and wind could be seen drifting ominously toward some of the most beautiful marine preserves in North America.

The next morning, hundreds of disaster responders seemed to have materialized out of nowhere, along with large tractor-trailer rigs filled with cleanup equipment and helicopters to locate the oil slick. The federal Superfund program for oil cleanup, established after the debacle that spilled millions of gallons of crude into Prince William Sound in Alaska when the *Exxon Valdez* struck a reef in March 24 of 1989, was accessed to pay for the concentrated effort. Federal and state agencies did not want a slow disaster response this time.

Meanwhile, television news crews and helicopters from the three major networks descended on our community en masse to assess the spill. The governor of the state and some of his top lieutenants flew in by helicopter to demonstrate the state's concern for this vitally important region. I was summoned for an impromptu meeting with then governor of the state, Booth Gardner, while television cameras recorded our brief conversation. The next thing I knew, I was being interviewed by television news crews on a daily basis and being asked questions like, "How well do you think the Coast Guard and disaster responders have responded to the spill?" It was my brush with Andy Warhol's "fifteen minutes of fame." It was also a demonstration of how modern technology takes news, amplifies it, and expands on its importance to a fault. It contributes to our sense of things out of control.

Thanks to this rapid response and the cooperation between our tribe, the U.S. Coast Guard, state, and the federal authorities and agencies that respond to dangerous spills, much of the damage that could have occurred was prevented. After several weeks of frenzied insanity, some semblance of normalcy returned to our community. We were no longer the lead five o'clock news story in the Pacific Northwest, and all the helicopters, television crews, eighteen-wheelers and strangers left town.

Sadly, since I began writing this book, a far more devastating oil spill has occurred off the Gulf Coast of Louisiana, destroying sea birds and causing damage to marine plant and sea life all along the coast. Caused by a fire onboard the British Petroleum–owned oil platform known as the Deepwater Horizon, it has been designated the worst oil spill in U.S. history. Fortunately, the oil well has been capped. However, it remains to be seen how seriously the delicate marine life will be impacted.

Thankfully, the natural world seems to possess a resiliency that sometimes surprises people. Consider, for example, how quickly the area around Mt. St. Helens in Washington State has recovered since the volcano's massive eruption on May 18, 1980. However, the BP oil spill, like the other examples I have discussed, is evidence of man's tenuous relationship with the natural world. And while this recent event may be more benign than first thought, no one really knows the long-term damage that is occurring to the environment because of humankind's industry and, very often, his carelessness.

Far removed as all of this seemed from ministry and my seminary training, I was learning something about God's creation and our relationship to it. Everywhere in the world, there are increasing signs of distress in the natural world. Much of it is caused by the inevitable conflict between human population growth and the stresses placed on the resources of the natural world to support it.

This has led to an increasingly contentious political and scientific debate as to what it all means, the magnitude of the problem, and who is responsible. There is, however, another aspect to nature's current state of distress that seems to have eluded the current debate, most likely because no one really knows how to factor it into the political equation. It has to do with evident geologic stresses within the earth itself. For example, the U.S. Geological Survey has been monitoring the number of seismic events taking place across the world. On average, as many as 50 earthquakes occur every day and amount to as many as 15,000 per year. What is particularly noteworthy is that their numbers are increasing and, in some cases, so is their severity, like the recent 9.0 that hit Japan.

It begs this question: is the natural world, like us, suffering from generational dysfunction? Does it have broken and missing pieces too? And perhaps even more profoundly, are its stresses related to our own? Most would probably argue, "No, it isn't. It is just part of the natural tectonic plate shifts taking place deep within the earth." There is a sense where this is true, of course. People who study such things have long known that tectonic plate shifts have been building up pressures deep within the earth that, from time to time, will eventually result in massive releases of energy, some with a magnitude like the earthquake that hit off the coast of Japan most recently. I grew up aware that there was a major fault-line off the coast of Neah Bay that could one day produce a tsunami similar to the one Japan experienced. There is some risk from natural world disruptions no matter where we live. However, the Bible implies that the creation wasn't always so disorderly. Since the Fall, it also has come under the curse of our sin. It is therefore subject to chaos, unpredictability, and tumult that, according to the Bible, will increase over time and in concert with humankind's rejection of God. I am convinced that this is what the Apostle Paul had mind in Romans 8:20 when he referred to all things God made as in a state of "frustration" or, in some texts, "futility," because of its connection to us and our dysfunction and that creation longs for redemption too. The text seems to suggest in the context that all of God's creation will be made perfect when we are. This has led me back to my theological roots and this application from Romans 8:19: "The creation waits in eager expectation for the sons of God to be revealed."

Just as sinful man is in desperate need of hope and restoration, the natural world is also broken and missing pieces and longs for rebirth. Through all of its disorderly manifestations, some caused by mankind's careless exploitation and some reflecting the curse following the Fall, creation seems to be mirroring the human experience. In the process, it is calling out to us with an important message. This message seems to include one with which most people are familiar, a cry for responsible management of the resources of the natural world. But in all of its disorderly manifestations, creation is also pleading with humankind to turn back to God, to rediscover our need for Jesus. Our turning from Him is causing the natural world to increasingly become distressed and even disruptive. In that sense, our moral pollution, rooted in our rebellion against God, is affecting the natural world more than our industrial pollution. That, fortunately, is not the end of it.

According to Scripture, Jesus is coming once again to claim His own and restore paradise lost. One of the signs of His coming is the very thing we see unfolding in our world today: increasing tumult in politics and upheavals in nature. In Matthew 24:6–7, we read, "You will hear of wars and rumors of wars, but see to it that you are not alarmed. Such things must happen, but the end is still to come. Nation will rise against nation and kingdom against kingdom. There will be famines and earthquakes in various places. All these are the beginning of birth pains."

The increasing number and severity of disruptions in nature reflect back to us our own state of brokenness and serves as a sign that our redemption is near. Like the discomfort a mother who is about to give birth experiences, the natural world's disruptions are reminding us that Jesus is coming again soon to restore all things. Thus, while the troubling behaviors reflected in the natural world are distressing, they are signs of the impending return of Jesus and a new and far better world to come. It is a bad news, good news kind of thing.

The good news for creation and all of us is that when Jesus died on the cross for our sins, He did not only redeem mankind. His death and subsequent resurrection was sufficient to pay for the restoration of *all of creation.* And thankfully, this includes the broken and missing pieces of the heavens and the earth. Someday, in accord with God's timing, the whole of His creation will be recreated in the perfection originally intended (see 2 Peter 3:10–13).

Until that amazing moment, as described for us in Romans 8:19–21, "The creation waits in eager expectation for the sons of God to be revealed. For the creation was subjected to frustration, not by its own choice but by the will of the one who subjected it in hope that the creation will be liberated from its bondage to decay and brought into the glorious freedom of the children of God." The earth will finally know peace when we do.

Chapter 21

A Stranger in Our Midst

——— ⟨∾∾⟩ ———

Foxes have holes and birds of the air have nests; but the Son of Man has no place to lay his head.

Luke 9:58

I learned a vital lesson about Jesus's character and the style of His ministry to the most needy and abused by life. It was a lesson learned as a result of some young volunteers who came to serve in our community and their engagement with my tribe.

About the time I became fully involved serving on the council, our small congregation began to experience growth. In part, this was due to a gift my denomination had provided to help us begin planning a new facility. In anticipation of this occurring, several years before my election to the government of the tribe, I had asked the tribal council for a small area of land on which to build a permanent church building. They agreed to lease to the congregation a portion of land one block off the main street.

Swampy and densely populated with skinny evergreens, along with ferns and thick underbrush, some of the locals thought the land unsuitable for a church building. As a young boy, I had managed to get lost somewhere in the woods behind the proposed site. It took me and a boyhood friend hours on an increasingly darkening day to work our way home through the substantial undergrowth. That was a long time ago. Now, many years later, I was faced with a different kind of challenge. Could

239

I find someone to clear the land? One of the local contractors told me a bulldozer would become mired in the mud trying to clear the site. He was not interested in the job. As it turned out, the appearance of the land assigned was deceiving. A Cat operator from a town adjacent ours looked at it, decided it was firm enough, and easily cleared the site.

We were soon able to begin construction on what turned out to be a beautiful four-thousand-square-foot church set amid a forest of young saplings and natural flora. A covered walkway next to a large cross sat in a small courtyard next to the church led to the entryway. Inside the entrance, a foyer with a cozy fireplace and comfortable chairs made an ideal setting for welcoming guests and hosting small-group Bible studies. Skylights connected the foyer with an intimate worship area that included a large cross-shaped window at one end of the sanctuary. Hosting retreats and servant work groups was accommodated by including in the design commercial showers and a multipurpose room with a well-equipped kitchen. Complementing the natural wildness of our setting were rhododendrons and flowering trees strategically placed around the property. The new church was another illustration from God that He could take my limited expectations and what seemed a least-likely location and provide a great place for worship as well as volunteers.

Whenever our church hosted a team of volunteers, I took time from my council responsibilities to spend the week with them. Our little congregation soon became adept at hosting summer adult and youth group volunteer teams from all over the country, arranging places for them to stay and organizing projects like repairing roofs, painting houses, or fixing fences— usually for those elders and single moms in our community least able to do their own handiwork. One of our teams even built a smokehouse for curing fish. Another constructed an outhouse, yet another, a small house for a homeless man.

Usually there was risk in having outside church groups serve the community for a week of work. You never knew with any certainty the degree of their maturity or how well they would perform the tasks assigned. Then there was always the possibility that an accident could happen. In all of our events, we tried to ensure appropriate adult supervision to accommodate all the risks. Fortunately, we never had anything more than minor cuts and scrapes, and most of the volunteers were fun to have around.

Many evenings following a hard day of work were spent on the beach. There, in the idyllic setting of expansive sand beaches, with a bonfire backlit by the golden sun sinking slowly over the western Pacific horizon, our volunteer workers would linger long into the evening enjoying fellowship. On some evenings, we would take the entire group to Cape Flattery. The walk along a steep trail through a dense forest of fir, spruce, and cedar trees, some dripping with moss, was a highlight.

At one point along the path stands an unusual tree that has been there forever. Dead or nearly so, it sits in the middle of the trail with its ancient roots exposed and weathered by the many hikers who, through the years, have carefully maneuvered around its desolate form. Amazingly, five separate trees, like the fingers on a hand, split off from the main trunk, each one ascending straight up thirty feet or more.

Down the trail a little farther, a nicely constructed viewing platform marks one corner of the United States. Standing on the raised area and looking out across the quarter-mile body of water known to locals as "the gut" is a view of Tatoosh Island. As often as I have made the walk down the steep trail to this very familiar place, my mind always comes back to my favorite memories of times spent fishing there.

Every now and then, caught up in the emotion of the moment and pride in my heritage, I would find myself trying to explain to anyone within earshot what it was like to take my little fishing boat beyond the island to catch salmon. "Look, over there you guys; do you see that island? Right near there is where I could catch a hundred or more salmon in a day." More often than not, the excitable teens and their adult leaders, fixated on the incredible beauty around them, ignored everything I had to say. That was fine with me. I was used to it. I was very happy to see them having a great time. After all, I was their host, and many had come a long way to serve in our community.

These moments were some of the best of times, for sure. More importantly, for all of the fun and fellowship of each event, there was always a God-feel to our time together. For one, we never had a bad week of weather, which was amazing along the northwest coast where fog and rain are typical. More importantly, no one got seriously hurt, and there was always some experience that provided a special God-lesson for the participants. One stands out in particular.

One year, one of my summer volunteer work teams scheduled servant projects in our community the same week that a similar-size youth choir from Seattle had planned to come to our town to perform nightly concerts at one of the other churches. It was a coincidence, but the circumstances as they unfolded would provide a unique teaching opportunity.

While my youth were hard at work repairing senior citizens' porches, painting, fixing, or cleaning one thing or another, the Seattle youth choir could be seen walking around the community, enjoying their free time between evening engagements. Some of my younger volunteers grumbled among themselves even as they exchanged pleasantries with the Seattle youth. As the week drew to a close, one of the tribal elders from the community came to invite my servant youth to a community party honoring our military veterans. It turned out the Seattle youth were also invited.

As the dinner and festivities progressed, the master of ceremonies announced, "We have some special guests from Seattle with us today who have blessed our community the entire week." None of the volunteers would admit it, but you could see a look of disappointment come over them as the leader of the Seattle area youth choir was asked to come forward to introduce his young people. The young people from Seattle rose from their chairs to applause. This was followed by effusive words of praise from those in the audience who had heard and been blessed by their concert.

Meanwhile, the body language evident among my volunteers all but said, "Hey, what about us?" Or maybe it was more like, "When can we leave?"

Recognition concluded, there was a pause for more announcements. My volunteers, increasingly restless and feeling slighted, were now shifting noticeably in their seats. I sat there fidgeting but somehow managed to choke down my last morsel of food. Uncomfortable with this unfortunate state of affairs, I tortured myself with the thought, "Maybe they thought we were all one group." I knew I would have some difficulty trying to explain to the kids the evident mistake and maybe have to find a way to lessen their disappointment and negative impressions by explaining the likelihood of the two groups being confused as one.

Right in the middle of my mental agony, the master of ceremonies, who had served on the tribal council with me, looked over to where I was sitting and said, "We have another group of young people who have been working very hard all week in our community. Reverend Johnson, please come up here and introduce your young people and tell us where they come from."

I nearly fell off my steel folding chair. Makah hospitality had not failed! I felt an immediate rush of relief as I pushed away from the table and made my way to the front of the dining hall, trying all the while to appear as if I had never doubted for a moment this would occur.

What followed was a beautiful expression of traditional Makah hospitality. To the great surprise of the youth and adults, and me obviously, a tribal elder called each one forward by name to receive recognition along with gifts of hand-carved or hand-woven Makah art and crafts. One by one, they arose and went forward as their names were announced. I remember thinking, "How did they know my volunteers' names?" Later, I learned that a member of the community had gone to all of the work sites and had asked the job site coordinator for the names of each of the youth. Families blessed by their work provided gifts as their way of thanking them for their assistance.

As each of my volunteers went forward to receive something of value, I could sense the change in their demeanor. Gone was their restlessness and disappointment. Smiles replaced the tension, and I knew they felt appreciated for their efforts by the people they had come to serve. They had been afforded a unique opportunity to experience the traditional native way of recognizing and honoring guests who had served well in the community.

Afterward, much relieved and grateful for the example set by my tribal elders, I gathered the volunteers at the church to explain what had transpired at the tribal community hall and how it related to the Christian faith. I shared how it was part of the tribal culture to be hospitable and to give thanks in return for services provided. More importantly, it would have been demeaning for the tribe not to do so. In cultures throughout the world, there exists a delicate balance of mutual reciprocation, an unwritten contract, if you will, that must be maintained between the giver and the recipient. Ideally, both must come away having gained something of value from the other. It is a matter of preserving each other's dignity.

Unfortunately, I have had occasion to witness well-intentioned volunteer teams traveling great distances to serve the spiritual or physical needs of a Native American community without assuring ahead of time local endorsement or affording the opportunity for them to return traditional hospitality. To ensure this occurs requires planning from the inside out. Otherwise, there is the likelihood that time in the community, whether teaching Bible school or doing work or even bringing in a celebrity, will be viewed with suspicion or even resentment. Since the community has not participated in the planning or the invitation or been afforded a means to give something in return, there is little local buy-in. At worst, some residents stand off among themselves and gripe about the outsiders who invaded their community to do work they could be doing for themselves. Or they may simply feel ashamed or embarrassed that they are judged so needy that people from outside their community had to come and do something for them.

This lessens the potential value of a servant event. More importantly, it is out of sync with Jesus's model of ministering to people with broken and missing pieces. We see the contrast in his approach to us, beginning with His choice to be born in the most humbling of circumstances—in Bethlehem to Joseph and Mary—and in choosing to be raised in the out-of-the-way, down-on-itself town of Nazareth. Most importantly, we see it in the manner in which Jesus carried out his ministry: He was always the stranger in need of hospitality. As recorded for us in Luke 9:58, Jesus characterized the whole of his ministry this way: "Foxes have holes and birds of the air have nests, but the Son of Man has no place to lay his head."

This is further reflected throughout His earthly ministry. How often is it that we see Jesus needing a place to stay, His feet washed, a cup of water to quench His thirst, or food to eat? Perhaps more importantly, how often does Jesus seek these things from the most marginalized, poor, and down-on-themselves in-dividuals? Even in His death, He had to have the assistance of a stranger to carry His cross and another man's tomb for His burial. His coming into our time and place in this fashion to live among us and to humble Himself in this way is not what we might have expected of the eternal Son of God, the Creator and Sustainer of all things.

Nevertheless, it is this aspect of Jesus's character, His hu-mility, His willingness to endure poverty, and His being a stranger in need, that is so effective in breaking down the walls of our guilt and shame. Entry into our hearts begins not by over-whelming us with His powerful presence or forcing us to believe in Him but with a gentle invitation to enter our lives. In Revela-tion 3:20, we read, "Here I am! I stand at the door and knock. If anyone hears my voice and opens the door, I will come in and eat with him, and he with Me." For those who receive Him, Jesus graciously imparts the most important gift of all: eternal salvation and membership in the eternal kingdom of God the Father.

Jesus' willingness to leave His heavenly home, take on human flesh and blood, and live among us as one in need— even suffer in our behalf—becomes the bridge to all, especial-ly those who have had to endure terrible circumstances. This aspect of Jesus's character would have special meaning for a friend of mine who had endured a horrific ordeal in a dark and dangerous place.

CHAPTER 22

That's My Star!

---◦◦◦---

A narrow window may let in the light; tiny stars dispel the gloom of night. A little deed a mighty wrong set right.
—Florence Earle Coates

A few years ago, following my years of service as pastor/ tribal leader, I met Linda Martin, a lovely Christian woman with a story that in some ways was a little like my own. Albeit, far more dramatic than mine. She too had experienced things in her life that left her with broken and missing pieces. What is more, her testimony about an encounter with Jesus was having an extraordinary impact on many in her native country of Canada. It was, however, a story born of grave danger caused by an evil man. The unusual circumstances could have easily led to her death. Her painful journey through shame and depression in the aftermath led to thoughts of suicide. Her willingness to share her story of how Jesus met her deepest need has helped many people understand the power of Jesus to fix the most broken of people. This is why I share her story here.

I first met Linda while serving as the executive director of the Lutheran Association of Missionaries and Pilots U.S. As I got to know her, I learned that Linda, a Cree woman from the native community of Muskrat Dam in northern Ontario had grown up without the amenities most of us take for granted. However, that was the least of her challenges.

From the day of her birth, Linda was not expected to live. Complications with her respiratory system seemed beyond modern medicine. Believing she had little chance of survival, a doctor advised her parents to take her home, where she would most certainly die.

At the time, home for Linda was Muskrat Dam. It was little more than a remote fishing camp that had been settled by her father and a few other native families in the 1960s. In this sparse wilderness, starkly beautiful in its pristine setting, were neither roads, stores, cars, phone service, televisions, nor anything resembling modern civilization and thus little hope for modern medical care to ease her passage from life to death.

There was in her little community, however, one intangible: the transforming power of love.

Living in Muskrat Dam was Linda's great aunt, the source of that love. Although I have been to her little village, I never had the privilege of meeting her. However, what she did suggests that she was an extraordinary person. Refusing to accept the doctor's dismal prognosis, this woman took it upon herself to faithfully hold, feed, and care for Linda day after day. There seemed little likelihood that her efforts would do Linda much good. Nevertheless, Linda's aunt refused to be deterred, continuing her daily regimen of lovingly attending to the child.

Miraculously, her constant attentions accomplished what modern medicine could not. The fragile little child, whose life had begun with a doctor's dire prognosis, began the tenuous crawl out of the dark shadows of frailty and imminent death to health. It was a marvelous transformation. More than that, it was a miracle, and it would not be the last.

Before long, Linda grew into a normal, healthy child who began immediately discovering a world far different from our own. Imagine her world: a remote fishing camp situated next to a river winding its way through a vast wilderness of poplars, birch trees, and pines—a place where few outsiders ever venture except for the occasional hunters and fishermen who would fly in on float planes. What these visitors experienced as an ideal, albeit temporary, place to hunt and fish, Linda's father saw as a place to live a traditional native way of life.

Possessing wilderness survival skills, Linda's father was one of a rare breed of conventional native men who still possessed the raw skills needed to make a living in the old way. That meant knowing how to build a cabin from the materials found in the natural surroundings, track a moose for days if necessary, harvest fish from the lakes and rivers, and make do with what was around you. And then one had to be able to do all of this in the face of the often brutally cold winters where snow arrives as early as September and temperatures in December typically plummet to 40 below zero or more.

Naturally, her parents began passing their wilderness survival skills on to Linda. By the time she was six, she was routinely walking five miles to check rabbit trap lines. At night, she slept on the ground in a bed made of fir branches. Later, she slept on the floor of the small cabin her father built. Since there were none of the amenities of modern civilization or laws to interfere with their style of life, clock time and the "time is money" philosophy or learning the English language had little relevance. The only language Linda knew was the Severn-Cree dialect spoken by her parents. Deriving its name from the Severn River that meandered by the community on its way eastward across northern Ontario where it eventually emptied into Hudson Bay, the Severn-Cree dialect was part of a much larger linguistic family. Before long, other Cree families began to trickle in to homestead the area too, making the small enclave of native people a community.

This did not go unnoticed by Canadian governmental authorities. Intent on insuring that the children in the community received an education, authorities contacted the parents and informed them that their kids would have to be enrolled in public school.

For native children living in remote places like Muskrat Dam, this meant having to leave home to attend residential school in far-away places. This, of course, destined the children to a life without parental guidance or protection.

The residential school system was unique to native people in North America. Founded in the late nineteenth century in both the United States and Canada, the system had originally been designed to "civilize" and educate the Indian out of the children. Keeping them away from their parents' influence for long periods was part of the strategy. There were often tragic consequences. A letter in a little museum on what is now the campus of Haskell Indian Nations University in Lawrence, Kansas, expressed a father's death-bed plea to have his child return home before he died. His request was denied, and the man died without ever being able to say goodbye to his child.

Even more tragically, many native children were subject to severe punishments and even sexual abuse by unscrupulous teachers, sometimes in schools affiliated with Christian denominations that operated the schools for the government.

Unfortunately, this happened frequently enough in Canadian residential schools through the years that eventually a lawsuit was filed on behalf of the victims, resulting in monies being awarded to them. In addition, there were official apologies by the churches involved as well as by the Canadian government.

Thankfully, measures such as these are helping to alleviate the past injustices and facilitate healing. However, the damage done to many of these children, now adults, is not so easily forgotten. The wounding, especially resulting from sexual abuse is an invasion of the most sacred of places in the human soul, often resulting in deep and lasting pain and the victim distressed for much of their lives. (Something like this occurs when men in the military are exposed to horrific combat that robs them of innocence and leaves them with post-traumatic stress syndrome.) High rates of suicide are often a consequence. In some instances, the abused victim from these residential schools becomes the abuser, insuring that the offense occurring in one generation is repeated in the next.

When this occurs, secrets, shame, bitterness, and guilt often become a part of a family or a community system, and if no intervention occurs to break the cycle, it almost always leads to tragic consequences, not only for the immediate family but the community as well.

Fortunately, Linda never attended one of these residential schools. They were discontinued by the early 1980s. Instead, she was assigned to live with a foster family in nearby Bearskin Lake, a mostly native community a short plane ride from her home. Although it was less intimidating living among other native people in similar surroundings, Linda missed family, friends, and her familiar places.

Eventually, the intensity of her melancholy led to an on-again, off-again education pattern. It was school for a while and then, when homesickness became unbearable, a decision to return home. In spite of her sporadic education, Linda still managed to learn to read English without having to learn to speak it. In her world, the relevance of any kind of education was in question. At the first opportunity as a young teen, she quit school altogether and returned home.

This might have been the end of her story except that some government official apparently had been tracking her progress or lack thereof. He determined that she was too young to drop out of the educational system. He decided that Linda should return to school as a ninth grader. This time, however, the school was farther away and situated in a predominantly White community with all the usual trappings of civilization: paved roads, fast-food restaurants, strip malls, and lots of cars and traffic lights.

It was a difficult adjustment once more. Linda had little exposure to the refinements and offerings of a modern Canadian city except during a brief visit with an aunt in Winnipeg. All she remembered about that occasion was her first-ever Popsicle freeze. Then, she knew she would be leaving soon. But now in her new setting, everything seemed so intimidating. Everyone spoke English, she was behind in her classes, she had no friends, and she struggled with understanding the daily classroom assignments. Every day seemed to last forever.

Overwhelmed by mounting feelings of homesickness and inundated with the growing sense that modern education was irrelevant, Linda decided once again to quit school. She couldn't have been happier than the day she boarded a plane for her home in the wilds of northern Ontario. She had given education a try. It didn't work for her.

In the familiar surroundings of her community once more, Linda contemplated her fitful journey through the education system. The outside world had been a strange and frightening place, and schooling seemed so unrelated to life in the wilds of northern Ontario. Then a disturbing thought began to nag her. While public school had been difficult, the books Linda had learned to read had become a means of solace in her aloneness. Sometimes they even opened up new vistas and unlocked in her a natural hunger for knowledge. In the process, she had discovered talents she little knew she possessed. Not only that, her recent exposure to the outside world had removed some of her fears of the unfamiliar. All things considered, she was not certain her present circumstances were all she wanted. Maybe education did hold promise for a better life.

Acting on her awakened interest in learning, Linda decided to give public education one more try. Before long, she came across an opportunity for a second chance at a school located in the city of Kenora, Ontario, not far from the U.S. border. It was, however, as far from home as she had ever been. She decided never the less to enroll in a two-year program offered at the school. "This is my last chance," she thought as she prepared to leave family and friends once again.

As she boarded the small plane that would take her away from her loved ones, she felt once more the intense loneliness she had always experienced at times like this. But this time, her renewed resolve thwarted any vacillation. Soon, the small twin-engine plane's motors were revving up, their sound echoing far off into the silence of the north. As the plane accelerated ever faster and then lifted off the gravel runway and into the morning sky, Linda looked intently out the window of the small plane as her little community quickly receded in the distance and then faded into the nothingness of the greens and browns of aspens and Arctic pine. Within minutes, the steady drone of the aircraft's engines and the endless landscape of forest and lakes passing below left her drifting sleepily off into memories of the life she was leaving behind. Eventually, the familiar places she had known gave way to flat plains and the first signs of civilization not far off. As the little aircraft droned steadily on to her new place of the unfamiliar, she contemplated her future in the strange world she was about to experience. Out of nowhere, a new thought came over her. For the first time, she was leaving home by her own choice, not because of some government fiat. A few hours later, the small aircraft touched down in the modern city of Kenora.

Linda settled into her apartment in Kenora and soon became engrossed in her studies. Just as she thought might happen, the old feelings of loneliness reappeared. This time, however, instead of fleeing for the solace of home, Linda began looking for companionship, someone or something to help fill the loneliness. Unfortunately, and this is where the story takes on a familiar pattern for so many native people separated from their people and their culture, she found it in the wrong places. Her new friends had their own way of dealing with the intense loneliness of their lives. They liked to party, and soon, Linda was introduced to the bar scene. It was exciting and seemed to dull her lonesomeness. She was entering a dangerous environment for a young girl. It didn't take long for her to discover this.

One evening, while bar-hopping with one of her acquaintances, a stranger who had been drinking by himself in the bar offered to take them to a party at the home of one of the regular bar patrons. It promised to be a continuation of the good times. As soon as the girls climbed into his car, however, they knew they had made a terrible mistake. Instead of driving in the direction of the party, the stranger accelerated his vehicle in the opposite direction—too fast for them to open the doors to leap to safety.

Initially horrified and stunned into inaction, the girls were unable to think what to do. Finally they protested, "This isn't the right way. Please, take us back." Their fearful protests were met with angry threats: "Shut up, or else!" Overwhelmed by the sheer magnitude of their predicament, they sat in shocked disbelief, all the while struggling to make some sense of their circumstances.

The road out of town seemed to stretch out forever into a menacing kind of darkness. How much time had passed? Where was he taking them? How could this be happening? Time and space seemed to compress. They tried to imagine a way of escape, but the speed of the car made it impossible.

Finally, after what seemed an eternity, their captor turned off the main highway and sped onto an isolated gravel road, leading to a trail. Their intense feelings of vulnerability intensified even more now that they seemed to be arriving at the stranger's destination. Suddenly the car came to an abrupt stop at the end of the road. Freshly fallen snow on the trees gave a surreal sense of peace and beauty to the otherwise sinister scene.

The driver angrily shouted at the girls to get out of the car. Linda's companion seized the moment to make her escape. The man lunged for her but missed. Seeing her companion escape, Linda tried to flee. But by now the man had recovered and managed to grab her, forcefully dragging her, despite her desperate pleas, down the snow-covered trail to a cabin hidden in the foliage of the woods. Its ramshackle, weathered form took on a menacing, evil appearance in the subdued lighting of the forest.

The next thing Linda remembers was being shoved through the door of the dingy little cabin, which her captor then secured with a rope so that there was no way of escape. She later related, "I watched him intently, overcome by the thought that this is where I might die. There was no way out for me. Somehow, in those terrible, awful moments in the presence of this evil man, I realized how much I wanted to live and to see my family again. And then I wondered, 'Who will ever know what happened to me?'"

What followed were moments of extreme terror and trauma as Linda's captor grasped her in a vicious headlock and then proceeded to abuse her, all the while explaining that his father used to inflict the same kind of things on him. Horrendous as it may seem, the evil man derived some kind of pleasure, maybe even some kind of revenge, by inflicting pain on his victim. At times, the pain was so excruciating, Linda could barely move her eyes back and forth.

In the midst of her horrific ordeal, she discovered that if she avoided any reference to his childhood and kept talking about anything else, her captor would become less agitated. She tried to imagine his motive. Was he a serial killer or on his way to becoming one? Most certainly, he was an abuser from an abusive family. Whatever he may have been, every moment in the presence of this evil man seemed to dim any hope she would survive the night. There seemed to be no way out.

But then something caught Linda's attention, something barely perceptible out of the corner of her eye. Through a small place in an otherwise dingy window, a brilliant light shone into her dismal prison. Where was it coming from? Why was it so bright? Amazingly, it seemed to be emanating from a distant star. For the moment, it distracted Linda from her desperate ordeal. The light from the bright star, shining through the window into the dingy cabin, inspired memories of the stories of Jesus she had heard as a child from her grandmother, stories of hope and promises of God's deliverance in time of need. However brief these stories from God's Word may have been, they were the only Sunday school lessons she had ever known. Incredibly, what little Word of God she had heard then was just enough for her present situation. God made His presence known in this evil place. In her despair, Linda's soul cried out, "O God, if you are real, would you save me? I'll do whatever you ask of me."

In the early hours of the morning, her life in jeopardy, a strange thing occurred. Her abductor nodded off into a state of unconsciousness. Her anxious plea had been answered. Sensing her opportunity, Linda managed to unloose her bonds, all the while glancing furtively toward her tormentor, fearful that at any moment he might awake and punish her more severely, perhaps even kill her for attempting to escape. As soon as she managed to get loose of her bonds, her heart pounding from the tension, she quietly but deftly moved toward the door, mindful that any noise, like the cabin floor creaking or the sound the door might make, could wake him out of his stupor. In quiet desperation, she struggled to untie the rope holding the door closed but somehow managed to unfasten it. Then, Linda carefully pushed the creaky door wide enough to slip out into the dark night. As she did so, she could not help but glance one last time at the man who had been her tormentor and might have been her killer. Slumped over in his chair, he looked strangely impotent in the pale light of the cabin.

Sensing the immanence of freedom, Linda dashed up the snow-covered trail as fast as she could through the woods and safety. Exhausted and in pain, her breath visible in the cold night, she caught a glimpse of light emanating from a cabin. Fearful that her tormentor might even now be gaining on her, Linda rushed to the door and burst into the house. The startled patrons were surprised to see a beaten, frightened native girl standing there. Out of breath and too bruised and hurting from the abuse, Linda asked only to use their phone to summon a cab for a ride home.

What these homeowners must have thought of this disheveled and desperate girl we will never know. They did not ask any questions, and Linda who had been traumatized, offered them no explanations. For their part, however, the surprised patrons were more than willing to allow her to use their phone to call a taxi to transport her back to wherever she had come from.

The days and weeks that followed were terribly difficult. Linda's feelings wandered all over the emotional landscape. On the one hand, she struggled with guilt and shame, blame and anger. At other times, she imagined it never happened. For a time she hated all men, distrusting any male relationship. Realizing her father was a good man brought her some sense of restoration. Nevertheless, through it all, she could not bring herself to call the police to tell them what had happened. Doubtful of how they might view a native woman's story, she wondered, "Why would they believe me?" Then, the terrible moments of intense guilt and shame would return. Linda was growing increasingly depressed and at risk of committing suicide.

One night, however, while crying herself to sleep one more time, Linda experienced something like a warm presence filling her room. Whatever its origin, for the first time, she felt safe and secure. Contemplating this unusual phenomenon, a message began to form in her mind. It went something like this: "Okay, Linda, I saved you. Now what will you do with me?" Linda immediately recalled how, in the moment of her peril, she had desperately cried out to God to save her. Then she remembered her promise that if God delivered her, she would do whatever He asked. It was a bargain born of desperation, and God had answered her cries. Had He now come to collect on her promise? Lying on her bed, surrounded by a sense of God's presence, Linda prayed, "Dear Jesus, I accept you as my Savior."

A God she had not known had intervened to deliver Linda in her hour of greatest need. His presence, triggered by the strange light from a distant star, had sparked the few memories of Scripture she had learned as a youth. This God had saved her and determined from all eternity that her life would be a blessing. He would transform her darkness into light and hope for many others who endured similar pain. Linda's life was about to become a beautiful tapestry God was weaving for His glory and honor.

Of course, it takes time to heal damaged emotions, and Linda had much to learn about God's power to bring healing. Shortly after her profession of faith, during a time when she was once again visited by disquieting and shame-inducing memories of her experience, Jesus re-entered her thoughts one more time. He said something like this: "Linda, I have always loved you and know and understand what you have been through. I, too, experienced shame and dishonor. I, too, was made to be naked before men and the world."

Linda thought of Jesus' humiliation, His suffering, crucifixion and death. She visualized Him being beaten, stripped of

His clothing, and ridiculed before a crowd. Then she saw Him nailed to the cross. It looked like the end of pure goodness and love. Satan had foolishly thought the same thing. It was, however, at the cross that Jesus took on Satan and defeated him. It was through Jesus' sufferings, shame, and death that He overcame great evil and darkness. It was through His shared experience of humiliation that He could offer understanding, comfort, and hope to Linda in her shame and anguish of soul.

The impact was liberating. Linda concluded, "I realized that God's own Son knew what it was like to know my pain and shame. The fact that He had endured what I had experienced meant that He knew what it was like to be me." In a devotion she wrote for Lent she shared, "I believe that Jesus became fully human so that He could demonstrate to us that He understood what it is like to be a finite human where pain seems to be a good part of our lives. I also believe that Jesus had to experience this depth of suffering in order to have victory over it so that you and I can have victory over our painful experiences today." Hebrews 4:15 declares, "For we do not have a high priest who is unable to sympathize with our weaknesses, but we have one who has been tempted in every way, just as we are, yet was without sin."

Since that time, Linda has moved beyond her trauma to a place where God has been mightily using her story of faith to touch the lives of people similarly affected by abuse. Her transparency in relating her story has been liberating for others. As a result, people contemplating suicide or living secret lives of desperation and loneliness are finding healing through her testimony.

In the meantime, Linda, in spite of all of her fitful starts and stops in school, has earned a masters degree in biblical counseling. Eventually, she met and married Rick Martin, a teacher assigned to her community of Muskrat Dam. (The government had since built a small school in the community) Today, along with her husband Rick, who team-teaches alongside her, Linda brings a message of hope and healing for wounded souls.

Underlying this amazing couple's message is this: when a person permits Jesus to come into their lives, He can take the most awful of experiences and transform them into powerful witnesses for His kingdom. Satan knows this and desperately seeks to keep people so focused on their shame and bitterness that they are prevented from experiencing Jesus's power to fix the broken and missing pieces of their lives. Satan knows what a great threat severely broken and missing people can be to his domain once they experience the liberating and transforming power of the Holy Spirit.

One night a few years ago, I was walking along with Linda and her husband Rick beneath the Nebraska night sky. Only moments earlier, Linda had completed a presentation that my organization had helped organize for some native men and women. Several of the attendees were so moved by what she had to say that they wanted advice in dealing with their own hurt. After a time of counsel and prayer with them, Linda had joined us in heading back to our hotel. As we walked under the starlit sky and gazed into the heavens, Linda suddenly turned to us and said, "That's my star." For a moment, I did not know what she meant. Then I realized that she would never forget how God used the light from a distant star shining through a dingy cabin window to call her out of her pain and into a relationship with Him. How fitting, I thought, that it was a star that marked the birthplace of Jesus, the God-Man who became one of us so that He could shine in the darkness of our lives and give us hope.

CHAPTER 23

Missionaries, Miners, and Misfits

⤙⦿⤚

Jesus answered him, "I tell you the truth, today you will be with me in paradise."

Luke 23:43

As a tribal leader, my oversight extended to virtually all aspects of community life, and this included dealing with difficult people who happened into our town in one way or another.

Situated at the edge of the land, our community was a magnet for people who had exhausted their welcome everywhere else. One day, a man motored into our harbor in a twenty-foot sailboat. He reminded me of the late stage and screen actor Darren McGavin. In his early sixties, the man seemed pleasant enough. His little vessel, however, had the appearance of a shack on the water. It was obviously in need of a refit.

Shortly after his arrival, he announced to an elderly widowed lady whose late husband had been a well-respected pastor of one of the churches in our community that God had told him that he was supposed to take her as his wife. In a bizarre courting ritual, he began leaving sacks of groceries on her doorstep.

Terrified by his unwanted attentions, she came to my office one day and desperately pleaded with me to do something. She was not a tribal member, much less a Native American. I suppose I could have told her my limited jurisdiction would not permit me to do anything for her, but she had a long history of working in our community. I felt it right to intervene on her behalf. As leader of the tribal government, I assigned local law enforcement to check on him to insure he not bother her any more. Fortunately, he didn't. Not long thereafter, I watched as his ramshackle little sailing vessel motored slowly out of the harbor to his next port of call, no doubt feeling his mission for God had failed.

Another man arrived in our harbor in a surplus World War II U.S. Navy minesweeper. A hundred feet or more in length, the dilapidated wood vessel had seen better days, even if those better days had been during the tumultuous years of World War II. Like the previous vessel, it looked much in need of repairs. Worse, it tended on occasion to list precariously to one side or the other. It soon became apparent that the only thing keeping his vessel afloat were bilge pumps constantly pumping water.

Having seen enough, the U.S. Coast Guard inspected the vessel and immediately directed the owner to take up anchor and move his boat to some place where he could have repairs made. This man and others like him were misfits, drifters who went from place to place, staying nowhere for long.

People like those I have described who end up on the fringes of civilization fit into a category known by some long-time northerners as the "Three Ms": missionaries, miners, and misfits. As a fisherman/missionary and self-described broken-and-missing-pieces person, I incorporated a little of all of these in my personality, so I can understand why missionaries, miners, and misfits are attracted to the fringes of America. The reasons are fairly basic.

For the miner, or in some cases the fisherman or logger, there is often the promise of abundant resources. Usually that means great fishing or hunting, few rules, and lots of opportunity.

Misfits are people who generally feel they don't belong. They may have experienced some great disappointment in their lives, or maybe they have worn out their welcome everywhere else. Living in isolation, on a boat or in a small cabin in a remote community, is a way of avoiding, maybe forgetting their past. A few may be escaping responsibilities or even avoiding the law. Others may be looking for something they lost or never found. Maybe the wild holds the cure for a broken life.

The third *M* stands for missionaries, the person I eventually became. We have it as our motivation to minister to the misfits and miners or to the many indigenous native peoples who, for thousands of years, have lived in these remote areas. Some of us have been lost once ourselves and now have come to reach out to others like us.

My community at the end of the land fit the profile as a "Three M" destination. Our town seemed to draw people short on luck and long on disappointment. In later years, after I had been named the executive director of the Lutheran Association of Missionaries and Pilots U.S., the non-profit Christian ministry I serve today, I had occasion to meet many others on the edges of America. As part of my responsibilities with the ministry, I would often travel to southeast Alaska, where we had a number of mission sites in very remote areas. Most of these were accessible only by floatplane or boat. Our ministry in this region of Alaska was made possible because of a ministry boat we operated called the *Motor Vessel CHRISTIAN* (*MV CHRISTIAN*). The vessel's design, even its conception, seems to have uniquely qualified it for ministry to people living on the fringes.

The vessel skipper at the time I began my leadership of the organization was Pastor Ken Olson. Along with his wife and first mate Nancy, the two made regular visits to a remote community known as Meyers Chuck. With few full-time residents, no roads, and only trails to connect the few cabins that seemed to cling precariously to the edges of the land, this was clearly a place most suited to those intent on solitude. On the other hand, it was also a place of incredible beauty. Surrounded by rocks jutting out of the sea and majestic, snow-covered mountains in the distance, Meyers Chuck made for an ideal place to escape life in the lower 48.

Whenever the Olsons set off from the island of Wrangell where they made their home to visit Meyers Chuck on the *CHRISTIAN*, they took the time to call on a man I will call "Joe." A reclusive loner, Joe lived about as simple a life as you could in a small, wood-frame cabin behind the back slough of Meyers Chuck. Once, during one of my many excursions to Alaska, I had occasion to meet him and see his cabin. Struck by its small dimensions and stark simplicity, I found myself wondering how anyone could live there for very long and not go crazy, especially during the long, dark winters. His cabin was without electricity, indoor plumbing, or any other amenity. Moreover, its dark and dank interior was hardly large enough for the lounge chair he apparently slept on or the wood stove that helped to bring warmth to the long winter nights.

Except for the times when Ken and Nancy motored into the small harbor on the *CHRISTIAN*, Joe had few visitors. Aware that he was alone and could use some friendship, Ken and Nancy made sure that he always felt welcome aboard the *CHRISTIAN*. Coffee and friendly conversation were an integral part of their times together.

Through the years, Ken and Joe developed a degree of trust and mutual respect. Ken would share his faith, often within the confidential confines of the *CHRISTIAN*. Sometimes people like Joe would reveal tragic instances of abuse, the loss of a loved one, or some other difficult experience they never felt safe to share anywhere else, especially not in their own small communities where rumors and repercussions could spread rapidly, often with devastating effects. The boat served as a safe place for people with broken and missing pieces to tell their stories of lost and broken dreams. Ironically, the *CHRISTIAN* had its own history of nearly lost and broken dreams.

Originally designed and built by the Nichols Brothers boat yard on Whidbey Island, Washington, the sixty-five-foot, hundred-ton steel hulled vessel had a hull design that made it resemble some of the purse seine vessels that fished in southeast Alaska. However, the *CHRISTIAN* was specifically designed with hospitality in mind. It was comfortable, practical, seaworthy, and had adequate room in its spacious stateroom for twenty or more guests to sit in comfort around tables. Then there was its unusual name, a name that identified both its mission and the One who inspired it.

Its unusual name, *CHRISTIAN*, had originally been inspired by a least-likely man, a toughened old sailor who had been skeptical of Christianity most of his life. Sick and dying, his eternal destination hanging in the balance, he experienced a deathbed conversion. Not long before he died, he heard that the ministry vessel was being built for ministry to Lutheran youth in the Puget Sound area. Having had a long love affair with the sea and now with Jesus, he was pleased to learn that the vessel's purpose was to honor the Jesus, who had so recently bestowed upon him eternal life. Out of gratitude for the second chance he had been given, he gave the vessel a brass ship's bell with the name *CHRISTIAN* inscribed on it in honor of the One who had saved him. The name has stuck with the vessel ever since. More importantly, the *CHRISTIAN* has seemed to reflect the character of the person from whom its name is derived. This is reflected in the unusual events that have been a part of its history ever since.

The vessel's design and construction was originally inspired by pastors with a vision to provide a place where youth could experience Christian fellowship in the natural beauty afforded by the marine environment in the Pacific Northwest. However, not long into its ministry, it fell on hard times when the churches sponsoring it could no longer afford payments or operating costs. With the mounting debt, a decision was made by its managers that the only solution was to sell it. The vision of a boat for God's glory had seemingly come to an end.

Just when all seemed lost, Seattle-area businessmen, led by attorney Bill Ruthford, stepped forward, managing to buy enough time to delay the inevitable. In a short period, they managed to raise $110,000, which was enough to pay off the debt. The new caretakers, led by Mr. Ruthford, then determined the vessel should be moved to Alaska. There, it could become part of a new ministry under the auspices of the Alaska Synod of the Evangelical Lutheran Church of America, led then by Bishop Don Parsons.

The vessel, named by a dying man who had received a last-minute second chance, had received a second chance of its own. Soon, the *CHRISTIAN* was on its way to Alaska where it would once more be used to serve as a means of light and hope. Things seemed to be going well. Or were they?

There is an old adage that goes, "A boat is a hole in the water in which you pour money." This is a true saying, and more than one wife has likely entertained thoughts like this concerning her outdoor-fishing-enthusiast husband, especially so when considering things like moorage costs, rising fuel prices, insurance, and engine maintenance. In the case of the *CHRISTIAN*, there were the additional costs of affording a skipper and first mate.

The Lutherans in Alaska soon realized that they could not sustain operating costs, either. Once more, its future as a ministry boat in doubt, it seemed as if the *CHRISTIAN* would have to be sold.

That is when our ministry stepped in. For a nominal fee, our organization took responsibility for the vessel. We then hired Pastor Ken Olson to be the skipper. Ken had been one of the visionaries for the boat and one of its first skippers. The vessel had been given another chance. In a way, so had Ken Olson.

Ken had recently endured some painful disappointments in his life. His marriage had failed, leaving him broken and discouraged. He decided he could no longer serve his pastorate and soon resigned in order to move to southeast Alaska, where his father had once served a congregation. Perhaps the move to a place familiar to him in his youth would enable him to gain some perspective on his life so he could figure out what God wanted of him. Ken's life began to take on new meaning when he met Nancy, who, like him, had also endured a divorce. Upon being introduced, they soon discovered common interests. With an engaging personality and a love for the outdoors, Nancy was a good match for Ken. It was not long before their mutual interests and love led to marriage. Not long after that, they became a husband-wife team serving aboard the *CHRISTIAN*. It was a second chance for them of another kind.

Soon, the vessel of second chances with a new skipper and first mate became a familiar sight throughout the isolated coastal communities in southeast Alaska. The *CHRISTIAN* established a reputation as a place for hospitality and kindness while serving as a beacon of light and hope for those living out their lives in lonely isolation. This brings me back to the Olsons' ministry with Joe, a man with broken and missing pieces living alone in his isolated cabin in the back slough of Meyers Chuck.

It was Christmas Eve 1996 when Ken's and Joe's lives became intertwined in a momentous struggle. Ken and Nancy had decided to spend the holidays with friends in Meyers Chuck, where they owned a small houseboat on the back slough not far from Joe's shack. I had been with them only a few weeks before in Wrangell, Alaska, where they had a home facing the harbor. My visit was motivated in part by my need to find a replacement once Ken retired. He was in his 60s, and even though he was in better physical shape than many people much younger, I felt compelled to discuss with him his future plans. Finding a pastor with U.S. Coast Guard certification to operate a one-hundred--ton vessel like the *CHRISTIAN* would not be easy. I needed some lead time.

There were other issues on my mind too. I was still trying to come to terms with my grief resulting from a terrible mishap that had occurred six months earlier when one of the planes operated by our ministry crashed high on a mountain side near Nome, Alaska. An occasional volunteer pilot with our ministry, Tom Liederbach, had been killed in the accident. Tom and his wife, Hildy, were special people. They had been longtime summer volunteers who often used vacation time to do whatever we needed to facilitate Bible schools. On the day before the accident, Tom and I had worshipped alongside one another during a church service in Nome. Almost as an aside, the pastor concluded his message by reminding his congregation that sometimes God calls men to give their lives for the cause of the Gospel. I thought it an odd comment at the time since that had not been the focus of his message. Then, Tom went forward to receive the Lord's Supper in the confident assurance that Jesus had died for Him and given him everlasting life.

Afterward, Tom, Hildy, and a friend, Mr. Ron Jones, and I went to lunch at Fat Freddy's, a popular restaurant in Nome. Located directly across the street from the terminus of the famous Iditarod dogsled race, the restaurant had a reputation for good food and served as a popular gathering place for the locals. While enjoying lunch and looking out on the sparkling Bering Sea, resplendent in the noon-day sun, we discussed our plans to fly with Tom the following day to pick up kids from the remote Inupiaq (Eskimo) community of Shishmaref. His intention was to fly the kids to Salmon Lake Bible camp, an hour or so drive from Nome but a much longer distance from Shishmaref. Ron and I planned to stay and visit people in the community until he returned later that evening to pick us up. After further discussion and at the last minute, Ron Jones and I decided it would be best to put off our trip for a day or so. Ron had need of something he could not readily access until the following day. In any case, delaying our trip to Shishmaref for a day would not affect our plans that much.

That Sunday evening, Tom flew our Cessna 206 with several of our volunteer teachers to Salmon Lake Bible Camp. The isolated little Bible camp had a crude but useable runway next to the equally humble camp buildings. Perhaps thinking about the concluding comments made earlier by the pastor in the morning service, Tom shared with his passengers as they flew to the Bible camp that "he was ready to meet Jesus his Lord whenever the time came."

The next morning, his pre-flight procedures completed, Tom was lifting off the tarmac at the Nome airport and on his way to pick up the youth in Shishmaref. The weather that morning was not ideal but certainly well within Tom's competency level. About the time Tom was lifting off, I had found a quiet little café in Nome to have my morning coffee. I noted the low clouds and mist that hung in the air around Nome. It reminded me of the Northwest coast where I grew up. By my second cup of coffee, Tom had to have been well into his flight plan and approaching what would be his final moments of life on this side of eternity.

Unfortunately, Tom's flight path led him into a box canyon that was part of a mountain range known as the Kigluaik Mountains, located on the southern side of the Seward Peninsula. When it became apparent to him that he had made an error, he made a desperate attempt to rise above or to maneuver his aircraft around. The engine tachometer recovered at the crash site high up on the mountainside, revealed that upon impact, the engine was revving at maximum rpms.

Having driven that morning to Salmon Lake Bible Camp, Ron Jones and I were with Tom's wife when a fast moving truck approached the camp around noon and a man quickly exited. He went right to Hildy and explained with anxious voice that Tom's plane was overdue. Did she know his flight plan? Not only that, the emergency locator transmitter on his plane had been sending a signal that had been picked up by another plane that was flying in the vicinity of the Kigluaik Mountain range. Could he have forgotten to turn his emergency transmitter off? His failure to arrive in Shishmaref and the ominous signal from his emergency transmitter were the first indications of serious trouble and the beginning of a desperate search for the missing aircraft. Ron Jones and I were with Hildy in the late afternoon when an Alaska State Trooper pulled up outside the place where we were awaiting word. The officer, somber and burdened by the sad news he was bearing, announced the awful news. They had located the plane. It was in pieces and located high on a nearly inaccessible part of the mountainside known as Mosquito Pass. There was no chance of survival.

Tom's death was obviously devastating for his wife and family. I struggled within myself for a long time afterward. I was saddened for them. At the same time, I knew that Ron and I could have easily been on that plane with Tom except for a last minute decision. I thought, "Why, God, did you allow this to happen?" It is a question we often ask when something like this happens, especially to someone serving God at the moment of their death. Through the years, this tragic accident has served as a reminder to me that our lives are truly like an arrow shot through time and space; ever so brief in a mere moment in God's eternity. In Psalm 39:4 David prayed, "Show me, O Lord, my life's end and the number of my days, let me know how fleeting is my life."

Six months later, I was still trying to come to terms with the accident during my visit to Wrangell to see the Olson's. However, I had a sense of comfort because I knew the circumstances leading up to the accident. Tom seemed to have been uniquely prepared to meet Jesus that day. I was therefore confident that Tom had entered the eternal presence of Jesus. He had given his life for the sake of the Gospel while doing something he loved to do.

Several weeks following my early December visit with Ken and Nancy, the usually wet and cloudy weather in Meyers Chuck turned uncharacteristically clear and cold. The majestic snow-covered mountains in the distance glistened in the brightness of the winter sun. Even the sea was calmer than usual for the time of year.

On Christmas Day everyone in the small community, including Joe, joined Ken and Nancy aboard the CHRISTIAN for a time of fun, food, and fellowship. Ken read the Christmas story to everyone. Later, they decided to go out and play a makeshift game of hockey on an ice-covered pond. He was especially anxious to try out the new ice skates Nancy had given him as a Christmas present.

The day after Christmas shone as bright and promising as the day before. Over a morning cup of coffee aboard the CHRISTIAN, Ken and Joe decided to take their skates to a large lake three miles distant. None of the others was interested. Soon, they set off together, skates slung over their shoulders, out to experience the beauty of the day.

The hike to Meyers Chuck Lake was no walk in the park. Just getting there meant having to traverse hill and dale through heavy forest and underbrush along a trail that winds over, under, and around stumps, fallen trees, and thick undergrowth. In the summer, you might meet a large bear along the way. People who made the hike then were advised to make a lot of noise and to carry bear spray - just in case.

As Ken and Joe hiked determinedly along the familiar path to the lake, they surely must have quickened their pace. The winter sun in these northern climes would set early. They wanted to make sure they had time to cross the lake and return on the trail in daylight. Soon enough, they came to the trail's end. In front of them lay an expansive, ice-covered lake. They surely would have conferred about its thickness and the best path for them to take to get to the other side. A minimum of four inches is generally necessary for safety. Their collective caution satisfied, they strapped on their skates and began the trek across the lake, managing to keep a safe distance from each other. They eventually made it to the other side. Their curiosity satisfied, the two men set off toward home. All seemed well, and it would not be long before they got to the other side. But on their return, a sudden, sickening sound of cracking ice underneath them provided warning of their impending demise. They had skated over a patch of ice too thin to sustain their weight. They could feel themselves sinking into the icy cold waters of the lake.

We do not know exactly what happened next, but here's what can be surmised. Apparently, the men broke through at about the same time. Although they were separated by a little distance, they were close enough to yell out to each other. The evidence suggests that both men struggled mightily to pull themselves onto the ice. During his struggles, Ken Olson somehow managed to take off his skates to use them like ice picks to pull himself up. It didn't work. The ice kept breaking off again and again with each desperate attempt. Somewhere into their struggles, the men began to feel the effects of hypothermia. Joe appears to have slipped into unconsciousness first. Ken lasted longer, but he finally succumbed to the cold. As a final gesture, he removed his gloves and left them on the ice to mark the place where they had fallen through.

I have often wondered about their last fateful minutes of struggle. Knowing Ken Olson, I suspect both men immediately understood the hopelessness of their situation. It is not hard to imagine that as it became evident they would not make it, Ken would likely have called out to Joe to remind him of Jesus's promise. I suspect that as the desperation of their situation became more evident, he would have reminded Joe that if he but trusted Jesus, Joe would inherit eternal life. And I imagine that Joe in his final moments would have accepted Jesus as his Savior. It is conjecture, of course. But knowing Ken as I did, I suspect my reconstruction of their last moments will be affirmed in heaven. In any case, by nightfall of that fateful day, Nancy and the others in Meyers Chuck realized something was terribly amiss. The next day, a search party discovered the place where Ken and Joe had slipped off into eternity to be with Jesus.

Months later, during a time when I was grieving Ken's death, I came across something he had written just before the drowning accident. It was part of a devotion booklet for Advent that all staff were required to contribute to as part of our ministry to our donors. I opened the booklet to re-read what turned out to be Ken's last contribution. It was based on John 1:12: "Yet to all who received Him, to those who believed in His name, He gave the right to become children of God."

In Ken's final devotion, he related a time when he was "holed up" in his little sailing vessel, the *Advena,* in a lonely harbor in southeast Alaska during a storm. Separated from Nancy and feeling very much alone, he began reflecting on the first coming of Jesus. He thought of his coming into the world as a kind of "homecoming," a coming "to that which was his own," meaning you and me as His children by faith.

He explained the biblical name for Jesus, "Emmanuel," which translated means, "God with us." He added, "Where God is present, the distinction between earth and heaven vanishes. We are blessed to know that God is always with us and has prepared a heavenly mansion that we will one day call home as we spend eternity with him."

I could not help but think of Jesus being present with Ken and Joe in their last moments of life and of the assurance of eternal life for all those who believe. I thought of the promise of a "mansion" prepared for us, a place for people like you and me and Joe. It is a powerful image of God fixing the broken and missing pieces of our lives, even at the last minute, through His son Jesus. For Joe, it would have been at the last minutes of his life, not unlike the thief on the cross or the old sailor converted on his deathbed who had given the *CHRISTIAN* its name in the first place.

CHAPTER 24

A Bridge to Opportunity

—◈—

Leadership is the capacity to translate vision into reality.
—Warren G. Bennis

Through all of my experiences as a pastor and tribal leader, I was gradually learning how organizations should function and the role of the leader in all of that. It seems to me as I look back on my experiences that God was really preparing me to help others to become useful in His service. In order for me to be used of God for this purpose, I needed to learn what it meant to be a servant-leader. Jesus was the pre-eminent servant-leader who was able to take ordinary men and turn them into extraordinary servants of His Father's kingdom. In the process of discipling these least-likely men, He had effectively taken the kingdom vision of God the Father and translated it into reality in the lives of the men He had selected to be His messengers. Chosen, trained, and equipped by Jesus, these men changed the world.

It is no small task to emulate Jesus's approach. Leadership as modeled by Jesus goes against our natural tendencies to seek power, recognition, or honor for ourselves. When given authority, some people are so seduced by power and position that they use it to lord it over people under them. When this occurs in organizations, it suppresses staff creativity, corporate teamwork, and organizational morale. The misuse of power, as in all abuses of power and position, results in fear and chaos. I did not want to be like that as a leader of my tribe, so I tended to go the other way and give people room to do their jobs—sometimes too much room. On several occasions, especially in my ministry, my tendency to put faith in people without carefully vetting their character or following my intuition when I sensed disloyalty led to divisiveness and acts of sabotage of my leadership. Overcoming my management deficiencies was no small task.

Then there was my long struggle with self-confidence. Ever since I had become a believer in Jesus, I struggled with self-limiting beliefs. These affected everything I did, including limiting my ability to lead others. How can you help others achieve their potential if you have not achieved it for yourself? Just as important, I struggled with vision for greater things in God's Kingdom. Think of my experience with the three Cheyenne men. How can you be useful to God if you lack the faith to believe He can achieve great miracles in the lives of people? Having a God-driven passion for people and faith to believe He can fix anyone is essential.

Through all of my experiences, both the good and bad, I was gradually learning to have a God-inspired vision and passion for ministry to people with broken and missing pieces. And ever so slowly, I was beginning to develop a confidence that He could use me, a characteristic I initially lacked that had inspired my odyssey through self-discovery in the first place.

Learning how to translate this emerging vision into reality was a difficult, albeit vital, next step in my learning process. How do you take a good idea and work with others to achieve a good outcome? For me, it begins with a servant attitude reflected in a commitment to create an organizational environment conducive to enabling the right people to express their talents. Often, the solutions to solving difficult challenges lie not in us but in others that God has gifted to work alongside us to achieve His purposes. The leader's task is to recognize this and facilitate those gifts for the good of the whole.

Working in concert with others to translate vision into reality was something I needed to learn in order to better serve God. But learning this while working as a tribal leader in a secular government setting to achieve economic goals? How could that help me learn this lesson? I was about to find out.

One day during my last term of elected office, 1991–1992, one of my staff came into my office to tell me that the Interstate 90 floating bridge on Lake Washington, a major thoroughfare connecting the city of Seattle with Mercer Island, had been badly damaged in a severe wind storm. Apparently, during repairs, portholes had been left open, and water from storm-driven waves began pouring unimpeded into the hollowed-out cells of the bridge. Several sections filled with water, had broken loose, and sunk to the bottom of the lake. Others had also come loose and initially threatened to drift into a new bridge under construction.

Eventually, all of the bridge sections were secured, but the city of Seattle and the Department of Transportation had a new problem: what to do with the remaining floating road surfaces. Each hollowed-out section was 300 feet long and 60 feet wide and weighed 6,000 tons! The city could not simply leave the massive concrete structures indefinitely where they had been secured in front of expensive homes on Lake Washington. Enter my tribe.

Our community was 120 water miles distant and had a need of our own. Seattle's problem was about to become our opportunity. The demise of the bridge in Seattle rekindled a long-dormant idea. Our community had needed a secure moorage facility for our salmon fishing fleet. Most of the forty or fifty salmon trollers that made up our fleet of commercial fishing vessels were at risk every year because of severe northeast winds that would funnel unimpeded through the Strait of Juan de Fuca between the Washington coast and Vancouver Island, often with continuous wind speeds of fifty and sixty miles per hour or more. Sometimes the boats would break loose from their mostly inadequate moorings. Others would drag anchor and end up on the beach or sink, leaving the tips of their masts sticking grotesquely through the surface of the murky waters of the bay. It was terribly costly!

Obviously, we needed a protected moorage, and we had needed it for many years before I came along. Unfortunately, the cost of building a secure marina was in the multiple millions. A sum we obviously did not have. Worse, no one had come up with suitable alternative strategies that would permanently fix the problem. In effect, we had a desperate need of the rebirth of a vision and an effective strategy to achieve it.

The events in Seattle reignited the vision and suggested a creative solution. Someone on our staff thought we could use the massive spans left over from the storm to create a moorage area by linking them together in an *L* shape, sinking them from the beach out into the bay, and constructing a marina inside the protected area formed by the massive spans. Finally, we had an idea to rally around. Lurking in the back of my mind was a question from Martin Luther I had learned during my seminary days: "What does this mean, and how is it done?" He might have added, "How much will it cost?"

We knew what it could mean. But the "How is this done?" was complex. Moreover, as someone wise in the way of harbor projects once told me, building projects on the water are usually double the estimates plus twenty percent.

Thanks in no small part to one of our chief consultants we were able to begin discussing how we could achieve our goals. Perceptive in business and marine science, Norm Down, a man who had served as a tribal planner for us in previous years, had the right blend of expertise in all the important areas for such a challenging project. Soon, he was contacting the appropriate people in charge in Seattle and inquiring about the possibility of our tribe taking the sections of floating bridge off their hands. It was a good question at an optimum time. Officials in Seattle were facing increasing pressure to have the concrete spans removed from their temporary moorage on Lake Washington. Our offer to take the spans turned out to be the right idea at the right time, except for one critical detail: the Department of Transportation could not just turn them over to us. The surviving bridge sections were considered "surplus property" and by law had to be put up for public auction. We would have to bid against other interested parties. They soon established that the bidding process should take place in Olympia, the state capitol.

Having to compete with other entities in a bidding process was intimidating. Accompanied by the key consultant who had been so instrumental in guiding the dialogue with the state, we arrived at the auction location in Olympia with little money and a lot of hope. Our optimism quickly dissipated when we realized our competition was well financed. The first six sections went for hundreds of thousands of dollars beyond what we could offer. We sat silent in the back of the room, discouraged. We wondered to ourselves if we would have any chance to bid for even one.

Finally, there were only six sections left. The man in charge of the auction asked if anyone else wanted to bid for any of the remaining six. There was a long silence. From the back of the room, we timidly raised our hand and said we would. He studied us for a moment and then after a long pause asked, "What's your bid?" "One thousand dollars," we replied. There was an even longer pause. Maybe even a chuckle or two. To our absolute surprise, however, no one in the room seemed interested in joining in the bidding. By the end of the day, we owned six huge sections at a cost of $1,000 apiece. I think they even gave us the last one.

However, ownership came with a huge logistical challenge. How do you float six concrete bridge sections, each weighing six thousand tons, 120 miles by water from the locks connecting Lake Washington to Elliot Bay and on through to the Strait of Juan de Fuca to our community? An even larger question before us now was if this was even feasible, since the bridge sections had never been designed to traverse through waves on open water we would surely encounter as we towed them to our community. We also wondered how the concrete sections, designed for fresh water, would react with salt water. Would they begin disintegrating? Moving them was also expensive. Tugboats large enough to pull massive structures typically charge by the hour. What if they had to wait out a storm along the way? Then what? Then there was the additional problem of securing them once they arrived. Only the U.S. Navy had anchors large enough to secure a six-thousand-ton floating concrete section once it arrived in the bay in front of our community. We could only imagine the horrific damage one of these floating bridge sections would do if ever one got loose in the bay. It could easily take out a dock or crush any boat in its way. We eventually contacted the U.S. Navy at the Bremerton Naval Shipyard to see if they might have surplus anchors large enough to secure them. They politely informed us that they did not. After some momentary discouragement and further efforts at problem solving, we finally ended up arranging to have mooring spikes driven into the rock bottom of the bay and cable the bridge spans to the spikes.

There was some advantage in the struggles we had encountered. The problems forced us to think outside the box and to bring in a multitude of our staff to problem solve. This meant convening the best minds from among our consultants, planners, forestry, and fisheries management staff and inviting them to discuss how we could manage the project. It was a huge undertaking that required the council, under my leadership, to create an organizational environment that permitted the best and most creative minds to contribute their ideas to solve the practical problems associated with our vision for a safe harbor. Everyone was important to the project, which, in turn, raised not only the energy levels of those involved but the corporate IQ as well. The morale of staff increased as people felt part of a cause vital to the community, one that enlisted them to become a part of the solution. We united behind a common vision to secure the fishing fleet for the good of the whole community.

The magnitude of the challenge had other beneficial elements as well. The fact that a small tribe had taken on a massive project involving what had once been a well-recognized structure in Seattle caught the attention of others outside our community. It was bold, it was challenging, it was positive, and it met a need for the tribe while helping the city of Seattle dispose of a problem. It was also cost prohibitive.

Our financial and planning staff was coming up with ideas to raise the funds needed to make our dream of a safe harbor a reality. One of my planning staff, Julie Johnson, an enrolled member of the Lummi tribe, was uniquely gifted in her ability to sell an idea to important government representatives. Soon, we were meeting in Washington, D.C., with key representatives of the Department of the Interior, the U.S. Army Corp of Engineers, our congressional representatives, and others to solicit their support. We were well received. Before long, we were able to generate the support we needed. None was bigger than that which we received from the federal agency that assists municipalities with projects like harbor development. The positive public relations the project generated and the effective work of my staff eventually enabled us to access the assistance of the U.S. Army Corp of Engineers.

All of this effort eventually culminated in a trip to Seattle to sign an agreement with the U.S. Army Corp of Engineers, committing them to build a safe harbor in Neah Bay. There, in the Seattle office of the U.S. Army Corp of Engineers, I signed the agreement committing my tribe to a partnership. Not long after this, planning for actual construction began. By the time construction began, my term had ended, and I was no longer living in the community. I had assumed my new role as leader of The Lutheran Association of Missionaries and Pilots U.S. A new vision would grow out of my relationship with this organization that would borrow from all of the lessons God had been teaching me through the years that I had served as pastor and leader of my people. The new vision would be far more critical than harbor development. It would have to do with assisting broken and missing pieces people in need of His grace to experience healing. And along with this, to begin to take responsibility for their lives as servants in God's Kingdom.

In a bit of irony, however, the Army Corps decided not to use the bridge sections for the harbor after all. They reasoned that the concrete bridge sections, as we had conceived it, would have to be cradled on rocks and could slip off in a storm, thus requiring ongoing maintenance—something they were unwilling to do. Instead, they opted to construct a rubble mount or rock breakwater. It turned out to be a good thing. The tribe was able to sell each of the unused bridge sections they had acquired at little cost for a profit of hundreds of thousands of dollars. The unexpected windfall from the sales of the concrete bridge sections generated additional funds that were then used to offset part of the cost of construction.

I learned some very useful lessons from this experience that would one day be applicable to my future ministry. The first was this: when you identify a way to solve a problem and circumstances favor action, move on it decisively. Very often, good ideas in a clock-driven world are time sensitive. When the bridge became a problem for the city of Seattle, we were the first ones in line with a creative solution. Had we waited, others would have stepped in, and we would have missed the opportunity.

The second is this: in order to take on a difficult but worthy task, it is important to learn everything you can about the challenge set before you, begin to understand why certain circumstances favor it—political, economical, practical, social etc.— and other circumstances that do not, and then design a strategy accordingly. If you do not know the things that favor the fulfillment of a goal or those things that do not, you do not know enough, and your efforts will likely fail.

The third: marshal all your energies, staff, and resources to take advantage of the opportunity. Had we not had the willingness to listen to the consultants and capable staff working for us at the time, we could not have achieved such an outcome. We needed all the available expertise to meet the challenge.

Fourth: hire the right people who can make it happen. Surrounding yourself with talented people is a tremendous asset to any successful venture, whether in the church or in the secular world of business. A difficult challenge always requires gifted people to take a vision and turn it into reality.

Having the right staff must be accompanied by a fifth leadership principle. As the leader, create a management environment that enables staff to freely express their talents without impeding others through personality conflicts. Staff must be able to feel that their opinions are valued. Failure to do so, or not managing any individual or department jealousies or hidden resentments within the organization, lowers corporate IQ and often diminishes morale as well. Through the years, I have seen how very talented people can work at cross-purposes to one another, often because of pride or jealousy. Contentious-ness in organizations results in the lowering of the corporate IQ and is like a wave on a pond, expanding in a negative ring outward from the source of the disturbance to all who would be served by the organization. Jesus, in His ministry, often had to contend with this dynamic among his disciples but effectively managed to head off potentially damaging conflicts. Learning lessons from the model of Jesus's ministry would serve me well in planning ministry strategy later.

Sixth: understand the importance of merging a compelling vision with a well-conceived strategy, one that will inspire and motivate people to work together for common cause. For many years, my tribe had needed a secure moorage facility. The vision suffered through the years because there was no effective strat-egy to make it happen. Without the motivation a vision and an effective strategy instills, the people who would be blessed by it languish in futility instead. Proverbs 29: 18 affirms, "Where there is no vision, the people perish." (King James Version)

Finally, I realized that a seventh and most important key to any worthwhile venture requires that the leader have a servant attitude, one who is not concerned with who gets the credit and is able to inspire others to express their ideas and utilize their talents to the best of their ability. This is no small thing. Our need to feel important can kill our capacity to effectively lead others to be the best they can be.

Not long ago, I read of a wise CEO who founded a successful technology company in Minneapolis. He had this as his philoso-phy: "If you do the right thing, trust people and spread the leader-ship, the right things would happen." John Scully, former CEO of Apple, said it this way: "Winning organizations are those that give individuals the chance to personally make a difference."[31]

---

[31]   Crouch, *The CEO's Little Instruction Book*, 98

Communities, churches, tribes, individuals, and even nations are often their own worst enemies in addressing needs and solving problems desperately in need of a vision and effective leadership to turn it into reality. Tribal cultures, especially with their long history of dependent relationships with the government and lacking necessary resources, struggle with many problems that cry out for a vision and an effective strategy. Very often, in the midst of problems needing unity and wise counsel, tribal communities become divided against one another.

Sometimes, as in the crabs in the bucket story, communities even stifle their own people from achieving greater leadership, often because of internal jealousies, family rivalries, self-interest, and factions representing special interests. Think how this is reflected by the present state of our Congress and how it has affected our ability to solve the great problems facing our country today. During my years on the tribal council, I was the subject of several recall petitions to remove me from office at times when my creativity was at its best. Sometimes the intensity of the divisiveness was almost too much to bear. I wanted to give it all up on more than one occasion. Even these problems had a God-intended purpose.

My struggles taught me something else about servant leadership. A leader has to be able to persevere under adverse circumstances in order to effectively lead others. Consider the opposition that Jesus faced. People who should have looked to Him for all that He had to offer rejected Him and eventually subjected Him to humiliation, sufferings, and death. Yet, Jesus persevered through it all and accomplished all that He set out to do in saving us from sin, death, and the devil.

I needed to learn perseverance to be of use to God. This would become evident in another unusual opportunity that surfaced. Just before my final term on the council ended, I began to see a way for us to overcome our own worst tendencies toward dependency. It came in the form of a new opportunity offered by the U.S. government.

Just before I completed my final term of office, the U.S. government approved an initiative to help tribes attain more responsibility for their own fiscal affairs. The program, called "Self-governance", promised greater autonomy and self-direction. It seemed a great opportunity for our tribe, a way, in a sense, to finally free ourselves from dependency and fulfill our own destiny. I would soon discover, however, that not everyone in my community shared my enthusiasm for this. In a series of events surrounding my efforts to integrate our tribe into this new initiative offered by the government, I was about to discover that we often become so used to dependence that we fear the consequences of freedom.

CHAPTER 25

Escape to Freedom

———————— ⚉ ————————

If a person fails to attain freedom, spontaneity, a genuine ex-
pression of self, he may be considered to have a severe defect,
provided we assume that freedom and spontaneity are the objec-
tive goals to be attained by every human being.
— Erich Fromm, *The Sane Society*

Through the years, the U.S. government hired a host of bu-
reaucrats to oversee its relationship with Native Americans. The system had evolved from where it began with the
War Department to become one great bureaucracy known ap-
propriately as the Bureau of Indian Affairs, a subsidiary of the
Department of the Interior. The progression through various
government agencies assigned to oversee Indian affairs reflected
the dire circumstances Indian nations were facing as a result of
government policies. It was subdue them by force first (the War
Department), acquire their lands second (the Interior Department), and then make them dependent on the government (the
Bureau of Indian Affairs).

Confined to usually resource-poor reservations that afforded little employment potential, subject to rules to live by, and
left without adequate means to insure a good education for their
children, Native Americans became increasingly reliant on the
government for everything. It amounted to programmed dependency, and its affects were crippling.

Further adding to the challenge, the system of managing Indians became entrenched with career federal employees with a vested interest in keeping the system in place. It meant that Native Americans had been deprived of the freedom and spontaneity that often inspires creative problem solving and had little help to break free.

However, by the time I was active in tribal government, a tribally driven initiative the U.S. government was willing to implement known as "Self-governance" promised to provide more economic freedom for tribes across America to shape their own destinies. Practically, it meant that those participating in the program could prioritize the spending of dollars formerly allocated by Congress for the Bureau of Indian Affairs according to their own priorities. This was a form of self determination, the essence of freedom and independence.

When I first heard that this new program was offered, I saw the benefits immediately. We moved quickly to become one of the first tribes to take advantage of this initiative. We soon entered into negotiations with the federal government while holding a series of downtown meetings with the community to explain the advantages. Few attended. We sent out mailings summarizing progress toward final agreement with the government. No one objected.

Then, just before Christmas, almost a year into negotiations with the government, the council officially acted at my direction to approve the contract with the U.S. government that would make us a "self-governance" tribe. It meant almost two million additional dollars to our budget. I remember sitting in my council office one December morning shortly after our action, pleased with our accomplishment and my leadership in helping to get the initiative approved. As I leaned back in my chair and looked out the window overlooking the bay and distant Vancouver Island, I must admit feeling pleased with myself. We had taken a giant step toward self-actualization and freedom as a tribe. At least that is what I thought.

Unfortunately, my exhilaration was short lived. I barely had time to savor the accomplishment when someone on my staff came into my office with some disturbing news. A clearly distraught member of my staff began, "Don, I have really bad news. There is growing discontent in the community regarding the council's action." I had heard this rumor too, but I thought whatever negative things people were saying about our decision to become a self-governance tribe would be little noted and unlikely to amount to anything. The agreement with the government had too many positive benefits. But I could not have been more wrong. Some concerned citizens in the community had gone door to door with a petition and had convinced many that the council's action would lead to the abrogation of the federal government's trust relationship with the tribe, thus ending federal recognition of the tribe and resulting in loss of benefits. In our negotiations with government representatives, we were assured that there was no chance that this would happen. Underlying some of the discontent was the additional fear that we did not have the ability to manage the money ourselves. It was one more example of how people used to dependence and acting out of fear tend to cling to the familiar slavery, not because it is better but because it seems safer than the uncertainty and responsibility that comes with freedom. The explanation offered by a tribal member, reported in a local newspaper covering the controversy, was, "We are not ready to assume control [of our financial affairs]."

The community's fear-based concerns were, of course, unfounded, at least as far as I was concerned. And why would I believe any less? Throughout my life since I had become a believer in Jesus, I had gradually been leaving my familiar with all of its attendant fears. Leaving my familiar for the challenge of the unknown had been a key to my walk out of darkness and freedom to be what God intended. Nevertheless, the people spreading the bad news got enough signatures to overturn the council's action. I was shocked and dismayed. Some of my relatives had signed it. I thought to myself, "How could our community do this? How could my aunt sign this? It means loss of jobs and freedom to shape our own economic future!"

Had I thought this through more carefully, I would have realized that my tribe's response mirrored my own reluctance to leave the reservation when I was a teen. At the time, I could not comprehend the possibilities a new community and school would afford. Nor could I imagine myself in a different world with a far different cultural environment. My fears caused me to do everything I could to find a way to stay where I was, even though in retrospect, leaving the familiar places for the unknown was the key to freedom in every other area of my life.

Now, many years later, my struggles with freedom and independence and my familiarity with the story of the Exodus should have helped me understand that the community anxiety was another example of an oft-repeated story throughout human history, reflected in the Old Testament story of Israel's bondage to the Egyptians. Once the people of Israel had been freed from their slavery to the Egyptians and were led miraculously across the Red Sea, they were soon overcome by fear of the unknown. Exodus 16:3 illustrates their fears: "If only we had died by the Lord's hand in Egypt. There we sat around pots of meat and ate all the food we wanted, but you have brought us out into the desert to starve this entire assembly to death." The familiar slavery was, to them, more appealing than the freedom that God was offering.

The referendum reversing the council's decision had thus become not only a rejection of my leadership but a directive for me to call the U.S. Office of Self-Governance in

Washington, D.C., and say to federal authorities we preferred to go back to the familiar dependency. To me, it was like declaring we wanted to be slaves once more. I was depressed and discouraged. We had spent a whole year negotiating a fair deal with the government. It promised so much good. How could I explain my community's reluctance to enter into this initiative to government officials and that we did not want to receive the funds we had negotiated? Embarrassed and discouraged, I delayed making the phone call for as long as possible.

Finally, when things seemed at their worst and time was running out, several local citizens came to my office to tell me that many people had been rethinking their vote. They wanted another chance to hear my side of it. Maybe there was hope? Maybe we could turn this around? I acted quickly to convene a public hearing downtown. I prayed, "God, please give me the words to say." Then I presented my case once more before the community, carefully choosing my words and explaining why this would be a good thing for the tribe. I remember my critics in the front row, staring me down and asking questions that they thought might be embarrassing or confounding. At times, the dialogue was intense. I answered every question with care. Finally, after three hours of continuous discussion and debate, I concluded my appeal by taking a full glass of water. I held it up for all to see, "This is our available funding if we assume self-governance." Then spilling half of it out, I concluded, "This glass half empty is what will be left of our budget if we return the agreement back to Washington, D.C. Which do you choose?"

There was a long moment of silence among the three hundred or so citizens gathered in the confined space of the same hall where I had brought my servant youth to be honored a year before. Finally, from the back of the room, someone shouted, "We have heard enough. Let's vote." There was a quick second, accompanied by rousing cries of, "Yeah, let's do it."

291

My critics, obviously disappointed, sat in silence. This was followed by a call for a show-of-hands vote. It was decisive. By more than seventy percent, the citizens voted in favor of self-governance. It was a tremendous triumph. I could not have been more proud of them or relieved for myself. The increased dollars available would be of critical importance to the harbor development project that would take place in the succeeding years because it meant we now had additional resources to afford the right staff and some of the funding needed to make the project viable. More importantly, the community had risen to the occasion and taken action to support their freedom and independence, and that would create new opportunities for the future. My leadership at that time might have been the most important of my entire tenure on the council. It eventually led to more job creation, and it enabled the tribe to take more responsibility for securing their own destiny, expressing their own talents and abilities in the process. As a result, it helped to raise the corporate IQ of the government of the tribe.

As I looked back on that experience, I realized it was a microcosm of my life. Throughout my life, God had been working through my many circumstances to take me from my own slavery and self-limiting beliefs to the freedom to be all that He made me to be. Through it all, His intent seems to have been to raise not just my expectations of self (mental health), but my spiritual IQ as well (increased faith). More often than not, His most effective work in transforming my life was in taking me from my familiar to the unknown, where exposure to different circumstances could permit Him to reveal Himself and bring healing to my life.

My trust gradually grew out of these encounters. Hebrews 11:6 says, "And without faith it is impossible to please God, because anyone who comes to Him must believe that He exists and that He rewards those who earnestly seek Him." God had been fixing me all along, and that was why I now could be useful to Him in helping others to become all that God intended for them to be.

Perhaps this was the most important lesson of all. True freedom is not independence from God, our natural human tendency in a fallen world. Freedom in God's kingdom is always related to our dependence on Him. In a faith relationship with Jesus, we find the capacity to be the kind of people God intended for us to be—that is, forgiven, transformed, and unleashed to be of use to Him in a world in desperate need of healing. Thus, my call to faith many years before was a call to freedom through a relationship with Jesus and a call to fruitfulness in God's Kingdom. Following Jesus meant learning to trust him to take me from my self-defeating behaviors and my insistence on control of my life to dependency on Him to provide His grace and power to be the kind of person He intended for me to be. The Apostle Paul affirms in Galatians 5:1, "It is for freedom that Christ has set us free. Stand firm, then, and do not allow yourselves to be burdened by a yoke of slavery."

It was not long after this experience as a tribal leader that I was called to serve the Lutheran Association of Missionaries and Pilots U.S. (aka Lutheran Indian Ministries) Becoming a part of this ministry would require that I leave my familiar once more. But by this time, I had learned vital lessons that would be useful in helping others experience the freedom God had given me.

CHAPTER 26

The Master Mechanic

It is perfectly true as philosophers say, that life must be understood backwards. But they forget the other proposition, that it must be lived forwards.

—Soren Kierkegaard

After many years in my community, I was feeling a pull to go back to school to pursue a doctorate and maybe teach at a college somewhere, ironic goals for someone who had failed first grade and struggled through high school, college, and seminary. Nevertheless, I had a growing conviction that my future was in teaching and that all that I had been learning about leadership and my family history were part of a larger plan God had for my life.

However, like so many things since I had become a Christian, I did not know what my desire to teach meant, or even how it could be accomplished. Frankly, much of what I had come to understand as God's will for me has always unfolded a little at a time and in ways I least expected. And more often than not, His latest revelation for my life was revealed in the direction of the unfamiliar. Of course, things were more understandable looking backward. Nevertheless, through all of my years of service in my hometown, I had never lost my sense of God's purpose, even when my life as a tribal leader seemed focused more on the mundane than the eternal.

Then, one day, I received an inquiry from a small ministry that worked primarily with isolated native communities in Alaska and Canada. The ministry employed single-engine Cessna 185s to ferry summer volunteers to these communities to teach one-week Bible schools. I was intrigued by the possibility of serving in the capacity they wanted, that is, someone who could visit congregations and share their story.

This type of ministry was not exactly what I had in mind for the long term, though. I was more interested in teaching leadership skills in some college setting. However, becoming a part of this organization would enable me to locate to a city of my choice where I could pursue a doctoral program while also serving in the capacity they desired. I eventually ended up selecting a suburban community near St. Paul, Minnesota. It was central to almost anywhere I needed to go, and there was a seminary nearby offering a doctoral program that would fit my educational objectives.

Voluntarily leaving my hometown thirty-three years after I had first left kicking and screaming proved difficult once more but in a far different way than the first time. Since returning as pastor to my hometown, I had been deeply invested in my community's politics, education, and spiritual life. During that time, I had advocated for the tribe, shared its grief in times of sorrow, and rejoiced in its celebrations. I had been there for the people and, just as important, they had been there for me. In truth, I had received far more from all the experiences afforded me in my community than I had been able to give back.

This contributed greatly to my conflicted feelings as I set about preparing to leave my community for a second and perhaps final time. It was difficult explaining to family and friends my desire to leave to pursue educational goals. Hadn't I been educated enough? My father, then in declining health, tried to dissuade me further by saying, "I don't think you have to be educated to talk about God." During a time when his health was in evident decline, what he was really trying to tell me was that he did not want me to leave home. I did not know how to explain to him that there was an even more important reason for me to leave. It was a still quiet voice deep within, one that I had first heard so many years before in the shadow of the Space Needle in Seattle in 1962. I had met Jesus for the first time and had promised God I would do whatever He wanted. I did not realize at the time that this meant entering the ministry, which I fought, or accepting a call to return to my tribe, which was unusual. Or that following Jesus might mean a journey toward self-discovery that would eventually reveal my and my family's deepest wounding and our struggles to manage the pain. Once more He would call on me to leave my familiar home for the unfamiliar.

Looking back with the clarity only hindsight affords, I can now see that my return to my hometown turned out to be a continuation of the journey of self-discovery that had begun in Montana with my unusual meeting with the three Northern Cheyenne men. My encounter with these men inspired the question, "How was I like them and their broken car?" It is a question answered throughout a lifetime, of course, and getting to the truth of it was often very difficult, made all the more so because all of us are a composite of a long history of things often hidden in our generational history or buried deep within our subconscious. Combined with our tendency for self-deception, this history obscures the truth about ourselves. As my story reveals, what traumas may have occurred to our parents and grandparents during their lifetimes often play a significant part in our development.

In all of my nearly twenty years of living and serving in my hometown, God had afforded me unique opportunities to see up close my generational heritage and that of the people who shared my history. They had experienced the same stresses as I had, and that was reflected in the broken and missing pieces of their lives. In the writing and telling of my story, however, I realized that we are not alone in sharing pain and disappointment. All people everywhere are alike in that way—all of us with broken and missing pieces and in need of repairs of one sort or another. So are the nations of the world and ultimately the natural world. My insights into time management and technology reveals the role they play in affecting all people, sometimes amplifying our worst tendencies and accelerating the consequences of our choices.

My involvement with the natural resources of my tribe afforded me an unexpected as well as up-close view of the natural world and its linkage to our behaviors. Declining runs of wild salmon, pollution of the oceans, and other natural world disruptions helped me to understand how all of God's creation, including the whole of the universe, is broken and missing pieces as well and mirrors our human dysfunction. And while we can and should do all we can to limit pollution and damage to eco-systems, we may not be able to reverse damage already done. Nor can we fix the hidden stresses deep within the earth that result in earthquakes and volcanic eruptions. These geologic events, random and disorderly manifestations within creation, mirror humankind's increasing dysfunction and remind us that creation also longs for rebirth. Even the house-size asteroid that strayed with little warning to within 6,000 miles from Earth in June of 2011 is a sign that our world and universe exist on the edge of unpredictability, potentially resulting in disastrous calamity.

Ultimately, only God can renew His creation and end its disorderly manifestations, and He will not do that until we are transformed to newness when Jesus comes again. As biblical revelation affirms and the native people of America have long understood, mankind's and the natural world's fates are linked.

Until God, in His time, acts to restore paradise lost, the earth and the political instability of nations will grow increasingly disruptive; events accelerated by technology and the accumulation of information at exponential speeds will cause time to appear to go by even faster, with increasingly dangerous consequences. And of course, our anxiety-driven responses will likely have dramatic impacts on people's values and beliefs and practices. Out of all these things, I am convinced that God can speak to us most clearly of our need for Him. He certainly spoke to my heart out of my concerns for the future of man.

And therein lies my greatest insight in my journey with God: my discovery of the gracious willingness of Jesus to take the individual, no matter how broken or tragic his or her life circumstances may have been, and transform the circumstances into good. It can take a while for us to recognize this, though. When I began my journey with Jesus, as my story reveals, I did so while carrying a lot of emotional and spiritual baggage, all of which eventually translated into a lack of faith.

Amazingly, God chose to reveal the scope of my desperate need for His grace through the least likely of messengers: Medaris Bad Horse and his companions—one more proof for me that God often reveals things in our lives in unusual ways, in ways we least expect.

Placing God's action in the context of my story, I began to think of Jesus as the Master Mechanic of the Universe, who, through the work of the Holy Spirit, is able to gather our broken parts and missing pieces, fit them together, and make us roadworthy once again. Ultimately, He renews us in body, soul, and spirit so that we are fit to live in the new heavens and the new earth He is going to renew at the end of the age. A wonderful new world is coming.

Perhaps the most unlikely of all, God sent Jesus, His Son, to accomplish our redemption through enduring the cross with all of its pain and shame. From before all eternity and for the love of all of His creation, Jesus, the Son of God, entered the time and space and the earth that He had created and willingly took on human flesh and eventually was betrayed, accused, abused, abandoned, cursed, and killed. And like Medaris Bad Horse, His body bore the scars of a hard life. However, Jesus's wounds were not caused by a carelessly lived life. Rather, they were the result of taking upon Himself the punishment for our sins. Isaiah 53:5 states, "But He was pierced for our transgressions, He was crushed for our iniquities, the punishment that brought us peace was upon Him and by His wounds we are healed." In this way, Jesus confounded the dark plans of Satan by turning the tables on evil. These were all key truths for me.

The day before I set out for St. Paul with my family, I took my boat out on the ocean one more time. I felt a deep sense of sadness as I stepped into my little boat, primed the engine, turned the ignition key, and set a course out and around the island in the bay for the open ocean, just as I had done countless times. My last fishing day seemed made to order for someone about to leave it all behind. It was one of those beautiful, warm, sunny days, and the ocean was uncharacteristically placid. Even a few fish were biting.

Not far away was Tatoosh Island, the place where I had faced grave danger several years before when the wind and waves arose so suddenly. It was a place where I gained an insight about God's foreknowledge and His presence with us in all of our circumstances. But already that was a distant memory. Mostly I thought about the grandeur of sea and sky and the incredible rock formations rising so majestically out of the sea, and I remembered back to the many times I had caught fish in just this place. How could I leave all of this beauty for a distant place? Maybe an uncertain future? Then I had this even more discomfiting thought: "Would I ever do this again?" It was a disturbing question.

The truth was, I never felt closer to my tribal heritage than when I was on the open sea in a small boat, facing wind and waves. Fishing for salmon was one of the activities I enjoyed most. Moreover, leaving it all behind seemed so much like abandoning a little bit of me. I wanted to hang on to this moment on the sea. Once more, I wanted to hang on to my familiar.

It is, of course, the dilemma we are all faced with in this world. There is so much beauty all around, and we become so identified with our favorite places and the people and experiences we share them with. Leaving them behind is always difficult. But life is at best fleeting, a continuous leaving of the familiar for the unfamiliar. Even the aging process is a reflection of leaving one place in our lives for another. Nevertheless, we cling to the familiar things of this world as if they should last forever, often reflected in the longing for the less-complicated "olden days," or the familiar tunes from another more-hopeful bygone era or maybe, as in my case, finding enjoyment in my favorite fishing places. I suspect that one of the reasons that I enjoy going to vintage car shows is partly that cars from the 1950s and 60s remind me of a familiar, less-complicated age when car designs reflected individual creativity and unbridled imagination. I think all of these things ultimately reflect a longing for eternity and permanence, for security and things lovely and beautiful.

I hardly realized it at the time, but as I tried to savor every moment of my last fishing day, God was providing me another insight into our broken world, our lives, and His forever plan. The world is also constantly leaving what once was for the unfamiliar. It does not have a good feel to it, though, as it goes through turmoil. There is increasing darkness in the world of men and evident disruptions in the earth and on the land, and even though there are grievous troubles among nations that seem to worsen with the passage of time, from a biblical perspective, these are signs of redemption not far off. There is great hope for the future. The good news is that the reality to come is so much better than the things we cling to here. The places God is preparing for His children are of indescribable beauty and harmony between man and creation, magnificent places of forever relationships born of love. The perfect circle of life representing the unity of all things created is about to be restored. What is more, it is made possible because of all that Jesus did on the cross. The cross, once a curse, is the Sacred Tree made alive once more.

In His suffering, death, and resurrection, Jesus subverted the devil's evil intent and unleashed Light for all people everywhere. For us, it means that in spite of all the pain and suffering we experience and observe in the world, God has acted in history to provide light for our darkness. John 1:4 says, "In Him was life, and that life was the light of men." As the title of my book suggests, He can and will fix the broken and missing pieces of people's lives, both in the here and now and for all eternity. We need only to acknowledge our sin and our need for Him to come and fix the broken and missing pieces of our lives. Amen! Come Lord Jesus!

Bibliography

1. Armstrong, William H. *Warrior in Two Camps*. Syracuse: Syracuse University Press, 1978.
2. Baum, Frank L. *Aberdeen (SD) Pioneer Press*. December 20, 1890.
3. Bonhoeffer, Dietrich. *The Cost of Discipleship*. New York: MacMillan, 1963.
4. Boorstin, Daniel J. *The Discoverers*. New York: Random House, 1983.
5. Brown, Dee. *Bury My Heart At Wounded Knee*. New York: Bantam, 1973.
6. Crouch, Van. *The CEO's Little Instruction Book*. Tulsa, OK: Trade Lite Books, 1996.
7. De Mallie, Raymond J. *The Sixth Grandfather*. Lincoln, NE: University of Nebraska Press, 1984.
8. Di Silvestro, Roger L. *In the Shadow of Wounded Knee*. New York: Walker, 2007.
9. Dobbs, Michael. *One Minute to Midnight*. New York: Vintage Books, 2009.
10. Friedman, Edwin H. *Generation to Generation: Family Process in Church and Synagogue*. New York: Guilford Press, 1985.
11. Gilman, Rhoda R. *The Story of Minnesota's Past*. Saint Paul, MN: Minnesota Historical Society Press, 1989.

12. Hobhouse, Henry. *Seeds of Change*. New York: Harper and Row, New York, 1985.

13. Johansen, Bruce E. *Forgotten Founders*. The Harvard Common Press, Boston Massachusetts, Copyright 1982.

14. Makah Cultural and Research Center. *Portrait in Time: Photographs of the Makah by Samuel G. Morse, 1896–1903*. Neah Bay, WA: Makah Cultural and Research Center/Washington State Historical Society, 1987.

15. Marshall, Joseph M. III. *The Day The World Ended at Little Bighorn*. New York: Penguin, 2007.

16. Metaxas, Eric. *Bonhoeffer: Pastor, Prophet, Martyr, Spy*. Nashville: Thomas Nelson, 2010.

17. Neihardt, John G. *Black Elk Speaks*. Lincoln, NE: University of Nebraska Press, 1961.

18. Scientific American, *A Matter of Time*. Special Edition, Vol. 16, Number 1, 2006, Scientific American Inc., New York, New York.

19. Twiss, Richard. *One Church Many Tribes*, Ventura, CA: Regal Books, 2000.

20. Underwood, Chuck. *The Generational Imperative*. North Charleston, NC: Generational Imperative, 2007.

21. Wright, Nigel Goring. *A Theology of the Darkside*. Downers Grove, IL: Inter Varsity Press, 2003.